What Brothers Do

Michael Everett Brown

Cover Photo Title:Five More Found, New York City, 2001.
Credit: Copyright Joel Meyerowitz, Courtesy Howard Greenberg
Gallery

"What Brothers Do," by Michael Everett Brown. ISBN 978-1-
60264-682-7.

This book is dedicated to my wife, Janet. The true love of my life, the editor of this book, and a breast cancer Warrior. October 14, 1958-September 30, 2016

With special thanks to renowned photographer Joel Meyerowitz for his efforts to preserve the historical significance of the 9/11 terrorist attacks through his book, *Aftermath: World Trade Center Archive.* He literally had to fight City Hall to get the masterful shots he curated for his book and I am grateful for his permission to use the striking shot that now graces the cover of my own book.

Introduction

EVERYTHING OF VALUE takes effort.

Reading takes effort, forces thought and therefore gives life more value and meaning. A book is a time machine. It doesn't change with the opinions of the day or tell how it should've been. A book tells how it was.

Since the beginning of humanity, we have protected what is ours—what has value. When your village was attacked, the community would come together to fight off the attackers and rebuild.

What Brothers Do is the same kind of story—our village being New York City.

Read *What Brothers Do*. And if you are able, read it with a New York accent.

Climb upon my shoulder and let me take you through this amazing journey. Discover what a hero firefighter and person my brother Patrick was. Discover how the great community of first responders came together when the village was attacked. Read. You will laugh, you will cry, and you may even get pissed off.

It was what it was.

Our village survived and rebuilt, but the scars still run deep—nearly 20 years later, which is why I had to re-launch this book. *We cannot let an entire generation come into this world and not understand why this attack was so crucial in world history.* It was not an attack on New York; it was an attack on the United States of America using the World Trade Center, a huge symbol of the success of our Republic as a target.

The attack proved the bizarre nature of the terrorists' long, careful plan--something so preposterous that even the most evil American mind could not fathom it—to attack our prosperity and spirit. Thousands of casualties later, beyond those who were incinerated, crushed or even worse, jumped to their deaths, there were 343 FDNY heroes, many more police and other first responders who also lost their lives—conducting the greatest rescue effort ever known to man. The only good that came from this tragedy was the resulting unity of the American people.

Our country still mourns, and we still bear our scars in our hearts and minds. *What Brothers Do* is about healing—it is an ongoing process.

Postscript...

Since I wrote this book, I've lost my partner, my editor, my one true love of my life, my Warrior—Janet. If I were granted the opportunity to relive 30 years without Janet, I would decline.

She died from a 13-year battle against breast cancer and not once did she consider herself as a cancer *survivor*. Janet was a *Warrior*. During that time of cytotoxic nightmares, multiple major surgeries and radiation treatments, Janet, graduated magna cum laude from UNLV school of business, volunteered for American Cancer Society, and even became a tap dancer. Two nights before she passed, she said she would save a spot for me next to her in heaven. She fulfilled my life. She and my brother inspired me to write our story.

Recently I was diagnosed with cancer. It appears that this cancer is directly related to my time on "The Pile" at Ground Zero.

This third round of loss—my brother, my wife and my life as I KNEW it, seems to be a 360-degree circle of loss, mourning and negotiating with what's left of life. It's tragic, at times funny and always, it's real—that was the message of *What Brothers Do* and the message that I will try to forward into what may be my final book,
N of 1.

We responders, the survivors, the downtown Manhattan residents and all our families and friends assumed that the attack ended on 9/11/2001. We now realize that the attack continues with the toxic time bombs that are growing inside each of us. We are Americans, we are fighters, we are all in this together, and *we never forget.*

As I participate in the World Trade Center Health Program for my cancer treatment, I feel even more connected with the families who have "survived" 9/11, the people like me who are battling for their lives, and even more inspired by my memories of my Warrior, Janet.

Read my book and others like it and teach the young who are now living with the aftermath, how to feel and fight. Don't let them forget what happened—or who we lost.

Life is not fair but it's worth it.

I will give advice to anyone who is diagnosed with cancer--be a Warrior like Janet—do not let anyone make decisions for you. It is your body, your mind, your life.

Take strength from those who went before you—you'll need it in the days ahead.

Chapter 1

Where were you when the towers fell? The question has been asked millions of times—with just as many answers. For some, the memory is muddled by the passage of time and activities of daily living. But for others, that morning remains just as sharp and vivid and indelible as all those happy milestones in life: winning the big game, first great love, first shared orgasm, first child's birth, acceptance into the fire department, graduation from medical school.

What do I remember about the day the world changed?

Everything.

I WAS WORKING THE 6 a.m. shift in a Las Vegas emergency room. I was 47 years old, six foot one, with the physical features and mannerisms of the New York fireman I once was. In my spare time I lifted weights, played softball, was even known to have a beer or two at the game; in fact, I referred to the beer I brought for the team each week as "my talent." Life was so good. It was very good. I thought I was one of the luckiest people alive.

Just one week before, I had walked in on Troy—one of the ER nurses—while she was putting nicknames on the lockers in our new doctors' lounge.

"Hey, Troy—what's my name?"

"Downtown Brown."

I protested. "I don't want to be Downtown Brown."

With the label maker ready in her hand, she said, "So…who do you want to be?"

I couldn't remember the last time anyone had asked me that question. It took me a little while to come up with an answer and, jokingly, I told her. After a few clicks of the label maker, Troy slapped it on my locker.

MICHAEL E. BROWN, MD
MASTER OF THE UNIVERSE

On September 11, 2001, I wasn't the master of anything. I was just trying to hold it all together until I got backup when the 10 a.m. doctor came in. For the first four hours of my shift, I was the only doctor for our 48-bed ER. That's not as crazy as it sounds. There are always people just stuck in ER beds. Most are waiting for an open bed upstairs, some are waiting for beds in a mental hospital, some are waiting for tests and, on a rare occasion, some are just waiting to die. Along with Troy, two other nurses, Ellen and Lois, were also working that morning. We were part of a little gang of friends that not only worked together but also hung together after we punched out. All three had good attitudes despite the stress of the ER.

Our emergency room is designed like four small ERs, with sections divided by halls and corridors. People are in constant motion from one section to another taking care of patients, searching for supplies or just wandering around. I encountered Troy in one of the hallways carrying an IV bag of meds.

"I still don't believe this is happening. Are you all right?" she asked.

"I'm all right, but I don't know how my brother is doing ... "

With the exception of the acute-care area, all the other treatment rooms had TVs attached high on the wall, and every one of them was blasting the news that our country was under attack. Troy hurried on to her patient; I went on to Skid Row.

SKID ROW WAS THE nurses' nickname for a group of rooms used to isolate patients with infectious diseases. This area had become the residence of the unwanted and unwashed. There were the few poor souls who truly couldn't control their behavior and had no other place to go, but most of those who populated Skid Row were abusers. They abused alcohol, crank, crack, heroin, GHB, X, their significant others, their parents, their kids, nurses, the hospital housekeepers, the security guards, the doctors—society in general. On the way to Room 37 I passed Room 38, whose occupant was an intoxicated thirtysomething female tied down to the bed. She'd already managed to kick a security guard and tried to bite a nurse.

"DOCTOR, DOCTOR! Get your fucking ass in here now! You have no fucking right to hold me here!"

She was doing a great impression of Linda Blair. The staff had placed restraints on all four extremities, and she was trying to spit on any unfortunate person that got too close. This woman had tried to stab her husband with a kitchen knife. Because she had an altered level of consciousness (she was drunk as shit) and may have had a psychiatric problem (trying to kill people when she got drunk), the police offered her two options: the hospital or jail.

"DOCTOR, DOCTOR! Get me my fucking lawyer! I don't fucking belong here!"

My brother was in one of the World Trade Center towers. Every time I looked at a TV, I saw people falling out of the sky.

I got only as close as the doorway. "Absolutely, you don't belong here," I told her in agreement. "You belong in jail."

I moved away just as her spit hit the door. Ellen was waiting for me.

"She's a real beauty, huh?"

From Room 38, I heard, "NURSE, NURSE— I want my nurse! Where's my fucking nurse?!" I leaned close to Ellen. "At least she's not yelling for her fucking doctor."

"Yeah, thanks, Mike," Ellen retorted, rolling her eyes. Then she got serious. "Have you been able to get through to New York yet?"

"I can't even get through to my sister—and she lives on Long Island. You know that Jennifer and Amie are right there in Lower Manhattan..."

"Oh my God, that's right!"

Jennifer and Amie were good friends of ours— also nurses. I had seen them just four days earlier at a wedding in Rhode Island. Steve Traub, the groom, was a former partner of mine; he'd met Nikki, a nurse, in our ER. While the newlyweds were on their honeymoon, Jennifer and Amie were spending the week in Steve and Nikki's downtown apartment. The happy couple had moved from Las Vegas to Manhattan a year earlier so Steve could do a fellowship in toxicology at Bellevue Hospital.

They hadn't left for their honeymoon yet, and I was certain that Steve had headed to Bellevue's ER after the towers were hit.

"I'll call Steve at Bellevue," I said to Ellen, heading toward the front desk.

"Hey, Doc!" Ellen called after me. "What about the patient in 37?" The female patient in 37 was suffering from the effects of long-term methamphetamine abuse, which eventually turns normal people into flat-out schizophrenics. Her complaint: there were miniature heads with little dicks emerging from under her kitchen sink to beat her up and steal her food. I handed Ellen the chart.

"If you see any little heads running around, smack them with this."

As I took off for the front desk, I heard my name come over the PA speaker. *"Dr. Brown, you are needed in Room 26."*

With a sigh, I turned toward 26. On good days the female nurses call it Bush Gardens; on bad days they refer to it as the Tuna Boat. Patients seen here often prove wrong the advertising slogan "What happens in Vegas, stays in Vegas." I arrived to find a 40-year-old woman in active labor with her first child. She and her husband had tried one more time to get pregnant, and now she was having the baby— at only 17 weeks' gestation. The TV screen was showing images of both towers burning, debris flying and people hurling themselves out of windows, preferring death from the impact of an

80-story fall to death from the ever-intensifying flames and fumes.

"Doctor, please do something!" the frantic husband pleaded.

The head of the fetus was already showing, and the tiny body soon followed. The child was moving his extremities and guppy-breathing. As Master of the Universe, I was helpless in trying to explain to these people that the child they so desperately wanted was nonviable outside his mother, and that their decision to take a vacation in Las Vegas had nothing to do with this outcome. With the World Trade Center burning in the background, the no longer expectant but now guilt-ridden parents watched the death of their child with horror. Through the fetus's thin chest, we all watched the heartbeat of their dreams and prayers thump up and down, falter...then finally give up. I looked away, only to have my eyes fixed on a replay of the South Tower being struck by an airliner.

"Dr. Brown to Bed 8, stat!"

Bed 8 is one of the 16 acute beds in the ER; it's also in the vicinity of the main desk. As I passed by, I quickly told the clerk, "Debra, please see if you can get through to Bellevue Hospital in New York. See if you can get hold of Steve Traub."

A gangbanger was lying in Bed 8. He was young—19 or 20, Hispanic, covered with gang tattoos. He also had a small hole in his abdomen.

Both Troy and Lois were setting up IVs. I donned a pair of latex gloves.

"I'm Mike Brown, one of the ER docs. Who shot you?"

He responded immediately. "I don't remember." He also could not remember his name, where he lived, his parent's names or his phone number.

It still fascinates me how such a little hole made by a bullet can kill so fast. A gunshot victim can be having a conversation with you one minute, and the next he's dead. I didn't have enough time, patience or sympathy to put up with his macho crap. I moved nose-to-nose with him.

"Who would you like me to call when you're dead?" His eyes opened wide. He started talking. I yelled to the front desk. "Hey, Debra—get the surgeon on call."

"I'm on hold with Bellevue. You want me to hang up?"

I needed to talk with Steve Traub; this gangbanger needed to go to surgery.

"Yeah, hang up, call the surgeon."

Katie, a tall, pretty paramedic, rolled another customer into Section 1. She and her partner off-loaded a male patient onto Bed 4 just as Lois showed up to get a report from Katie's partner. Katie rushed over to me at Bed 8 with a pre-hospital EKG.

"Hey, Doc Brown, brought you a hot one. Fifty-six-year-old male with two hours of chest pain; short of breath and diaphoretic. Little change after three nitros and 10 mgs of morphine. Looks like an anterior wall."

"Sure does," I agreed as I scanned the EKG. I yelled over my shoulder, "Debra, please call for a stat EKG—Bed 4."

Putting down the EKG, I saw Katie's concerned eyes. "Hey, Doc, don't you have a brother who's a New York City fireman?"

"He's a captain."

She pointed at the burning towers on the TV. "You think he's in there?"

I nodded my head and moved to Bed 4. John, the patient, had the fear of God in his eyes, as if he were about to walk toward the light. Lois was taking vitals, starting a second IV and placing him on the cardiac monitor. I shook his hand.

"John, I'm Mike Brown, one of the ER docs. We're going to take good care of you. When did the pain start?"

"It started last night, but I thought it was heartburn," he said. "It seemed to subside until about 6 a.m."

"Did it wake you from sleep?"

"No. I was up all night."

The EKG tech placed the leads on John.

"John, do you have a history of any medical problems?" I asked.

"No."

"Taking any medications?"

"No, none."

"You smoke?"

He hesitated. "Yes."

Lois approached. "What do you need, Mike?"

"Heparin and Tridel."

She quickly headed to the medication room.
The PA system sprung to life yet again with
Debra's familiar voice.

"Dr. Brown, physician call at the front desk."

The tech handed me John's EKG.

"Is it bad?" John asked.

"You're having a heart attack. There's a blood
clot in one of your main coronary arteries
preventing blood from getting to..."

"Dr. Brown, physician call at the front desk."

John's face was sheet-white. I spoke quickly.

"John, have you had any recent trauma,
surgeries, bleeding problems?"

He shook his head no.

"We have medication that can dissolve the
blood clot and open up your artery."

"Dr. Brown, physician call at the front desk."

"The problem with this type of medication is
that it will dissolve every blood clot in your body.
If you have a clot in your nose, you will bleed some;
if you have a clot in your brain, you will have a
stroke and may die."

Fearful, covered in sweat, John asked, "What do you think?"

"Your heart is dying and we need to save it."

The thrombolytic was ordered. I returned to the front desk way too late to get the call.

"Debra, repage the surgeon."

"Sure, Dr. Brown, but that wasn't the surgeon," she shrugged.

"No? Then who was it? It wasn't Steve Traub, was it?"

"It was the HMO doctor you asked me to page."

"I asked you to page him an hour ago!"

"I *did* page him an hour ago!"

I felt as if my wheels were about to fall off. I took a deep breath.

"I'm sorry I yelled, but this is what I need, and in this order: first, the surgeon; then the on-call cardiologist; then the HMO doc; then Steve Traub."

"Sure, Doctor, whatever you want."

The charts of the new ER patients that needed to be seen were accumulating on the front desk. I instinctively picked up several and was about to run off to evaluate these new patients when the phone rang.

"Dr. Brown, it's the on-call surgeon."

I took the phone receiver from Debra.

"Hello, Dr. Hanish, you're on call for us…Yeah, we're a little busy." As I was presenting the case, Debra informed me that both the cardiologist and the HMO doctor were on hold. I continued with Hanish. "Well, the patient is stable now, but you will need to take him to the OR…Yeah, I'm sure…Thank you."

I leaned over the desk and interrupted Debra, who had picked up another ringing phone.
"O.K., transfer the cardiologist."

Debra transferred the call from another phone. "That's who you'll have to speak with—because the other doctor hung up."

As I spoke to the cardiologist, I scanned the nursing notes of the people waiting to be seen. There was abdominal pain for a year; rash for a month; toothache; typical migraine and allergy to all meds except Demerol; too weak to go to work today; fibromyalgia flare-up. No one needed immediate medical care. I put the charts back on the desk and went in search of a TV to find out what was going on at the Trade Center.

I WENT OVER TO Room 17 in Section 2 where a few people had gathered to watch the unbelievable events unfolding in Manhattan. They were fixated on the TV, watching in stunned silence. Maria, a short Spanish nursing assistant with a heavy accent, rushed over when she saw me.

"Dr. Brown, you sure your brother's there?"

Pat was a captain in a ladder company; his firehouse was about a mile from the Trade Center. Even if he were off-duty, he lived just a few miles from the towers. If he wasn't here in Vegas visiting me, I told Maria, he was in the building that got hit first, the North Tower.

Another nurse came into the room and asked me to speak to a patient and her family in Room 28. The patient had been admitted by one of my partners who had worked the shift just before mine. She was diagnosed with pancreatitis. A CAT scan had been performed; they wanted to know the results. The nurse knew that this patient was not my responsibility, but the medical doctor in charge of her admission would not be in until late afternoon. The nurse handed me the CAT scan report. I could see clearly the results were consistent with metastatic pancreatic cancer—a death sentence. I walked into the room to find four family members huddled around the patient's bed. Their conversation stopped. All eyes were on me as I shut the door.

There is only one thing worse than having to tell someone that a loved one has died: Telling someone that *she* is going to die. I needed to concentrate to answer their questions about the horrors this woman was about to face. Right above their heads was a TV. My mind kept jumping to the horrors that my brother was facing at that moment. Contrary to what often happens on prime-time television, there was no magic pill or superstar surgeon that would burst into the room and save this woman from the slow, excruciatingly painful death that was her fate.

BACK AT THE FRONT desk, patient charts continued to pile up. I needed to get moving. The HMO doctor was on the phone and wanted me to send a critical patient home. I had spent an hour saving this man's life and, against all Vegas odds, I'd kept him off a ventilator. Now this jerk wanted me to send him home! The doctor responded by asking, "What do you expect me to do?"

I needed to see the new patients. There was a 35-year-old female who was having chest pain because her boss yelled at her; an 18-year-old male who wanted to go on methadone after trying heroin for the first time; an 85-year-old woman who fell and remained on the floor for three days; an asthmatic who smoked; a cirrhotic who drank; a schizophrenic who abused methamphetamine. They were all lying in wait. And here I was, a doctor whose only brother was somewhere in the World Trade Center. Maria tugged on my sleeve.

"Dr. Brown, Dr. Brown! The tower fell!"

"Maria, *which* tower fell?"

"I don't know . . ."

I sprinted back to the TV in Room 17. Lower Manhattan was now engulfed in a thick gray cloud. A monstrous, billowing tidal wave of smoke and dust was chasing thousands of panicked people trying to escape its path. As they ran through the streets, some were overtaken and swallowed up.

14

Then the camera went black. I couldn't believe what was happening. One of the Trade Center towers was *gone?* Thousands of people must have been killed. Was my brother one of them? Which tower was it? I was frozen. Another camera shot. Each fireman that ran by could have been Pat. I figured he was in the tower that got hit first, but which one was now dust? Then, a view from a different camera: I saw it—the tower with the big antenna on the roof, the one that was hit first, the North Tower—still standing.

"Run, Pat, run," I pleaded under my breath. "Get the hell out of there. Drop the equipment and take off. Get the fuck out…"

Maria was tugging on my sleeve again.

"Dr. Brown, you are needed at Station 1. You can't hear it?"

Debra's voice: *"Dr. Brown, you are needed in Station 1, now! Where are you, Dr. Brown?"*

Dr. Larry Pellegrini was waiting for me in Station 1. He was the 10 a.m. shift doctor, and someone had called him in early. There were several charts of new patients scattered on the desk, but the ER was in no greater chaos than usual. "What the hell is going on?" he asked me. There was neither an explanation nor help in my eyes, so he picked up five charts and rushed off.

Run, Pat, run!

"Mikey." Lois handed me a new EKG from John, the patient who was having a heart attack. "Mikey, he's having more pain."

And the EKG was showing more damage.

"Debra, get me that cardiologist on call."

"Didn't you talk to him already?"

"I need him again; please call him stat."

I wandered back to Room 17 and watched the black smoke pouring out of the North Tower. There were people and debris falling from the upper floors and smashing onto the sidewalks. I was called back to the front desk and spoke to the cardiologist. We transferred John to the cardiac-catheterization lab; they successfully opened his coronary arteries. At least someone's life was being saved. Lab and x-ray results were back. I had to make dispositions on a few of my patients...I started to go through the results and was halted by an overwhelming need to get back to Room 17. I dropped everything into one disorganized pile and headed for the TV.

Run, Pat, run.

First the top floors started to pancake—but they didn't stop. It all seemed to be happening in slow motion. My heart was screaming...the great tower, in a monstrous cloud of smoke and dust, was folding to the ground.

Run, Pat, run.

I slowly walked to the main desk and sat down next to Debra. But my mind was racing. If the order had been given to evacuate the North Tower after the South Tower collapsed, he would have escaped. He was a marathon runner. He had plenty of time to get out. As long as he tried to get out, he would have made it. He had to have made it. I looked up when I heard my boss, Dr. Paul Fischer. His voice has a very distinctive South African accent.

"Michael, Michael, go home. Clean up what you're working on and go home."

I gazed absently at him across the desk. Home? What was I supposed to do at home?

"Michael, go home—lend me your stethoscope."

I complied. Then I put my head in my hands to shut out the world.

"Dr. Brown, Bellevue on Line 2."

I lifted my head. "Thanks, Debra. How'd you do it?"

"ER to ER. Pick up the phone."

I grabbed the receiver. "Hello, Steve—"

"No, this is Bob Hoffman. How can I help you, Mike?"

Bob Hoffman is the director of the toxicology program at Bellevue. Ten years ago I had rotated through toxicology as a resident at Bellevue and hadn't seen him since—until four days ago in Rhode Island, when I'd had a drink with him at Steve's wedding. I remember thinking that I wouldn't talk to him for another 10 years, but here he was: my only source of useful information.

"Thanks, Bob. My brother is in the fire department and I'm trying to find him."

"What's his name?"

"Captain Patrick Brown."

"Mike, he's not here. I'm sure of it. We have an overabundance of doctors, nurses and volunteers. What we don't have are victims. Listen, I'll call around to the other ERs. If I hear anything, I'll give you a call."

I went back to staring at the charts in front of me. Both Paul Fischer and Larry Pellegrini were now standing over me. Dr. Pellegrini held out his hands.

"Give me and Paul three each."

Paul reiterated. "Give us your charts, tell us what needs to be done and go home," he said. "Don't worry, we'll cover you."

He didn't mean go to my house in Vegas. He meant go home—home to New York City.

Chapter 2

OUTSIDE IN THE GLARING desert sun, I turned and
faced the ambulance entrance. Several ambulances
were off-loading patients. There were the sick, the
not so sick, and the sick as shit—and I was going
the other way. Normally after my shift, I love to get
the hell out of there. But this time was different.
This time we were at war, and there was a chance I
wouldn't be back. I didn't have a clue what I was
heading into back home; yet I knew, in some
capacity, that I would be useful. I was going home
to find my brother and take care of him.

My wife Janet—five foot two, with long,
straight blond hair and blue eyes full of tears—was
waiting in the doorway. She threw her slender arms
around me. That familiar wide smile, her zeal for
life, was gone, replaced by trepidation. Our dogs
Blizzard, a white German shepherd, and Murphy, a
yellow Lab, were close by Janet's side. They
seemed to sense that something was very wrong.

Janet is five years younger than I am. We'd met
during my medical internship in New York; she

was a quality-assurance nurse at the hospital where I was training. It was years later when I found out that she had access to the house staff schedules and would mysteriously end up reviewing patient charts on the same floor where I'd been assigned. Janet had always sworn she'd never go out with a doctor. They were Type-A personalities, she said, unbearable. Then she met me. She liked that I was a fireman before I went to med school. I was different from most of the other docs she'd known—much more a firefighter than a doctor. I think that's what impressed her.

Internship was a bitch. On the medical floors you were on call every fourth day; in the critical-care units, where the sick as shit are trying to die, you're on call every third. Working 36 to 40 hours in a row without sleep was not rare. In the time since my training, they've changed the rules and made internship much easier—though I don't think making it easier has made better or happier doctors. That year of internship was the hardest year of my life, but I left with knowledge, strength, confidence and, best of all, I left with Janet.

THE NEXT 36 HOURS were spent straining my eyes looking for my brother on CNN and receiving calls from friends telling me that they'd seen someone who looked just like him. Phones, phone books and sheets of paper with numbers scribbled on them were spread out on the coffee table. I called everywhere, desperately trying to find information about Pat and get a flight to New York. I called FEMA, the Red Cross and the National Guard—no answer. I tried to contact the FDNY, downtown hospitals in New York, my sister on Long Island—all busy signals. The airlines were no help; all flights were canceled indefinitely. I could get a ticket, but the people who were already ticketed had priority. I would have to get on an ever-expanding standby list. The people who were stranded in Vegas were doing anything to get home. All rental cars had been reserved within hours of the attack. Train and bus tickets? All sold out. People were buying used cars, even new cars.

Months later it would be reported that the only planes cleared to fly just after 9/11, other than U.S. military, were private jets taking high-ranking Saudis out of the country.

I did get through to Steve Traub's apartment in New York and spoke to Jennifer. She and Amie were there, saw it all, and wanted to get home to Las Vegas in the worst way. They were stranded in Manhattan just as I was stranded in Vegas. It was becoming obvious that the only way to get to New York would be to drive my own truck. And if I did, Jennifer and Amie said, they'd gladly turn it around and drive it back to Vegas.

One number I didn't try was Pat's apartment. I knew he wasn't there. As the 50th replay of the towers being hit was showing on the TV, a message crawled across the bottom of the screen: FAMILIES OF MISSING FIREMEN CAN CALL THIS NUMBER FOR INFORMATION. *Busy. Busy. Busy. Busy. Busy. Busy. Busy. Busy. Busy. Busy. Busy.* Then out of nowhere I remembered the phone number from my old firehouse in Harlem—Engine 37. The last two digits of the phone number were *3* and *7*. Since Pat worked at Ladder 3, I thought if I replaced the *3* and *7* with *0* and *3*, I just might get lucky. It was worth a shot.

"Hello. Ladder Company 3."

Finally!

"Hello, my name is Mike Brown. I'm Patrick Brown's—"

"You're the captain's brother? You're the doctor from Vegas, right?"

"Yes."

"What do you need?"

What do I need? Wow! More than anything I needed information. The fireman on the other end told me that Pat was on duty Tuesday morning, and that he and 11 others from Ladder 3 were still missing. "Don't give up hope," he encouraged. "And please, call back anytime."

THE RELENTLESS NEWS FOOTAGE of the attack was finally getting to me. I needed a break. The dogs sensed distress and would not leave my side. I wearily got up from the couch; Murphy and Blizzard were excited to follow me into the yard. I sat in the fading summer sun while Murphy chomped on her bone and Blizzard chased her ball. I started thinking about last October when Pat was out here. He just called up one day and said, "Hey, Mike—I'm coming out for a visit." This was truly out of nowhere. To get Pat out of Manhattan was almost impossible.

When he arrived in Las Vegas, he seemed different somehow. Pat always had an edge about him, but that week he was at peace. I was the one with the edge. He didn't care for the casinos, didn't drink, didn't care if we went out to eat, nor did he play golf. I was nervous. How were we going to entertain him? Only after he went back to New York did I realize that what he'd assured me was true—he just wanted to hang out with his brother.

Pat, at 5-foot-10, was thinner than I'd ever seen him. Even though I had him by 50 pounds and three inches, he could still kick my ass. Although he was only 13 months older than I was, his hair had turned gray long before mine ever considered it. He had shaved off his mustache years ago; up until that time, people had difficulty telling us apart; we looked strikingly similar. I was in my weight room one day doing my thing: picking up heavy things and putting them back down. As usual, loud music was playing so I wouldn't have to listen to my grunts. With Pink Floyd blasting, Pat came in wearing small running shorts and an FDNY T-shirt. He walked over to the stereo and shut off the music.

"Mike—you ever try yoga?"

"Ummm, no."

He started doing these strange contortions, breathing heavy, breaking out into a sweat. "You should try it. It's a good workout and it's hard as hell to do."

Lifting a barbell, I said, "I believe you."

He then stood on his head and, with short, staccato breaths, said, "Think about it. You should give it a shot."

"No, it just doesn't look like a lot of fun."

What happened to the brother I grew up with? Did something take over his body?

I looked him up and down from his feet to his head. "Hey, Pat—how come you lost so much weight? You're not eating bugs or dirt as part of yoga, are you?"

He grunted at me.

THAT NIGHT, AFTER DINNER, Pat handed me a large manila envelope.

I looked at it blankly and turned it over in my hands. "What's this?"

"It's my will. I want you to take care of it. There's also a letter in there that tells you what I'd like to have done—you know, like, donate my organs and stuff."

"Get the hell out of here. I'll take it, but I'll never open it. You're going to outlive me."

I put it in my safe and locked it. I didn't want to think about it. But I knew in my heart that Pat had always lived in harm's way.

BLIZZARD BROKE THROUGH MY thoughts by dropping her slimy wet tennis ball in my lap. Her eyes were wide open and she was wearing a big dog smile while she impatiently waited for me to throw the ball. What else could I do? I threw the ball to the end of the yard, and in three seconds she'd retrieved it and was back again.

Pat called Blizzard and Murphy the luckiest mutts alive. He dubbed our yard "dog heaven." Janet and I had first spotted them at a shelter, and on some level I think they knew they were on death row. There was a yellow Post-It on Murphy's cage: SAVE ME FROM DEATH TODAY, SCHEDULED TO BE PUT DOWN AT 4 P.M. She'd been found wandering the streets of North Las Vegas a week before. Murphy looked up at us with sad brown eyes. Her time was up, and she knew it.

"How can we leave her here?" I said to Janet. She wrote Murphy's ID number on a piece of paper and we moved on through an endless maze of cages.

Across from Murphy was Blizzard, who was much too thin—her ribs showed through lusterless white fur. But she was a happy dog, jumping up to greet us as we neared her cage. Blizzard's owners had been evicted; they left her to die in a hot, stuffy apartment with no food or outside access. For almost a week, until the landlord finally showed, she had lived on nothing but toilet water. The shelter was required to wait one week to see if her owners would come back to claim her. By some crazy rule, she was scheduled to be put up for adoption the day *after* she was scheduled to be euthanized. What kind of sense did that make? She should have been isolated in another room to wait for her owners, but lack of space and divine intervention put Blizzard in the general population of dogs available for adoption, where we found her. Her owners never came to claim her—thank God— and after the required waiting period, we took her home to join Murphy.

I remembered how my brother-in-law once referred to them: "dead dogs walking." Just then Janet came into the yard as I was picking up the slimy tennis ball from my lap. "Why don't you call Eddie? He'll drive back with you."

Eddie—married to Janet's sister—was the CEO of Flex Plastics Company back in North Jersey. He was in Vegas for a trade show and was now stranded here like everyone else. I'd been planning to call him for dinner.

I picked up the phone. "Listen, Ed, I'm driving back to New York…that's why I'm calling. I figure it'll go like this: sleep tonight, leave in the morning."

Ed was speaking to someone in the background. He came back on the line with a request. Seemed that Bill, the company's vice president, and Darby, head of sales, were also stranded and wanted to join us on our cross-country drive.

"Not a good idea, Ed," I replied. "We'll be driving back in my Tundra. It's a pickup truck with a small bench back seat. It'll be a tough ride with two. Maybe we can do it with three, but four? Impossible."

Later that day I would have offers from other people wanting to make the drive to New York, but I knew that with Eddie, other than breaks for gas and food, there would be no stopping. My plan was to go straight through—more than 2,500 miles—in about 45 hours. Eddie could do it, but he wouldn't leave without his employees. As far as I was concerned, I had no choice. There would be a foursome heading back East in the morning.

THAT EVENING MY GOOD friend Ernie called. He and I had been planning to meet for wings and beer. Ernie was engaged to a beautiful, gentle woman named Lisa, a doctor he worked with in one of the quick-care clinics here in Vegas. They were in the middle of planning their wedding; it was obvious that he was going to ask me, over a platter of wings, to be in his wedding party. But now his concern was about getting me to New York. He offered to take off from work and drive cross-country with me. I thanked him and told him of the plans already made with Eddie. Before I hung up, I promised to call with any news.

Exhausted, I petted the pups, gave Janet a kiss and was heading for bed—when Janet stopped me.

"Mike, I want to go back with you."

I told her she needed to stay here. I needed her to take care of the house and the dogs.

That's not right," she pleaded. "I want to go with you!"

We went back and forth until I pointed at the TV, replaying footage of what used to be the World Trade Center.

"That's where I'm going," I told her. "I need you to stay here."

Chapter 3

THE NEXT MORNING WAS clear and sunny, like almost every other day in Las Vegas. I said my goodbyes to Janet. Her mood was hard to read. Was she was nervous *for* me or annoyed *with* me that she wasn't going? I threw my luggage in the back of my white Toyota Tundra, petted the pups and was on my way. I turned left on Flamingo Road and headed to Treasure Island to pick up Eddie, Bill and Darby.

That morning the Las Vegas Strip was abandoned, evidence that something was desperately wrong. The usual vacationers weren't wandering up and down the sidewalks; the volcano at the Mirage seemed to be erupting for no reason. The mega-resorts, with their individual themes, flashing neon lights, massive hotel towers and open casinos, were ghost towns. Millions of people plan, fantasize and play each year in this adult Disney World; now the thrill was gone. What mattered to everyone was getting home.

I pulled up to the entrance at Treasure Island. Its large pirate ships were abandoned, the entrance to the casino absent of its usual pirate greeters with their hearty, "Aye-aye, Matey, how can I help ya?" But Eddie, Bill and Darby were there with their luggage. The mood was hushed, serious. No one spoke unless there was a very good reason to do so. I gave Eddie a hug, and he introduced us all. Eddie himself was in his mid 50s, someone I'd always known to be strong, both in build and character. Bill was slightly built, glasses, probably in his early 60s. Rounding out the trio was Darby, in her 40s, with shoulder-length black hair. At that point I made one more futile attempt to talk Darby and Bill into waiting for the airports to reopen. The two simply loaded the bed of the truck with their luggage and squeezed into the back seat. Neither one cared to drive, and that was fine with me. Ed and I agreed that we would switch off whenever we stopped to refuel. With my cell phone next to me and the news on the radio, I turned the truck onto I-15 to head north out of Vegas. We were no longer stranded. We were on our way home.

I'd always loved driving my big white truck. It was quiet, sat up high and had a great audio system. I loved the power of its four-wheel-drive off-road racing package—though off-road to me was an unpaved parking lot, and the farthest I'd ever driven it at one time was 60 miles. I called it my Cadillac in the Sky. The beauty of the open road was a pure contrast to the horrific reason we were on it. There was very little traffic, and we were speeding through the desert, a calico landscape of hills and valleys.

Trying to push the most miles out of that first tank of gas ended with us getting off the interstate desperately in search of a gas station. There was a family in a station wagon following us; I guess they were low on fuel too. The road soon turned to dirt; it ended in a small parking lot in front of a small building. The area looked abandoned except for an elderly man—also small—who came out to greet us. It turned out he never missed a day of work. Flash floods, sandstorms, sickness, now even war wouldn't keep him from going to work.

"We have no gas here!" he announced pleasantly. "This is an Indian burial ground! Would you like a tour?"

"No thanks," Eddie answered. "We're in a hurry—but if I pass by here again, you're on. What we do need is gas. Where's the nearest gas station?"

"Well, if you get back on the 15, go south—"

I interrupted. "No sir. We need to go north."

"North, huh? Well…if you go north, you can try stopping in Joseph. I *think* they have a gas station in Joseph…"

The station wagon went south. We took our chances and headed north to Joseph.

JOSEPH, UTAH, IS A flat, dirty, dry town where the only noticeable activity was the dirt being kicked up by our tires. The town did not look friendly, but it did have a gas station. After giving the Tundra its well-deserved drink, we needed to drive to the general store to have ours. As we pulled off the dirt road into the general store's dirt parking lot, more dirt from the tires kicked up. It was tough to decide which was older, the store or the dirt. The general store—the town's only store—had one of those wooden screen doors that would slam shut despite any attempt to close it quietly. We all went inside. Darby got a kick out of reading the elapsed expiration dates on the packages of food. Bill and Eddie had already paid for their water and soda and were back at the truck when I heard the door slam again. Standing in front of me, arms folded and filling the entire door frame, was a six-foot-three resident of Joseph. His teeth had more color than the whole town. And he was obviously trying to look as mean as possible. I waited for Darby to pay for her expired food. She muttered to me, "What's this about? Is he just going to stand there?"

With a surge of adrenaline—and its effect of producing increased muscle—I replied, "Don't worry, Darby. He'll move."

Nothing was going to stop me from getting to New York. We had no time to waste on Mr. Joseph, who needed to prove his existence by demonstrating that he did not appreciate strangers in his town. I planned to walk right through him— and the look on my face conveyed my resolve. The minutes ticked by. Our eyes stayed locked. Suddenly, and for the benefit of both of us, he moved away from the doorway. We quickly walked past him and out to the truck. Eddie and I switched seats and, in a cloud of Utah dust, we were back on the road.

Bill and Darby were now sitting cross-legged, facing each other; Bill was reading a book he'd found tucked under the back seat about a rock-'n'-roll band being abused and taken advantage of by the music industry. The news on the radio became repetitive, full of rumors, hearsay, inaccuracies; we switched to CDs. The cell phone would ring frequently, and instead of it being someone calling to tell us that Pat was O.K., it would be someone asking how or where we were, or if I'd heard any news…

Somewhere between Marc Knopfler, Nanci Griffith and Tom Waits, Darby asked me where Pat and I grew up.

"Queens Village," I told her. Well, not exactly. "Actually, we started out in Hollis, Queens. My father will tell you that the reason we moved from Hollis was that Pat would come home from kindergarten with bruises. One day Pat came home and asked him, 'Daddy, what's a white motherfucker?' So we were off to Queens Village—which, by the way, was not that much better."

"Were you and your brother close?" Bill asked.

"We fought all the time," I said. "But yeah, you know, we were brothers. When I needed my older brother, Pat was always there for me."

Eddie changed lanes to pass a slower vehicle. He wondered if Pat always wanted to be a fireman.

He did—as far back as I can remember. "He used to hang out at the neighborhood firehouse all the time and go to calls," I said. "He and his friend Kevin had a setup at our house. They would listen to the fire radio, and when there was a call, they'd climb down a ladder that was propped up outside Pat's second-floor bedroom window. Then they'd race their bicycles to the fire. Sometimes they'd even beat the fire trucks there."

"How about you?" Darby asked. "Did you want to be a fireman too?"

"Nope, I had no ambitions," I said, laughing. "Pat was the ambitious one. I was the pain-in-the-ass little brother. I used to throw rocks at Pat's bedroom window and run away before he and Kevin could catch me—until one time, when I thought they were up there, I threw a few rocks…and when I turned to run, they were right in front of me. They dragged me into the garage where they had two very unsteady ladders hung up by nails. Pat and his friend spread and tied my arms to the lower ladder and put a rope around my neck and attached it to the upper one. If I moved, the upper ladder would fall and hang me. Don't you just love brothers?"

The cell phone started to ring; I fumbled with the earpiece. "Hello. Hey, Marc, what's up?"

Marc was a pediatric ER doc and a very close friend. He was at work and wanted to keep the ER staff updated on our progress. I knew that he wanted to be in New York too.

"Marc—how many? That's great news! We're in Colorado…"

Marc told me that rescue workers in New York had just found and rescued six firemen. They were starting to pull more out alive from different locations. The latest count was 17. Before I got my hopes up, I needed to confirm the story and, by this time, I knew how. I dialed the number. It rang twice; then I heard a weary voice: "Hello, Ladder 3."

The real story: The six rescued firemen were rescuers themselves. They had been caught in a secondary collapse and had jumped into a nearby fire truck to avoid being crushed to death. No, there had not been 17 firemen pulled alive from the collapse; so far since the 11th, as far as anyone knew, no one had been found alive.

"Don't give up hope," the firefighter encouraged me before he hung up.

Rain! Who thinks about rain? I live in a desert. Unfortunately, we were not in the desert anymore; we were in the mountains of Colorado, with night falling, and Eddie doing about 80 m.p.h. I was leaning my head on a pillow against the passenger-side window when I saw the first drop, then a second large spatter on the windshield, and then the sky opened up. The rain rapidly turned the road into a river, and I was glad we were traveling in a big pickup truck. The magnificent mountains on both sides of us disappeared in the darkness, and the only things visible were the rain, about 50 feet of road, and the lights from other travelers. One more sight that became visible from time to time out the back window: our luggage, floating on a few inches of water in the bed of the truck.

Eddie preferred to listen to the radio when he drove. The news reported that it was also raining heavily in downtown Manhattan. I closed my eyes and imagined what was going on where the World Trade Center towers used to stand. The rain would be turning the site into a dangerous pit of mud and muck, which would make it more difficult for the hundreds of rescue workers to conduct operations. I also imagined the surviving firemen on top of a steaming pile desperately trying to get to their men who were buried underneath. I imagined one fireman slowly raising his face, full of dirt and disbelief, to the sky. He stood in this position for several seconds while the rain washed off the grit, but it could not wash away the reality. Then he went back to work.

The rain in New York could also be a blessing. I hoped it might dampen the deep fires and clean the dust-filled air. But the most important thing about the rainwater was that it could provide sustenance for the people who'd been trapped now for almost three days. The rain needed to make its way down to my brother, who—please, God—just had to be still alive.

I must have dozed off. Suddenly I felt the truck come to an abrupt stop and immediately opened my eyes. Did Eddie fall asleep?

Wide awake and pissed, Eddie said, "For Chrissake, look at this. Why the hell do they have that lane closed? There's no one working!"

Construction workers had closed down one lane for miles—and left it closed. What had been an open road for us just two hours earlier had turned into a Midtown Tunnel–like traffic mess. Eddie was contending with the rain, darkness, fatigue and now stop-and-go traffic. The gas tank was about half full; I thought it was a good time to at least try to sleep. But it seemed that every time sleep would come, the phone would ring and unmercifully steal my one escape from this nightmare.

It was a few hours later when I felt the truck stop again. It was 1 a.m. We were at a gas station just west of the Nebraska state line. The rain had finally stopped; it was my turn to drive. Bladders were emptied, the truck was refueled, and we all bought some crap to eat on the road. Darby and Bill slid into their seats; Eddie and I shut the small back doors, locking them into their little torture chamber. I adjusted the mirrors, started the truck, slid in a

CD, slipped her into gear and headed back to Interstate 80. When we got to the highway, the road was straight, dry and empty. The sky had cleared and a generous moon was illuminating our surroundings. Eddie didn't have to say it. The look on his face said it all: *Don't you dare say a word about how magically the conditions improve when it's your turn to drive.* By the time we passed the WELCOME TO NEBRASKA, DRIVE SAFELY sign, the cruise control was set at 98 m.p.h. and everyone else was asleep.

Eddie opened up one eye. "Hey, Mike, you all right?"

"I'm fine. Go back to sleep and I'll wake you in 400 miles."

Driving was so much easier than trying to sleep. The soft sound of Nanci Griffith's *The Flyer* drifted out of the stereo speakers. I too was flying— flying past the cornfields of Nebraska, flying in my Cadillac in the Sky, flying back home to New York.

WE WERE SOMEWHERE IN Illinois when it happened. Eddie was at the wheel, Bill was reading the rock-'n'-roll book and Darby had just got off her phone with her family; it was early in the morning. The inside of the truck had begun to take on the odor of four non-showered adults on a cross-country trip. I was rolled up into a semi-fetal position facing the passenger window. Lack of sleep or the lack of any positive news was making me very shaky. The phone no longer just rang—it felt as if it had been wired directly into my brain. Electricity would fire into my cerebral cortex each time I received a call. More than anything else, I needed sleep.

The thought that I would soon be giving a eulogy for my brother had entered my mind. I finally fell into a deep, comatose-like sleep and was out for an hour or two. The phone exploded in my frontal lobe and I thought I was having a seizure. Controlling the tremors, I stuck the earpiece in thinking that this might be "the call." It was just someone wanting to know how and where we were. Awake again, I made a call to the FDNY family-information line. The fireman who answered the phone at the other end sounded just as tired as I was. Then, some news—Pat was no longer on the missing list! My heart skipped a beat.

"Can you please check again?" I asked him. "Captain Patrick J. Brown."

Pause. Silence. Then through the earpiece I heard the tired fireman say, "Oh, he's a *captain.* There are so many missing that they split the list into two. I was looking at the firefighters' list. Let me look at the officers' list…Yeah, he's still missing. Hey, listen, I'm real sorry."

He made sure he had my number and promised he'd call if there were any word.

Eddie turned to me and said, "Why don't you shut that damn phone off?"

"I can't," I told him. "It's the only thing that can end this nightmare."

Laying my head back on the pillow, I felt it come on. I didn't want to fall apart in front of Darby or Bill, and had done a good job of not doing so up to this point. There was nothing that was going to stop it now. It started out as a mild ache but quickly built into excruciating pain. I felt like the part of my life that was occupied by my brother was slowly being torn out of my very core. I rolled up in a ball—as much as someone six foot one could—and sobbed uncontrollably until there were no more tears to shed.

The Tundra needed gas. Thank God it was my turn to drive.

THE LAST GREAT TEST was before us: getting through Pennsylvania on Interstate 80. We hit that stretch of road late at night. It was pitch black and, just for kicks, there were obstacles placed all over the highway. Construction detours, quick lane changes, narrowed traffic lanes, single narrowed traffic lanes and traffic barriers that appeared to jump up out of the ground at us with—and some without—red warning lights. Eddie had no problem with the first half of this endless state. We stopped at a gas station and performed what had become our routine; then we loaded back into the Tundra. I turned the key, adjusted the mirrors, turned on the headlights and slid in a CD. But for the first time since leaving my house in Vegas, I suddenly felt it wasn't a good idea for me to drive. I knew if I asked Eddie to drive he would...but it was my shift. A quick look at Eddie told me that Pennsylvania had already beaten the shit out of him.

So I drove while everyone slept. This was a blessing for them. They didn't have to watch me behind the wheel. With my eyes open as wide as I could keep them and my face as close to the windshield as possible, I maneuvered the Tundra through the obstacles. To make it even more interesting, we were sharing this Interstate 80 pinball game with other cars and trucks—big trucks. There would be smooth straightaways to lull you to sleep; and then—out of nowhere—a camouflaged barrier forced you to jerk the wheel toward the shoulder; then another one—maybe with lights, maybe without—sent you swerving back to the regular lane. Throw in a couple of single-lane *S* curves for fun...then back to a smooth, sleepy straightaway. Twice we flew past demolished barriers, flashing red lights scattered along the roadside with the cars that had lost their game of I-80 pinball.

I started to experience hallucinations. The trees were turning into giant chess pieces. I kept driving. Ahead, in a small valley, I saw something that was not an illusion: several emergency vehicles tending to two overturned cars. In front of one car was a body bag. That was it. Enough. That was enough for me. I stopped at the next rest stop though the truck didn't need gas. We were close to Jersey now, and Eddie said he would take over—he knew the roads, he told me. I think he took over because he didn't want to die on that dark Pennsylvania highway.

WHEN WE FINALLY REACHED Eddie's plant in Elizabeth, New Jersey, it was 5 a.m. The weather was cold and damp as we unloaded the soggy luggage. Eddie was attempting to control his emotions as he turned to me. "Whatever you need, call me," he urged. "I don't know when I'll see you again."

"Probably soon," I replied. Eddie knew exactly what I meant.

I gave Darby and Bill a hug. It is amazing how much you learn about people after being stuck in a truck with them for 2,600 miles. Not once did they ever complain about being locked up in my back seat for two days. Not once did they say anything to me about falling apart in Illinois. Bill took the rock-'n'-roll book to finish. I was off.

Dawn was breaking when I made it to the George Washington Bridge. Driving across, I looked south to view the city for the first time. Where the Trade Center towers once stood, there was now billowing black and gray smoke.

It had been 45 hours on the road, with almost no sleep. But my purpose was once again clear. *Pat, I'm coming to find you.*

Chapter 4

I CONTINUED ON THROUGH the South Bronx in my big white truck. Something just wasn't right, not right at all. The crumbling high-rise projects—in the '70s, some city official felt it important to paint flowerpots on the windows so they'd look less vacant—that part of the South Bronx looked the same. The ever-present potholes that aged my truck, the heavy traffic, the narrow lanes—the same. How could everything here seem so normal, when in a neighboring borough just 10 miles south, there existed a massive pile of rubble and broken dreams that had changed the world?

This wasn't my first time on the Cross-Bronx Expressway. When I was a city fireman, I used this route to commute to work. My firehouse was Engine 37, Ladder 40 on 125th Street in Harlem; I cut through the South Bronx to get home from work. It was a pseudo-shortcut. Driving the familiar route brought back memories of my days as a New York City firefighter. My brother had been instrumental in getting me assigned to Engine 37, though at the time

44

I didn't know I wanted to be there. My thought at the time: Who would ever want to drive to Harlem—for work or anything else?

Every firehouse has its own personality; some even have nicknames. Engine 58, Ladder 26 is the Fire Factory; Engine 69, Ladder 28 is the Harlem Hilton. Engine 37, Ladder 40 is Life Begins at Forty.

The day I graduated from the fire academy, Pat was as anxious as I was to find out where I would be assigned. He pulled me aside.

"So what'd you get, Mike?"

"Engine 37."

"Great!"

I wanted to be assigned to a ladder company, but the only openings were in slow firehouses and, according to Pat, what I really wanted a busy engine company. As it turned out, Engine 37 was the busiest house in any of the five boroughs during the time I worked there. Other firehouses may have had more calls, but we had the most fires.

After the graduation ceremonies, Pat and I got into his old green Ford Pinto and drove to Harlem so I could introduce myself to the captain of Engine 37. It was a sobering drive through the neighborhood in northern Manhattan that would soon become my place of employment. My job prior to this one was as an engineer at Grumman Aerospace in Bethpage, Long Island. Harlem in the early '80s was a far cry from middle-class Bethpage and its neat, well-kept rows of single-family homes. Harlem was not a place for the white and unarmed. But Pat was fearless. He thrived in areas like this. "What's the use of being in the fire department if there are no fires?" he would say.

We drove through the littered streets, and I couldn't help noticing the unwelcome looks and bad-ass attitudes directed our way by the denizens of this notorious area of New York City. We finally arrived at an area with massive housing projects on one side of the street and dirty, decaying storefronts on the other. Pat pulled the car in front of a red brick building squeezed between two dilapidated storefronts. I was surprised when he pulled his Pinto onto the sidewalk.

I turned toward Pat nervously. "Why are you stopping?"

With a big grin, he said, "We're here!"

I looked around for a few seconds. "Oh, shit."

ENGINE 37 HAD THREE large garage doors, each with a thick yellow stripe used to guide the big trucks as they backed in. Next to one of these doors was a thick steel pedestrian door with a small window. Pat waited in the Pinto as I got out and walked to the door. On one side of the building I noticed a firehouse parking area: an alleyway guarded by a high steel fence with razor wire on top. There was no doorbell, so I pounded on the door with my fist. A face appeared in the small window and the door opened. A strongly built firefighter with a stern face filled the doorway. "How can I help you?" he inquired.

Still nervous, I replied, "I'm Mike Brown. I was just assigned here and came to introduce myself to the captain."

He looked me up and down for a long minute. "So, you're the new probie? O.K., come in. I'll tell the captain you're here."

The house-watch desk was inside the front of the building on the ground floor, and there was an office next to it. Captain Hartnet was sitting behind his desk with the presence and confidence that comes with being the captain of a hot fire company.

George, the stern-faced firefighter who had opened the door, introduced us.

"Hey, Cap—this is Mike Brown, your new probie. He came to introduce himself."

"To introduce himself?" Hartnet repeated. He appeared puzzled and impressed at the same time. He came out from behind the desk and shook my hand. "I'm Captain Hartnet. Welcome to Harlem."

The man who was to be my boss turned to George and said, "George, why don't you show Mike around?"

The inside of the firehouse smelled like diesel fuel. Engine 37, the hose truck, was at the far left of the firehouse; Ladder 40 occupied the middle of the floor. Ladder 40 was a tiller truck, the kind that has a seat on the back of the ladder for a man to steer the rear wheels. The third bay was empty. Next to the office were two small doors that opened out and protected one of the fire poles that extended up to the second floor. After a quick tour that included the big kitchen and the second-floor sleeping quarters, we returned to the front door. George shook my hand. "See ya in two days," he said.

I slid back into the small passenger seat of the Pinto and didn't feel sad to be driving out of there. As he drove, Pat enumerated the rules of a probationary fireman—in other words, how to act in the firehouse: 1) get to work at least an hour before your tour; 2) be in the kitchen to help prepare the meals; 3) eat fast and get to the sink to wash pots and pans before anyone else; 4) take out the garbage; 5) and most important—whatever you do—keep your mouth shut. Following my brother's wise suggestions worked out very well for me, and I found myself accepted by the best in the companies.

There were also a few rules I had to learn on my own. One of these hard lessons: Probies should not stand on the sidewalk outside the firehouse. Jim, a fireman from 40 Truck, would haul five-gallon buckets of water up to the roof and dump them on anyone standing in front of the firehouse. I was drenched a few times before I finally got the message. Like the time when I was standing outside getting a breath of fresh air, or the time I was taking the garbage out, or the time I was backing the truck into the firehouse after a call. He even got me when I was walking into work. There were days when he wasn't even working but would come in anyway— you'd get hit. You could almost hear the water falling but had no time to get out of the way. There you were, instantly dripping wet.

The brothers at 37/40 soon got tired of changing their clothes several times during a shift and plotted to get back at him.

Jim liked to read on the second floor near the fire pole that had its exit doors on the first floor. It was time for payback. The whole house was in on it. The doors to the pole were locked by sliding a broom through the handles. Then the house was turned out. Over the PA came *Ring! Ring! Ring!* Three bells is the signal for a fire that both the truck and the engine respond to.

The shout went out. "Everybody goes!"

With his adrenaline flowing, Jim ran to the pole and slid down—only to find the door locked from the outside. Confused, trapped now like a rat, he looked up to find eight firemen holding water buckets. He ended up using that excess adrenaline to escape any way he could and finally managed to kick the doors open. For a change, he was on the receiving end of a drenching.

But getting soaked didn't bother Jim as much as his need to get back at us. We knew it would be only a matter of time before he would exact revenge. Three nights later, his opportunity arrived.

It was 3 a.m. and Jim had the late watch. Everyone else was asleep as he turned the key and started up Engine 37. He charged the booster line—the one-inch-diameter hard rubber hose on the side of the truck—then draped it over the ladder truck and scaled the fire pole with the hose. He crept into the pitch-black bunkroom, and with an exuberant *"Woo-HOOO!"* he opened up the nozzle. Being awakened by a fire alarm is expected; being roused from a deep sleep by 80 gallons per minute of dirty water coming from a fire hose is something you never forget.

I miss 37/40.

LOST IN MEMORY, I hadn't realized how far I'd driven. I looked around to see green lawns and the shade cast by the large, lush old trees of the Northeast. And it was quiet. I'd made it to Westbury. I turned into my father's driveway and put my truck to sleep. Sleep was the plan for me too. My younger sister Carolyn and her husband Hector were living in my dad's house; they came out to greet me as I emerged from the driver's seat.

My father was still in a rehab hospital recovering from knee-replacement surgery he'd undergone two weeks prior. During the surgery, the bottom of his thighbone was sawed through, as were the bones beneath his knee. The old worn-out knee was removed, and the surgeon, with hammer and glue, pounded a prosthesis into the space.

Muscle and flesh were sewn back together, and—*presto!*—a new joint. Unfortunately, it wasn't *presto!* for my 83-year-old dad. He would not cooperate with the staff and refused to get out of bed "because of pain," he said. Everyone blamed his behavior on depression and gave him drugs, which made him an easier patient. What none of us knew then was that about a year earlier, during a preoperative workup for a total hip replacement, his chest x-ray had demonstrated a suspicious nodule. Instead of doing a workup for cancer, his doctor cleared him for two major surgeries. Turned out Dad wasn't depressed; he had metastatic lung cancer, and no one—including me—believed him when he said he was in excruciating pain.

Carolyn also looked terrible. Her diabetes, diagnosed when she was in her teens, was now kicking the shit out of her in her thirties. She'd lost a tremendous amount of weight. It seemed to me that the life and spirit were being slowly sucked out of her. And then there was her construction-worker husband, Hector, with his arm in a sling from a shoulder injury; he had fallen on his back at a job site.

When I stepped out of my truck on that meteorologically perfect September morning, surrounded by green, blissful stillness, I proudly became the head of my shrinking family.

In any crisis, you need to prioritize. Right now, more than anything, my priorities were shower and sleep.

Chapter 5

CAROLYN WAS GLAD I was back in New York. Her phone had also been constantly ringing. Friends and family wanted to help in any way they could; they wanted updates about Pat and the rescue effort. She had compiled a list of people who wanted to speak with me. I copied the names and numbers into a small spiral notebook and went upstairs with my wet luggage to find sleep.

My father's house seemed much smaller with the passage of time. A farmhouse more than 100 years old, its main support in the basement is a tree trunk. The upstairs bathroom is tiny, but at that moment it didn't matter to me how small it was. To me it was as grand as any in a luxury hotel. It had a shower, and I needed to wash two days of road and stink off me.

I went into my old bedroom, blacked out the morning sun that was streaming through the windows and collapsed into bed. I fell into a comatose-like sleep only to be jarred awake by vivid dreams that I was still driving and falling asleep behind the wheel. I was in this in-and-out state of sleep, not knowing the difference between dreams and reality, when I thought I heard the door to the bedroom open. The sound was followed by rapid breathing that increased in intensity and proximity. I forced my eyes open. There I was, nose to nose with a big black Rottweiler. He gave a low-pitched growl as he stared me down. I must have been in his bed.

"Brooklyn, Brooklyn, good dog," I whispered. "Don't bite my face off, Brooklyn." The sound of his name calmed him down, and soon he was in his bed lying next to me.

While petting Brooklyn behind his ears, I looked around at my old bedroom. This was where I studied, played music, sneaked in a girl or two and watched the world mature—or should I say, watched *my* world mature. There were so many unconnected memories scattering my thought processes; I think it must have had something to do with the real possibility of never seeing my brother again.

Whatever Pat did, good or bad, it was always with uncompromised intensity. If he had a goal, nothing—not even the distinct possibility of self-destruction—would stop him. Growing up in Queens Village got us both into a moderate amount of trouble, so my father moved us out to Westbury. I loved Westbury. I went back to high school after taking a year off, took up the guitar and eventually joined the Westbury Volunteer Fire Department. Pat hated Westbury. He refused to go back to school and eventually joined the Marines to go to Vietnam.

My father, a former Marine lieutenant, had to sign for him to get into the service because Pat was only 17 years old. The recruiter told them that since Pat was underage, he would have to enlist for a minimum of three years. So off he went Parris Island. After Marine boot camp and basic training, Pat came home even more intense than when he'd left. He was a fighting machine, a Marine, ready and willing to face the ultimate challenge and the ultimate sacrifice: kill or be killed. He was prepared to do anything for his country. Patrick John Brown was ready for 'Nam. So what did the Marines do with this physically and psychologically prepared patriot? They make him a clerk. He had scored too high on his aptitude test to be sent to the jungle.

So what did Pat do? He went nuts. He would come home on leave and refuse to go back to his desk job. He also drank with such intensity that trying to get him back to his base became a scary, sometimes impossible feat. When he found out that the recruiter had lied to him and that he could have enlisted for only two years rather than three, he went AWOL and returned to Long Island with plans to hunt down and kill that recruiter. Thank God Pat never found him. There were times when I tried to drive him back to the airport after his leave and he'd jump out of the moving car. This was not a good time in our lives. No one could control him, and it was all I could do to steer him away from harm, hoping he wouldn't get hurt—or hurt someone else.

Then out of nowhere he changed his focus of energy and started to use his skills as a clerk to write letters. He wrote letters to the Commandant of the Marines, to the Secretary of the Navy, to the Secretary of State, even to President Nixon. His orders finally came down. Everyone in Vietnam was trying to get the hell out, and it took almost a year for Pat to get in. Military intelligence! He was first sent to Guam for deployment, and while there he became a model Marine. Assigned to an engineering battalion, Pat ended up teaching the classes and was promoted to sergeant. His commander wrote that he was intelligent, cared for his men and was a natural leader. *A natural leader?* Initially, it made as much sense as the Marines making him a clerk. I don't know how many times I had to get him out of a bar and onto a plane so he wouldn't land in jail. I guess he needed the challenge of war to step up to the responsibility of leadership.

As a Marine in Vietnam, he was a fiercely dedicated warrior. We saw this in the middle of his first tour when he was given emergency leave to return to Long Island. My mom was in the hospital dying from metastatic breast cancer. They let him come say goodbye. It was so good to see Pat home, in one piece— or so we thought. His mind was still in Vietnam. If you made any noise around him while he slept, it would jolt him upright, wide awake, ready to kill. I didn't know what the hell was going on over there, but I was in no hurry to take my turn playing that draft lottery.

Pat rarely spoke of the war, but he was haunted by his memories of Vietnam. It showed in his eyes. He told me about one time when he was out on patrol with his men and they were getting heavy fire from one of the huts in a village. Pat ordered the others to wait; he crawled up to the hut and opened up with his M-16 on automatic. When he was done, there were no more bullets coming from that hut— there was only a dead family.

Another time he was on patrol in the jungle, three days of unbroken vigilance, surviving on a few cans of shit food. Out of nowhere he and his men came upon an Army helicopter base. They headed straight for the mess building and were just about to walk in when they were stopped by two clean and well-rested MPs.

"Where the hell do you think *you're* going?" one of them demanded.

Pat grabbed him by the throat. "Get the fuck out of my way," he muttered.

The other MP drew his 9mm and put it to Pat's head. This was followed by Pat's men aiming their M-16s at the MPs. An Army officer ran over. "Put down those weapons! Now!" he screamed. "If you Marines want to eat here, go wash that shit off you. If not, go eat in the jungle!"

Having no other choice, they showered and returned for a meal of nasty looks and nastier food. But it was better than eating shit from a can.

I know from experience that you never want to piss off my brother. He would hold it in until he got his revenge. Before leaving the mess, he unlocked one of the windows. That night when he and his men were in their sleeping bags near the helicopters, Pat sneaked away, crawled up to the mess building and climbed through the open window. As an engineer, one of his jobs was to blow things up. When he finished what he went in there to do, he crawled out the window and back to his men.

One of them saw him coming. "Hey, Sarge— what the hell are you up to?"

Pat grinned.

The Marine said, "Ohhhh, fuck."

What immediately followed was an earsplitting explosion—along with the annihilation of the mess building. The soldiers on the Army base thought they were under attack. They were panicking, running into one another, yelling, shooting into the night. Pat told me that he and his men laughed so hard they couldn't breathe.

Chapter 6

I CAUGHT MYSELF SCRATCHING Brooklyn and daydreaming. Shit, time for me to get moving. My first priority now was to visit my father at the rehabilitation hospital. Carolyn made me a strong cup of coffee and we discussed how we would deal with the unfolding horror. Carolyn would take care of my father and his house; Janet was in Vegas taking care of the dogs and our house; I would handle everything else.

Traffic was light that afternoon, and I soon pulled up in front of the cold brick building that housed the rehabilitation unit where my father was a patient. There was something a little strange and unfamiliar going on. It took some time for me to figure it out: people were actually being nice to one another. In the lobby, as I signed in, a woman pleasantly gave me the location of my father's room on the third floor; I walked into the elevator thinking that maybe this wasn't such a bad place after all. I shared the elevator with several other people, all very courteous.

Then I reached the third floor. Before the elevator doors were fully open, I knew why my father was depressed. His floor had little to do with rehabilitation and a lot to do with palliative care. It was full of people unlucky enough to be alive, and my father saw his future in these people. There were TVs everywhere—all broadcasting images of the World Trade Center attack. A kitchen table was set up across the hallway from the nurse's station, and around it sat the end results of a variety of disease processes. These once proud, strong and productive human beings were now imprisoned in decaying bodies. Their only crime—possession of a strong heart. These unfortunate souls were not able to feed themselves. They wore diapers, and they appeared demented from an organic process or by choice.

There is no rehab here. This is God's waiting room.

Those TVs were blasting, and the staff, patients and visitors watched the collapse of the towers no matter how many times it was shown. Each replay was like an ambush of ice balls to the head.

Then I saw him. In a corner room by himself, trapped in a hospital bed with his own TV blasting, was my father—John P. Brown, retired special agent of the FBI, professional baseball player in the New York Yankees organization, retired president of the Thoroughbred Racing Association, retired investigator for the Nassau County court system, New York State senior racquetball champion. He was motionless, staring at the TV with dull, flat, hopeless eyes.

"Hey, Dad," I called.

I heard an uncharacteristically frail voice come from him.

"Mike...*Mike.*" His face came back to life as if someone had plugged him back into a wall socket. While I hugged him, he continued. "Mike, I'm so happy to see you. How'd you get here?"

"I drove."

His mental status waxed and waned as he struggled to pull himself out of a drug-induced fog. During our conversation he kept bringing up the subject of his will. It seemed to be of less importance than the other concerns that day, but now I realize that he knew he was dying. On the TV, the South Tower collapsed. Again. With a look of horror he cried, "Pat was in there!"

I stood up and pointed to the North Tower. "No, Dad—he was in this one."

He leaned back with a look on his face as though he were watching it for the first time and, because of the drug- and depression-induced dementia, he was. What torture it must have been to watch for the first time, over and over again, your firstborn being killed.

He was relieved when I told him that I would take care of everything, and that the only thing he had to do was get himself out of this rehab hospital.

"No, Mike, I can't. It hurts too much."

Making eye contact directly with his soul, I said, "Dad, you need to get out of here. You understand what's going on?"

Nodding his head, he said, "Yes, I do."

He leaned back on his pillow, eyes on the TV as the North Tower fell once more. In a weak, dying voice he cried out softly, *"Pat!"*

SOON I WAS BACK in the truck, back on the road. I mentally added another priority to my list: get my father out of God's waiting room. Carolyn could not do this on her own. I called my cousin Don Brown and his wife Kathy and asked for their help. Don is about 20 years older than I am, and he—like his father before him—was a cop; he'd been a narcotives detective in Harlem just before he retired many years ago. He had opened a bar/restaurant in the city and kept in touch with Pat all these years. After September 11, Don was one of the first to contact me, asking if I needed help. When I called him and Kathy about my father, they knew exactly what I meant when I told them, "I think we may need to bust his balls a little."

THERE WAS A REPORT on the radio that they'd arrested two men trying to loot buildings around the

World Trade Center, and the National Guard was sent in to isolate the area. I knew that I was still going to get in there somehow, but now it would be more difficult. I knew that the Westbury vollies had been going down to help at the Trade Center, so I pulled into the parking lot of the Westbury Volunteer Fire Department. I'd heard that on the 11th, the Long Island Expressway was closed to all but emergency vehicles. As far as the eye could see, volunteer rescue and fire trucks raced down the L.I.E., heading to the city. It was as if the site were some celestial black hole attracting energy to counteract its negative properties. The site was the center of evil. It was attracting good people from all over the world to neutralize it.

I walked into the firehouse to find Steve, a friend, on duty. We exchanged greetings and began talking about what had happened.

"Yeah, Doc, we took the heavy rescue truck in. First they had us standby at a firehouse in Brooklyn; then they called us in." With a wry smile he continued, "When we pulled up, Rescue 2 ran over and took all our heavy rescue equipment and disappeared into the pile."

Another good friend, Doug Ingram, entered the room and was surprised to see me. "Brownie, how the hell did you get here?!" He gave me a bear hug and informed me that they were sending a truck into the city in a few hours—but that it would be stationed in Queens.

"I guess I'll have to find another way in," I told them.

"I don't know, Doc," Steve said. "They've closed down all access and don't want anyone but the city guys anywhere near that site."

I left my truck parked at the firehouse, grabbed my backpack—inside was the Harlem Hilton sweatshirt that Pat had given me—and walked three blocks to the Long Island Railroad station. I made more phone calls from the train. There was no new information, just more rumors. I called 3 Truck to ask if I could stop by.

"Ladder Company 3, John speaking."

"John, this is Mike Brown…"

"Yeah, Mike, what can I do for you?"

"Well, I'm coming into the city. Do you mind if I stop by?"

John sounded surprised. "Sure, Mike, anytime. Where are you?"

"I'm on the Long Island Railroad."

John gave me the cross streets where the firehouse was located. When I hung up, I immediately forgot what he'd just said.

The conductor walked by to punch my ticket, saw my final destination and said, "Stay on this train straight through to Penn Station."

"Thank you."

I'd always hated driving to Midtown and often took the train. It gave a person time to think.

I WAS CAUGHT UP in my memories again. After Pat was discharged from the Marines, he took up boxing and talked me into doing the same. I would take the railroad in and meet him at Gleason's Boxing Gym on West 30th Street—walking distance from Penn Station. We would beat the crap out of each other for an hour and then share half a gallon of orange juice. I never imagined how important that time together would turn out to be.

Pat was working for the Fire Patrol. The Fire Patrol was a salvage operation financed by insurance companies; it wasn't part of the New York City Fire Department. The men of the Fire Patrol would go into a flaming building and protect the contents from water damage. It was close to being a fireman—but not quite. For my brother, it was like being a guard at a harem.

Pat had taken the New York Fire Department test as soon as he was old enough, just before going to Vietnam. But the department proved as smart as the Marines and didn't hire him right away. He got a number on the hiring list. When he returned from Southeast Asia, he was informed that since he did not contact the department when his number had been called, he'd been passed up. It seems that being at war in a country halfway around the world was no excuse for not contacting the department. Pat was furious. To plead his case, he hired a lawyer—who did nothing but pocket his money. Pat ended up taking the test again and getting hired, but before that happened he took out his frustration in two ways: by consuming large amounts of alcohol, and by beating up anyone who was dumb enough to get into the ring with him. Like me.

I suddenly remembered the time when Pat asked me to drive him to get his car because it had been towed. To this day, I still don't understand why he didn't take a cab to pick it up; but looking back, I'm glad he made me come into the city. I drove my father's car from Westbury to Midtown—always such a relaxing drive for this Long Island boy. It was a gray day full of rain and traffic, and I had trouble finding the address he'd given me. As I pulled up in front of the brownstone, Pat came running out. The clothes he'd worn the night before were getting wet with the rain, and he was pissed off as hell.

"You believe this shit?"

"Huh?"

"Do you believe this?!"

"Pat, what happened?"

"They towed my fucking car, that's what happened. I pick up this broad and I take her back to her place. I was going to screw her, then leave."

"So what happened?"

"I closed my eyes only for a few minutes, and when I opened them it was daytime—and my car was gone."

As I pulled away from the curb, I said, "You know, Pat, you should have let me come up to check her out."

"Mike," he said with a smile, "she wasn't that good-looking."

The rain had let up a bit; Pat told me to make a right on Seventh Avenue. We were waiting at a light to make the turn when Pat noticed something.

"Hey, Mike—look at that."

"What?"

He pointed down the street. *"That.* You see that guy?"

About a block away and walking toward us was a tall man wearing a long black coat and hat. He was smoking a pipe and pretending to be reading a book. When someone would walk near him, he would body-check him—or her—with his shoulder.

"You see that, Mike?"

The light turned green and I turned right onto Seventh Avenue just in time to see this guy knock the groceries out of an elderly woman's arms.

"Stop the car!" Pat yelled.

"I can't—we're in traffic."

"STOP THE FUCKING CAR!"

I stopped the fucking car. A cab behind us laid on his horn. Well, that was until Pat got out and shot him a look from hell. The cab cut into the other lane and was on his way, but not before cursing at me in a foreign language. Pat grabbed a folding umbrella from the back seat, then ran to the sidewalk to confront the pipe smoker.

"Hey, motherfucker—you wanna hit me?" He started hitting the guy in the ass with the umbrella. "Come on, motherfucker!"

The guy tried to pretend that Pat was not screaming at him and hitting him in the ass with a folding umbrella. He pretended to read his book as he picked up his pace.

Now the situation was getting even stranger. Normally uncaring New Yorkers started to form a small crowd and began cheering Pat on.

"Don't let him get away!" someone yelled.

"Beat the shit out of him!" yelled another.

I was still watching this as I stood next to my father's car in the middle of Seventh Avenue when the pipe smoker turned toward Pat. *Oh, shit.* Pat grabbed the much taller man and threw him into a storefront window. Thank God it didn't shatter, but the guy fell to the ground like a bag of tools. Pat, still yelling, stood over him wielding the umbrella. The pipe smoker rolled to his knees and slowly crawled away from Pat. He got to his feet, started walking, then broke into a run down the avenue.

Chapter 7

"PENN STATION, LAST STOP," crackled a barely coherent voice from the train's PA system. The announcement jarred me back to reality. A few seconds later, the train screeched to a stop.

New York City. Wow, I made it.

Penn Station was the same as it had always been: same stores, same dirt, same rushing people, same noise. An announcement for a last call for a train going to Huntington on Track 19 brought a rush of people running toward that track. Things felt normal, things seemed kind of O.K. Then I walked up the long stairway leading out from under Madison Square Garden to the street, and the smell hit me. It hit me like a sharp left jab to the nose from my brother. Even though no one had smelled anything quite like it before, we all knew exactly what it was. It was the smell of concrete, smoke, asbestos, dust and the dead. It was the smell of broken hearts. It was the smell coming from the Trade Center, and it was everywhere.

The streets had less traffic and the crowds were thinner, but there was another big difference, and you had to be from New York to notice. Just as on Long Island, people were being kind to one another. They were actually concerned about strangers. No horns, no yelling, no in-your-face "I'm gonna get the better of you" attitude.

This was very strange.

I grabbed a cab outside the Garden, shut the door, and the cab driver pulled away from the curb.

"Where to?"

Shit! I forgot the address of Ladder 3.

I knew it was on 13th or 14th Street, but still wasn't even sure I should go there, so I told him, "14th Street and Fourth Avenue."

I was very hesitant about going to the firehouse. I felt as though I were intruding, and they had enough to worry about without me showing up. So when the cab made it to 14th Street and Seventh Avenue, I told the driver to let me out.

Here I was with no plan, but at least I was in New York City. There must be a way for me to get into the site. Instinctively, I looked to the sky for my bearings and felt a little silly to be reminded that the landmark I'd always used was no longer there, only a big hole in the sky. I turned south toward downtown and started to walk. I walked and walked. At one point I turned around and saw the Empire State Building over my shoulder, so I knew I was going in the right direction. Both the police activity and the pungent smell of broken hearts were more pronounced now, so I had to be getting closer.

Suddenly, there it was—Houston Street, a major east-west thoroughfare. And now a police blockade. There were hundreds of cops stopping any access to SoHo. I knew I was getting nearer to where my brother was, but there were barriers at every corner. First I attempted the direct approach and walked up to three police officers, as if I expected them to move the barriers for me.

Displaying my ID, I said politely, "Excuse me, officers, I'm an emergency medicine physician and I'm here to help. You need to let me through."

That didn't work at all, so I moved on to the next corner.

"Officer, my brother is among the missing. He's a captain in the fire department, so please let me pass. I drove all the way from Las Vegas. You have to let me try to find him."

"Sorry, there are plenty of rescue workers there already. If anybody can find your brother, it would be one of them. Besides, it's too dangerous."

One last plea. "I was a fireman for many years—believe me, I'm not going to get hurt."

The cop was now impatient. "I'm very sorry about your brother, but there's no way you're going any farther."

I thanked him for his time and headed west on Houston. I walked into a few little shops hoping that there might be a back door to exit behind the barricades. No luck. Then I noticed that the barricades on one of the corners did not fully extend to the next building. Feeling like a criminal staking out the area, I slowly moved next to the opening, waited for the perfect time, and started to slither through. Only then did I notice a few police officers heading my way, walking quickly, so I retreated in the other direction and headed toward Chinatown. With my heart pounding a little faster than I'd like to admit, I turned and started to walk back uptown.

Most of Manhattan is laid out on a grid, with avenues and streets running perpendicular. But downtown—especially in Greenwich Village—the streets have names, not numbers, and they all run into one another like a plate of Little Italy spaghetti. I wandered and wondered. More and more thoughts started racing through my head, and now I wasn't even certain if my brother's firehouse was even on 13th or 14th Street. A large brick building with papers taped up on its walls was several yards in front of me. It turned out to be St. Vincent's Hospital, and the papers were 8-by-11 printouts bearing the face of someone missing from the towers. Each piece of paper had the person's name printed, along with words like PLEASE FIND OUR DADDY. HE WAS LAST SEEN ON THE 93RD FLOOR OF THE NORTH TOWER. I was lost—but so was everyone else.

The Empire State Building appeared in the distance between two buildings; I headed toward it and came up to a firehouse. Engine 24, Ladder 5 had several firemen standing out front, so I approached a thin man wearing an FDNY shirt.

"Excuse me." He looked at me as if he might know me. "Excuse me, can you tell me where Ladder 3 is located?"

"No, I don't know where it is." He yelled to another man in a FDNY shirt.

"Hey, Sam—you know where 3 Truck is?"

"No, I don't."

I thanked them, continued north, and thought. *Shit, I must really be lost.*

I found my way up to 13th Street and headed east. Right after crossing Fifth Avenue, I was stopped by a typical New York female—tall and thin with pleasing facial features; long, straight hair; wearing the appropriate fashion of the day, complete with stiletto heels; in a major hurry; and with an attitude that says she is doing *you* a favor by stopping you to ask her question. Yup, a New York City girl, all right.

"Which way is Broadway!" she ordered.

"Well, this is Fifth Avenue, and Broadway is west of Seventh…" I answered.

She scowled in disgust. "No it's not!"

I knew that I was lost, but I was sure that Broadway was west of Seventh. Not completely convinced one way or the other, she strode off to the west in her painful shoes and I continued east. The next block I hit was Broadway. *Oh, shit. Broadway runs on a diagonal. Up in Harlem, Broadway is west of Seventh. Maybe I better try 14th Street before she comes back this way.*

It was getting chilly and the sun was setting when I made a right on 14th and into Union Square, a small park with a monument, a dog run and lots of benches. On that day, it was also full of lost people like me. The problem was that we were all lost—not in physical location but in time and space. A few moments of pure evil, and our foundation for reality was gone. There were candles and pictures spread throughout the park and no one was saying much except for a small group of people at one corner. They were protesting the President and advocating "a peaceful response" to the attack. *A peaceful response? What were they, fucking nuts?!* I bet to myself that none of their family members were missing. I wondered why no one was kicking the shit out of these assholes. I wondered if *I* should kick the shit out of these assholes. Then I realized that they all looked kind of foolish and irrelevant. No one was paying attention to them anyway.

Walking through the park of the lost, I could easily tell the difference between the people who didn't have a loved one missing from those who did. Everyone was sad as shit, but the ones who were missing friends and family had glassy red eyes, silent tears or telltale tracks on their cheeks where the tears had dried after mixing with city dirt. It was obvious that no one had been able to sleep or eat, nor did they care to do either. The one thing that made *me* different, I told myself, was that I had a mission. What suddenly worried me was that all these people probably started off with similar missions—and failed.

I continued to follow the rules of Brownian motion. I found myself heading back across 14th Street and passed an all but abandoned Virgin Record Superstore. Music was just another casualty; it had lost all importance. I headed south on Fourth, and at the corner of 13th Street, my search was over. Across the street was a small, two-story red brick building with two large American flags out front. The huge garage door was open and revealed the front of an older replacement hook-and-ladder fire truck. On the front of the grille was a large *3* that someone had fashioned out of white duct tape. There were firemen and civilians standing out front, and on both sides of the open door were numerous cards, posters, candles and flowers. To the right of the door, almost completely hidden by flowers, was what looked like a wooden bench. A passing young woman knelt down in front of the bench and relit one of the candles. She then gave each fireman a loving hug and continued on her way. As I worried about what to say when I got up to the group, I took a deep breath and crossed the street to the firehouse.

Chapter 8

FIREMEN ARE THE ARCHETYPAL strong, silent American males. They don't like to let outsiders know what they're really thinking. They're suspicious of strangers and open up only to close friends, family and other firemen who, over time, also come to be considered family. But that's a generalization. On an individual basis, I've known my share of firemen who were as safe as a pet crocodile—but even they would stop at nothing to drag you out of a fire.

So here I was, the last thing they needed, the civilian brother of their captain. There was a high probability that they'd lost 12 of the 25 men from their firehouse—12 of their brothers, 12 of their closest confidants. They cooked together, ate and slept in the same firehouse, played with one another's kids, helped each other move, fought the same fires, fought each other, froze together in the winter, went into burning buildings in the heat of summer, celebrated when they saved a victim and grieved with each lifeless body they recovered.

They drank at each other's weddings, drank after each other's divorces. And now, here I was.

The firemen standing in front of the firehouse were wearing work uniforms—dark blue T-shirts with a Maltese cross on the front and LADDER 3 over the top of it. The house nickname RECON was printed under the cross. As I walked up to them, I was greeted with that typical, guarded "What the fuck do *you* want?" fireman look. But before I could even speak, they saw the family resemblance and reached out their hands.

"Oh, shit—you're the captain's brother!"

"You're the doctor from Vegas? How'd you get here?"

All of them asked: "What do you need?"

I was offered everything from a place to stay in their homes to the use of their cars. Ladder 3 was a senior house, which meant that the average member had more than 15 years on the job. There was Tim Brady, who was hired the same year that I was. He had a large mustache and a broken heart from giving up hope. John Gates, about six foot three with a warm, friendly smile, was still holding on to the belief that someone would be found alive. Brendan Guillen, who was named after the Irish saint and traveler, possessed a unique accent: equal parts Irish brogue and New York street. He also had a quick Irish wit and an Irish temper. Brendan may have been transferred to Pat's company for, let's say, violent outbursts. But he was quick to remind me that he wasn't the only one at 3 Truck to act on impulse.

"You know, Mike, I was supposed to be the problem, but your brother was something," Brendan recalled. "One day we were going to a call and a truck was blocking us. Refuses to move out of the way. Cap runs up to the truck, and the guy tells him to go fuck himself. So he pulls this guy out of the truck and starts to beat the shit out of him, and it was *me* who had to stop him from killing the guy."

I met Jim Wind, a big man with a drooping mustache, barrel chest and a deep, thoughtful voice, never one to waste words. He in turn introduced me to Bobby Burke, "a good friend of your brother's."

Shaking my hand, Bobby said, "Mike, I'm your brother's best friend, and I'm here if you need anything."

Bobby, tall and thin with tight, muscular arms, was the only one in the group who was not wearing an FDNY T-shirt. His voice sounded so familiar, but I couldn't place it. Then a firehouse public-address page scored a direct hit to my central nervous system.

"Captain Brown."

For a brief moment, the randomness of my thought processes tangled with my space/time journey and mixed with irrational hope—for that very brief moment. The impossibility of the World Trade Center being attacked by two hijacked airliners was, in fact, impossible. My brother was just about to walk down the stairs and greet me with, "Hey, Mike, you didn't have to drive all the way from Vegas. I'm fine. See?"

"Captain Brown, you have a visitor up front." Again, another shot.

Dan Browne was the covering captain for Ladder 3. He'd been transferred there indefinitely until Pat was found and could return to work. Dan possessed some of the same qualities as my brother: he was quiet, he was intelligent, and he was fully aware of the volatile situation he'd been thrown into. He had many years on the job in the FDNY. Like everyone else, he had close friends now buried under the rubble of the Trade Center. But he couldn't fall prey to the roller coaster of despair followed by good news and then the crush of any hope over and over and over again. Dan Browne had a firehouse to run. When he saw me take that central nervous system hit as his name was announced, he quickly realized that I was not the only one reacting that way. From that point on, he told everyone to refer to him as Captain Dan.

He invited me to the kitchen in the rear of the building. "Where we can talk," he said.

We walked the length of the floor and into a small kitchen. Bobby silently followed. There were several men around the long, wide wooden table; I was introduced to them all and shook many hands.

They offered me a seat. Each one knew Pat, and respect they had for him was obvious.

A battalion chief, Richie Burban, told me, "Your brother and I did not see eye to eye, but we respected each other. He is one of the best firefighters I ever met."

Jim Ellson, a retired captain, worked with Pat at Manhattan's elite Rescue 1; they were close friends for more than 20 years. He was sitting at the table with a dirty fire coat draped over his knees.

"This is your brother's," he said. "It was found in the rubble this morning." Amazingly it was Jim's son, also a firefighter, who had come across it.

Reasons that the turnout coat had been found by itself were discussed. Some wondered if Pat had taken it off to be able to run up more flights of stairs, or maybe he'd given it to a victim, or it was an old spare coat that someone else had grabbed when rushing to the site. "The site" was what the World Trade Center was being called. None of the firemen were using the media's Ground Zero cliché. It was the site that had stolen a piece of the soul from every man in that kitchen, the site that had turned their eyes red and the air they were breathing into fire, the site that was keeping them up at night with the ceaseless, haunting question, *Why was I chosen to be on top of the pile and not under it?*

Bobby seemed to know a few of the firemen, and I just assumed that he'd been hanging out when

I came along. Dan took a seat across the table and handed me a cup of coffee. He spoke about the possibility of voids—spaces around which the buildings collapsed, leaving pockets of survival. As I'd suspected back in Vegas, Pat and the other members of Ladder 3 were operating in the North Tower. Currently the area of the North Tower was quite unstable: the last crew down there was almost buried alive when a wall collapsed on them. Those six firefighters jumped into a fire truck just as the debris fell and had to be dug out. This was the report that I'd received on the road from Marc— that they were finding a multitude of firemen alive.

"It's just too dangerous," Dan said. "We're waiting for a large crane they're bringing in before we can go back."

It was easy to figure out what Captain Dan was really saying in his calm, businesslike voice. *We have lost too many, and we are not going to jeopardize anyone else.*

Examining the turnout coat, Jim Ellson commented to me, "If there's anyone who could walk out of that place alive, it would be your brother Paddy." Several other firemen agreed.

Dan leaned across the table toward me.

"Your brother's locker is upstairs at the end of the room. The keys to his apartment and his car are in it. There's no rush, Mike. Take all the time you need to look at what else is in there."

All the time I need? That's my brother's stuff. I'm not going anywhere near his locker. He'll kick my ass.

Dan leaned in closer and asked, in that calm, steady voice, "Mike, what do you need?"

"I need to go to the site."

And without hesitation, with total understanding, Dan leaned back and said, "O.K."

Chapter 9

WE WAITED AS NIGHT descended over lower Manhattan. Voids, rumors and devastated families were the main topics of conversation. Dan came out to the front of the firehouse and gave Bobby and me an update.

"The crew down there now has been digging out a fire truck and doesn't want to leave just yet. We figure as the building came down, the men may have sought refuge in their rig."

He asked us if we wanted to eat. Eat? My stomach was so knotted up, there was no room for food. The last time I had anything solid to eat was somewhere in Pennsylvania. Bobby said he didn't want to eat either. I glanced over at him. Who is this guy? He'd been at 3 Truck for several hours. Doesn't he have a home? My situation was obvious—I had no place else to go. And why did I feel as if I knew him? One thing was sure: He knew my brother very well.

It was evident that John didn't have a problem with his appetite. He was gnawing on a fried chicken leg, hanging out with Brendan at the other end of the large front doorway. They came over to us.

"Mike," he said, waving his chicken leg at me, "sure you don't want anything to eat?"

"No, John, I'm fine," was my answer, but I was so far from fine. The delay in going down to the site was starting to worry me because the longer the wait, the greater the chance of being denied entrance. At any time, Dan could reconsider and tell me that it was too dangerous, or that he didn't want the added responsibility, or a battalion chief could show up and tell me the same.

"You sure, Mike?" John brought me back to our conversation. "I'll go get you a plate."

"No, but thanks." The words came from my twisted gut.

"Yeah, Mike, you better eat," Bobby urged.

I didn't need to eat. I needed to find my brother so I could go home. Then I would eat. I noted Bobby's concern that I hadn't had any dinner—but he hadn't either. The firehouse phone rang. A fireman from the house-watch desk yelled, "Barnyard, outside phone!" John put down the chicken leg and went to pick up the phone.

"Barnyard?" Bobby asked. "Because he eats so much?"

"No," Tim Brady said, "because his snores sound like animals."

Brendan added, "If you don't get to sleep before he does, you're up all night."

The firehouse phone rang again. A fireman named Dennis came over. "Mike, there's a John Presten on the phone for you. He says he's your cousin."

"My cousin? I don't even know a John Presten."

Dennis spoke into the receiver for a minute then turned back to me. "He says he's a fire captain from Los Angeles."

"You sure he wants *me?*"

Dennis patiently listened to the voice on the other end of the line once more, then turned back to me.

"He says you know him as Jay—Jay Mooney."

I did have a cousin Jay Mooney, but hadn't had any contact with him for about 40 years. When Pat and I were very young, Jay was like another brother. He and his family moved to California when he was 7 or so, and we never heard from him again. A few years ago I thought about tracking him down but never followed through. Now here he was on Ladder 3's phone, and quickly brought me up to date. Jay was now a captain in the Glendale Fire Department and, much like me, played softball and brought the beer supply to the game. He promised he'd come to New York very soon.

I hung up the receiver and went to stand by myself outside, in front of what was known as the captain's bench. When Pat was assigned to Ladder 3, he made some home improvements to the firehouse. Brendan told me that one day he and Pat were standing outside the firehouse when Pat turned to him and said, "What this house needs is a bench." Brendan's initial reaction: *Why the hell do we need a bench?* "Get the men," Pat told him. "We're going out." They all piled into the ladder truck, and it wasn't long before they found the perfect bench to set outside the firehouse. (Where they found it is a carefully guarded secret to this day.) It was hoisted up on the fire truck and, with hopes there wouldn't be a call, they drove back to 3 Truck through the streets of downtown Manhattan. In any other city, pedestrians would have taken note of a huge fire truck rolling through the city streets with a long wooden bench precariously perched on top, but not in New York. No one could care less that an FDNY truck was transporting a wooden bench through Greenwich Village—that's just how things are in New York. When they got back to the firehouse, they placed the bench exactly where it remains today, and firefighters and pedestrians alike have a place to sit and reflect outside 3 Truck's house.

Just across 13th Street is a coed dorm for NYU. The girls had posters in their windows that said things like THANK YOU FIREMEN, YOU ARE THE BEST! and WE LOVE YOU, FIREMEN! I was looking up and reading the posters. I was not looking at the college girls behind the posters—I was reading the posters, I swear. Then Brendan came over and stood next to me. To read the posters too.

"Doc," he said softly, "the first time I saw your brother was at a fire. We'd responded to a fire in a townhouse. We pull up. There's black smoke pouring out the first-floor windows. So here we are, about to force the front door, when it flies open— and out walks your brother. In a dinner jacket. Carrying an unharmed old man over one shoulder. He walks right past us and hands the guy over to EMS, walks away. Off to meet a date, we found out later." Brendan shook his head. "We're all standing there in shock. Then Lieutenant Browne turns to me, smiles and says, 'That's our new captain.' "

It was approaching 10 p.m. and the next crew to head down to the site was forming. Captain Dan came down from the second floor carrying two work shirts. LADDER CO. 3 RECON was printed on the front of both. He handed one to Bobby and one to me.

"Here, put these on. We just got word that the crew is heading back from the site. Find yourselves boots. We should be leaving soon."

He walked away before any of us could ask if they had found anyone. I felt proud to put on the FDNY work shirt and was reassured that, at that moment, I was exactly where I was supposed to be.

A very short time later, a van pulled up to the front of the firehouse; out poured six tired firemen.

Their eyes were flaming red. They were covered by thick gray dust, and their disappointment weighed heavy on them. No one had to ask if they'd found anyone. I was introduced as they hung their gear on the racks. A big man who looked as if he could turn over a fire truck single-handedly came over to shake my hand.

"I'm Mike Moran. It's good to meet ya. Do ya need anything?"

"No, no, I'm O.K.," I replied.

"Got a place to stay?"

"Yeah, I'll be staying at my father's in Westbury."

"Well, if there's anything you need—a place to stay, a car, money—you just ask me." He started to walk away, then stopped and said, "Your brother is a great man." Then he disappeared though the doorway that led up to the second floor.

Tim walked over to me and said, "Mike's brother, John Moran, is also missing."

We gathered all the hope we had left and loaded ourselves into Brendan's van. He drove, Dan sat beside him, and Bobby and I were told to sit on the bench seat. John (a.k.a. Barnyard), Tim and Dennis sat on the floor behind us. We headed toward the great hole in the sky. There was little traffic; the closer we got to our destination, even less. Then there was none. No people, no cars, buses, trucks—but what did I expect? It was war. Dan turned to Bobby and me.

"There are three checkpoints that we have to get through. Don't say anything and there shouldn't be any problems."

We knew what he was saying. Bobby and I, in our LADDER CO. 3 RECON shirts, looked like firemen—no, that night we truly *were* firemen. There was just one difference: we didn't have the red, hopeless eyes of the others.

The first roadblock was at Houston—mostly police. Dan showed his ID. We were through. As we progressed south along the deserted downtown streets, the van's motor was the only noise to be heard. The smell of broken hearts that I'd first noticed when I got out of Penn Station was getting stronger, the dust thicker. Up ahead through the haze was the second roadblock. As we got closer, we could see that the intersection at Canal Street was blocked by a Hummer with a mounted machine gun pointed in our direction. It was surrounded by military personnel with automatic weapons. Several of them came up to the van and stared hard at us through the windows. They also had flaming red eyes, looked tired, angry, frustrated, and as volatile as the gunpowder in their weapons. Dan rolled down his window as a soldier approached.

"Ladder Company 3, we're going to the site," Dan said as he showed him his ID. The soldier thoroughly examined it. *Oh, shit. What if he asks for mine? I don't think my hospital ID would be any help...*

"What about them?" he barked, nodding his head toward the group of us in the back. "I need to see their IDs," he ordered.

I had a moment of panic. *I've gotten this close. What should I do? Pretend to look for it?*

"They're my company, they don't need to carry their IDs," Dan said. "They left them at the firehouse like they always do."

I held my breath. There was a long pause as the soldier considered Dan's lie. His steely eyes once again passed over each occupant of the van. He took an extra long look at me. Finally, he spoke.

"O.K.," he said. "Go ahead."

The soldiers backed away from the van. I heard the sound of the engine dropping into gear, and we were on our way. I let out a long sigh of relief. At the next corner we encountered the third roadblock. We tensed. The sentinel there just waved us through.

Brendan pulled up next to what was probably the curb. It was hard to tell. The engine stopped. We all got out, slammed the doors shut, and then—dead silence. The gray dust was several inches thick and covered everything like a desiccated snowfall. On either side of the road were flattened cars piled 10 high on top of each other. Once-important papers were blowing in the wind, and the heavy dust was starting to fill our lungs. We were real close now.

"Before we start walking, a few ground rules," Dan stated. "We need to stay together. Brendan, stay close to Bob; Tim, keep an eye on Mike." Few other words were said as I walked next to my brother's friend Bobby. *So he's not a fireman? He must be a damned good friend of Pat's to want to come down here.*

The base of the great hole in the sky was filled with bright lights and smoke. As we got closer, more activity. A company of maybe five or six firemen crossed our path; then another group; then three more companies; then fire trucks and more companies on foot. Dan waited for Bobby and me to catch up.

"Now there's a lot of heavy construction equipment down there, so don't get yourselves run over." As we walked, Dan continued, "We may not get a chance to dig. We'll see when we get there; they might need us on a bucket line."

For some reason, I knew we were going to dig.

We continued on to the staging area that was in one of the few World Trade Center buildings left standing. To get there, we walked past tents with food, bottled water, even full sets of clothes. Volunteers manned these stations, ready to hand you as much as you could carry. There was a long row of ambulances; those waiting paramedics would give everything they had for just one victim to be found alive. We made a left past a small mountain of donated new white socks and walked into the building. It was lit by portable lights hooked up to generators. There were other groups of firemen in the process of obtaining equipment before going to the pile. I searched their faces for someone that I might recognize, someone I may have worked with—an old friend, a friend of my brother's. What I saw were faces of despair. There was one room that contained all kinds of equipment spread out on tables and in bins. Tim stopped. He cut a length of rope and tied it to the handle of a flashlight; then he hung the rope and flashlight around my neck. As a fireman you can never overestimate the importance of light.

I picked up a pair of work gloves. We made our way down one last dark alleyway filled with construction apparatus and fire department equipment. I stepped over fire hoses that would slither like snakes when water flow stopped or started. One suddenly sprung to life like a giant serpent, almost knocking Barnyard down. He grabbed it and threw it to the side.

Some members of Ladder Company 4 were coming the other way and stopped when they saw us. The men of Ladders 3 and 4 worked together at fires and knew one another pretty well.

Brendan called over, "How many are you missing?"

"Fifteen," came the answer.

Fifteen. Ladder 4 lost 15 men—from a house that had maybe 50. Nothing more needed to be said. They were devastated. We continued through the alleyway as the noise, smoke, dust and activity escalated.

We turned the corner, and there it was.

Chapter 10

THE SITE, THE PILE, the Trade Center, Ground Zero. Whatever it was called, no matter how many times I'd seen it on TV, I was still unprepared for the image I encountered at the end of that alley. It was like visiting the Grand Canyon for the first time— totally beyond description. The site was lit by hundreds, maybe thousands, of floodlights. There were two massive mountains of twisted steel. Their sides were made up of dagger-like remnants of metal that could easily impale anyone unfortunate enough to lose his balance while navigating the harsh terrain. Broken, mangled pieces of rebar protruded like thousands of steel snakes poised to attack careless passersby. The buildings' lacelike facades, part of what had given the towers their character, had crashed down from the sky and sliced into one of the mountains. These enormous shards had become unyielding and colossal barriers to our ascent. Hell had shattered the gates of heaven.

On one of the peaks were hundreds of rescuers. Most were firemen, but there were large numbers of police, ironworkers and rescue dogs. The other mountain was barren, as if daring anyone to climb it.

From Dante's burning plain, smoke rose through the twisted metal and emerged from pockets of death.

"Hey, Mike—look out!" Tim yelled. I didn't notice that a crane was about to back up over me. The crane's massive wheels passed in front of my face and brought me back to the dangers at hand. Dan shot Tim a look to remind him to stay close to me. We picked up shovels and pry bars that were lying in a pile of tools and started to scale the mountain. I was proud to be carrying a shovel with these brave men as we searched for the place to dig. We stepped over empty hose lines, fire department hand tools and heavy rescue tools—each one with its own history of saving lives, now scattered throughout the area, abandoned and useless. I was looking for one with WESTBURY FD written on it so I could bring it back to Long Island with me.

During the climb, the most disturbing images buried in the debris started to take shape: fire trucks. Just a few days ago, each of them had carried its crew into this hell. Engine 5, Battalion 6, Ladder 10—to look at them now was to have your heart ripped out.

"Mike, you O.K.?" It was Tim.

"Yeah...I'm O.K. Did you ever find Ladder 3?"

Tim pointed past the barren mountain. "Yeah, over there. It was parked next to Rescue 1."

Bobby reached us. "Mike, you all right? You know, we don't have to go all the way up. We can wait for them back down on the side."

I turned away and continued to climb. *Why was he was so concerned about me?* We'd never met before; I wasn't even sure he wanted to be there. I paused to let a rescue dog and his handler pass. Then it hit me. Bobby was there for one reason: to watch out for his best friend's brother.

Despite Dan's orders, Brendan, Barnyard and Dennis were far in front of us and seemed to be freelancing. They stopped only when they reached the top of the mountain. An I-beam lay flat across the top of the peak. One end gave way to a jagged steel cliff over a deep, steaming, serrated valley. Across the valley, rising up high above us—the second mountain. The men ahead of us were leaning over the edge and were about to climb down.

"STOP!" Dan ordered. They were looking at a fire truck that formed part of the cliff. "That rig was thoroughly searched already! Get back up here and stay together!"

There was obvious tension between the survivors of Ladder 3 and the covering captain. The men had already experienced a lifetime of disappointments in just the past few days. Firemen—like doctors—see death all too often. Civilians and fellow firemen die in fires, accidents and collapses, but this was different. It never took this long for resolution. In other building collapses, firemen would tear the shit out of the structure until the person was saved or the body recovered. This time the progress was painfully slow. The men were frustrated; Brendan seemed to have become desperate. Dan had seen his share of death, buried many close friends over the years. And he knew most of the missing guys very well: before being promoted to captain, he was a lieutenant in Ladder 3. But what made Dan different from the others in our crew was that he was responsible for his men. He was fiercely determined not to lose anyone else, even to injury.

Bobby and I made it to one side of the mountain and Dan climbed over to us.

"You see that pile over there?" He pointed to the abandoned mountain. "That's the North Tower. We're standing on the South Tower." He continued. "The last time anyone heard, your brother and 3 Truck were operating on the 40th floor of the North Tower. There's some talk about a collapsed stairway that may have created voids where someone may have survived."

I asked Dan, "How come we're not over there?"

"Too dangerous. Remember—we almost lost six men there already." He pointed to the shattered gates of heaven. "That large crane I told you about? The one we're waiting for? It'll remove the facades before we can go near there again."

Dan moved away and Brendan walked up. "Mike, where do you want to dig?" he asked.
I raised my arm and pointed to the mountain that was the North Tower.

But I couldn't go to the North Tower. If I were alone, maybe I would have tried, probably would have gotten myself arrested. Here, I was a guest. I couldn't repay Dan for getting me into the site by getting myself killed. The headlines would read ONLY ONE KILLED DURING RESCUE EFFORT: DOCTOR FROM LAS VEGAS. These thoughts were the only rationalizations that eased my mind. I knew that if I were the one under the debris of the North Tower, the only way that they could ever stop my brother from getting to me would be to shoot him.

We scattered and searched for the best place to start. We climbed over the rebar snakes, around the escaping smoke and down into the many small holes that had been left abandoned by the rescuers that came before us. Dennis found an area that had a very faint scent of death sneaking up through the debris. It appeared that the scent was rising from underneath a long I-beam that once held up the South Tower. Now it was this massive immovable object that held us away. With our hearts as much as with our hands, we started to scrape our way under the I-beam. We could have been on our way to finding a void that contained someone who was dead—but it might also hold someone who was alive. We could be digging for a dead body that would have given a family the chance to put their loved one to rest; or we could be digging over a smashed refrigerator filled with rotting meat. Who knew? But we were doing something.

I'm no construction worker, but even I know you can't dig through steel. There was nothing that looked like much of anything else. There was the dust, of course. Also recognizable were papers, carpet fragments, cables, but there was nothing that resembled a desk, chair, coffee cup, picture frame, telephone, office door—nothing. It was steel and entropy. I would try to loosen it up with the shovel, use my hands to fill a bucket with dust and pass it over my head to a man on a bucket line that probably also smelled the death. Barnyard was digging next to me and hit my shoulder.

"Check this out." He handed me a pamphlet that was almost completely intact. The title: *Living Safe in a Dangerous World.* I passed it over my head to the bucket line and watched every person on that line pause, read the title, then pass it to the next person.

Brendan invaded my little space. "Mike, where'd you learn how to dig?"

Barnyard also paused to observe my technique. "What do you do for a living?" he asked.

"I'm a physician," I grunted.

Barnyard yelled over the noise. "A what?!"

"I'm a DOCTOR!"

Brendan and Barnyard grinned at each other. "That explains it," said Barnyard. "Here, this is how you dig." John drove his shovel into the steel and entropy while he and Brendan chanted, "DIG motherfucker, DIG motherfucker, DIG motherfucker, DIG!"

The ball busting didn't bother me; in fact, it made me feel accepted. My frustration with our lack of progress was building, so I dropped my shovel and started to push against the massive steel girder. What bothered me were these motherfucker I-beams. They were everywhere. As irrational and as stupid as it must have looked, using every bit of my strength and with a face full of dirty tears, I had as much chance of moving this motherfucker I-beam as we thousands of rescuers had of finding anyone alive.

I was standing on I-beams to help position the lights. Eventually I made it to the top of the mountain, balancing on the girder that jutted out over the steel valley. Columns of smoke surrounded and sometimes briefly engulfed me, but I didn't budge. From this magnificent vantage point, I could see everything.

Over to the right were a group of police officers digging in a large hole. In the middle of them was a young female police officer. She was digging with the strength and passion of anyone there; her uniform was covered with dirt and her beautiful blond hair was matted with gray dust. The ironworkers did most of the real cutting. Anytime there was something heavy to cut, they were there and well-appreciated for their efforts. They whirled around with oxyacetylene torches like Samoan fire dancers. We kept an eye out for them as much as we did for the crane cables swinging overhead. I could see one of these fire dancers passing in a trench far below—his torch almost roasting Bobby's gonads.

The rescue dogs were doing whatever was asked. I watched as these intelligent, determined creatures climbed up the hills of broken razors without any protection on their paws. They looked as exhausted as their handlers. A battalion chief would call over a handheld radio: *This is Chief F, I need a dog at the southwest pile.* The answer: *"Chief F, do you need a live dog or dead dog?"* I guess even rescue dogs have their specialties.

Oh, those handheld radios. They were everywhere, and all blasting like boom boxes on a Brooklyn beach. They were full of chief chatter. *"This is Chief A. Go ahead Chief A, this is Chief B. Chief B, blah blah blah, Chief A this is Chief B, blah blah blah blah, Chief B this is Chief C, blah blah*

blah blah blah, This is Chief A, Chief C, What the hell are you talking about?"

This went on and on until there came a *"Mayday, mayday!"* A collapse—a crew had fallen into a hole of fire. The work and the noise stopped. Everyone turned their attention to where the mayday had come from. The chief chatter stopped and was replaced by the voices of captains and lieutenants. We all listened to radios as the drama unfolded. Fire hoses and ladders were rushed over. Then, finally, a collective sigh of relief: all the men were pulled out safely. Everyone got back to work. The construction noises ratcheted up and the chiefs were back on the radios.

There was a crew digging above the area of the fire truck that was embedded in the cliff. They called for quiet. *"This is Chief C, silence...silence."* All work halted as we held our breaths. They brought listening devices over and were snaking them near the fire truck. Did someone hear something? Yes? Wait—was that...? No. Another false alarm. More disappointment. The work started back up a few minutes later.

I saw Tim pulling on some electrical cable, so I went down to where he was and pulled too. I asked him, "Why is Ladder 3 called Recon?"

He explained that at one time their nickname was West Point because you needed to know somebody to be assigned to Ladder 3. They changed it to Recon after a fireman from another company got separated from his crew in a burning building. He called for help; a member of a top rescue company went in after him. He got lost too. They finally sent in Ladder 3, who found them and got them both out. "Since then, we're Recon."

Bobby joined us to help move lights, tanks, hoses and anything that needed to be moved. We were trying to pass down a large tank when Brendan came up to us and told Bobby, "If the captain comes by, flash your light at me." Then he scaled down the side of a cliff of twisted steel and was gone. Bobby and I just looked at each other; then we tried to find Dan. He was several yards down in one of the razor gullies; when he spotted us, he started to head our way. Bobby did his best to flash the warning light and I did my best to block what he was doing from Dan, who was furious by the time he finally made it over to us.

"Where the hell is Brendan?" Bobby and I stood silently like two young brothers trying to protect the third from getting in trouble. "He was just here! I saw him with you!" Dan accused.

Bobby and I looked at each other. Bobby started to improvise, weaving and gesturing to distract him. "Gee—you know, he was right here a second ago. *Right here, Dan.* Mike, wasn't he right here a second ago? We were just talking to him. I just said to him…"

Dan was not amused.

"Huh! I guess I was just having a conversation with myself! Dan, that is just the damnedest thing! I swear he was right here!" He threw it over to me. "Hey, Mike—Mike, did Brendan tell you where he was going?"

Dan turned to me now, mad as hell. "He…he…" I stammered. I was dropping the ball. Bobby gave me a little incline of the head, c'mon, Mike, that's it, keep it up, keep it going. Just then Brendan's head popped up from behind some twisted metal as he climbed back over to us.

"I was right over here!"

A good leader knows which battles to pick. Dan shot Brendan a look. That was enough.

DAWN WAS DOING ITS best to break through the smoke and dust over the site. Dan ordered us to take up; it was time to go. Bobby and I could not agree more. We grabbed our equipment and started down the ominous pile of twisted metal. We would soon be replaced by yet another crew with, maybe, some regained false hope. Dan stopped me from slipping down an I-beam, and as I was getting my balance he said to me, "Coming here to dig is as much for therapeutic purposes as it is for anything else. All these men need to do something—anything. They know it's almost hopeless, but at least they're doing something."

In the end, after eight long hours and all the physical exertion and mental effort, we were able to dig down maybe two feet into the mountain. While walking out, Tim and I were lagging behind. As Tim continued on, I stopped, turned and faced the site. After the agony of watching the North Tower collapse and intuitively knowing that my brother was in it, the frustration of not being able to get a flight out of Vegas, the exhausting nonstop 2,600-mile drive, the failed attempt to get to the site with the Westbury Fire Department, getting lost in Manhattan, having my way blocked at Houston Street by police, then finally finding Pat's fire company, I'd arrived—only to discover that it was all useless, all of it. And I, my brother's great savior, was also useless. Tim noticed that I'd stopped and yelled to me.

"Mike—you all right?"

Alone, with flaming red eyes and covered in thick dust, in the shadow of this hopeless hell, I looked up to the great void in the sky.

Goodbye, Pat.

Chapter 11

WE RETURNED TO THE firehouse with our eyes on fire, disheveled and disheartened, covered in dust and dirt and that smell of broken hearts. I felt it appropriate to wash up in the 3 Truck's slop sink that was in the basement. I had no basement; I no longer had a foundation. The rules had changed. This is America. We were the strongest nation in the world. Where was that protection that we'd paid all that tax money for? Where were those great leaders that we'd elected to office and promised us everything? I guess when you're constantly feeding your own interests with both hands, you have to drop the ball.

Barnyard was passing when he saw my head in the sink.

"Why don't you go upstairs and take a…"

I looked at him and he read my mind.

"Don't give up hope—at least not yet," he said.

I put my head back under the faucet and let the cold water run over it. The wet sting of the frigid water flooded my face and reminded me that I was alive. I attempted to cough out the dust from the site, but it was as futile as trying to remove the site from my mind. The rules had changed, but I hadn't. On that night last October when I accepted Pat's will, I accepted the responsibility too—and there was no way that I was going to drop the ball.

I did what I could to restore some of what then had become irrational hope and started to make calls. Janet was getting more upset that she wasn't with me. She was worried about me. I didn't tell her that my head just came out of a slop sink. She said she felt isolated, useless and frustrated. Since the airports had reopened, she could easily fly to New York. She didn't understand that the only calming thought I had was that she was taking care of the dogs far away from the destruction and confusion of the city. Bobby had already moved his family out of Manhattan to Long Island because of the real possibility of a second attack. Waiting for the attack became a main reason for us to hang around the firehouse. If it was going to happen, it was going to happen here and I wanted Janet there in Vegas.

I called my sister to discuss how bad things were, but she already knew. I called Marc in Vegas and gave him an update. He told me that he was going to try to get to New York. I knew this was not going to sit right with Janet, but what could I do? Marc had family upstate and understood that I was going to be busy; if he made it here, he would be on his own. As I headed to the front of the firehouse, I knew that my father would need to be given any news in person. That was my next priority.

It was a pristine New York City fall morning, and outside waiting for me were Brendan and Bobby. It was a morning that normally would be full of potential—bright sunshine and cool, crisp, clean air. It was full of potential all right: unfortunately all negative. Shift change was at 9 a.m., and Dan thought it was a good idea for me to hang around and meet some of the other members of Ladder 3. People started coming by again, leaving flowers, and some of the young women were giving the firemen hugs. With tears of sadness and appreciation in their eyes, these beautiful girls were throwing their arms around the firemen.

If there was one thing that I looked like that day, it was a fireman. Wearing an FDNY work shirt still covered with some dirt, smelling like the Trade Center and with the same red, morose eyes, what else could I be? And how could anyone turn down this affection? There I stood, and *bam!*—out of nowhere, a beautiful woman would be throwing her arms around me, telling me how sad she was, thanking me for being there. A number of these women knew my brother, and when they found out who I was, they would stare at me, start to cry, then give me another hug. They kept coming. It got to the point that I felt guilty about *not* being a fireman. If I told them why I was there, they would cry more. And to be honest, fireman or not, this affection did make me feel a little better. I was talking to Tim and it happened again.

When the girl walked away, I said, "Tim, you know, I feel uncomfortable getting all this attention. They think I'm a fireman. It's not right. I'm family of a fireman."

Tim grabbed my shoulder as if he were palming a softball and gave me a little shake. "Mike, don't worry—you're part of our family now."

ONE OF THE FIREMEN coming on duty that morning was Lieutenant Steve Browne. He was about my size, strongly built, with one of those wide open, honest faces and a friendly demeanor. The way he and the other firemen interacted, it was easy to see that Steve was not just respected but also truly liked.

After introductions, Steve said, "I wish I knew your brother better. We worked opposite tours so I never worked with him. We used to relieve each other, and in that short time I knew that he was unique. He'd do anything for his men." He took a long breath and stared unseeing across 13th Street. "I still don't believe it." After a moment he turned back to me. "Ah, Mike, how you holding up?"

Granted, I looked like shit, but I was still vertical. "I'm O.K."

He pointed out Pat's car parked by the curb. It was an old Honda Civic, silver—more like battleship gray—covered with dust and looking as if it hadn't moved in a month. Pat hated cars, preferring to jog or ride his bike around town. Steve had to go to roll call, but before he left, I asked, "So how many Brownes are in this place?"

With a smile Steve answered, "Seems like a lot. You must have met my brother Dan."

Engine 5 pulled up in front of the firehouse and a few guys went inside. Out of the corner of my eye, I noticed a fireman pointing me out to an elderly black woman who had arrived at the firehouse with her three-year-old grandson. She waited until Steve left, then walked over to where I was standing.

She leaned over to speak to the child. "This is Captain Paddy's brother." The boy told me that Paddy was his favorite fireman, and his grandmother said that Pat would make him feel important. Pat would let the boy climb on the fire truck and talk about things important to a three-year-old. She then looked at my face. Noticing the close resemblance, she started to cry.

A fireman from Engine 5 interrupted. "Sorry, we got a run." He then shook my hand. "Just needed to tell you that your brother saved my life. About a month ago. Just doing his job." Two loud blasts from Engine 5's air horn sent him running. He called to me over my shoulder, "He's a great man! If there's anyone who can make it out of there, it'll be him." He got into the massive fire truck as it pulled away with lights on and sirens blaring.

I turned to see a young woman crying. She was in Pat's yoga class and said she could not go to class without breaking down. Moments later a photographer showed up to take my picture; he told me that Paddy had saved his wife's life when their apartment went up in flames a year and a half ago. Pat found her unconscious; he dragged her out of the fire and resuscitated her.

Shortly after the photographer left, a well-dressed businessman speaking low and slow, pulled me aside to tell me how Paddy had saved his life as well.

"Didn't pull me out of a fire, but I was dying all the same. Paddy got me into the Program." He paused and stared at my puzzled expression, suddenly wondering if perhaps he'd said too much. "You did know he was in the Program, right?" I shrugged, not quite following. As he continued, I figured out that the Program was another name for Alcoholics Anonymous. He went on. "I had nothing till I met your brother. Now I have a good job, I'm happily married and have two sons and a daughter— good kids too. If it weren't for Paddy Brown, I would be dead."

If it weren't for Paddy Brown, I would be dead.

I would hear this recurring theme from so many different people, from all walks of life. The stories would have continued that day if Dan hadn't came by to say that his brother Steve wanted to speak to me in the office, and that my brother's locker is right next to it. "No hurry to go through it," he assured me, just as he had the night before in the kitchen. "Take all the time you need."

No hurry? No need? As irrational as it was after spending the night on the pile, I was still not ready to concede that Pat was dead. But I knew I should be the first to go through his locker.

I took a slow walk up the concrete stairs to the office. It was silent. No jokes or laughter or sounds of locker doors being banged closed, no conversations of future plans—just thick sadness that hung heavy in the air. The office was at the end of the small locker room. It had the same old green metal lockers that I remembered from Engine 37. They were tightly packed, some half open, others with clothes draped over the doors; half of them had a piece of white loose-leaf paper taped to their doors. There was a name written on each piece of paper. As I walked slowly past, the names came into focus: FF COYLE, FF OGRAN, FF DEWAN, FF McSWEENEY. The names continued: FF MALONEY, FF GIORDANO, LT DONNELLY, FF McAVOY and, at the end of the row by the office door, CAPT BROWN.

Rank has its privileges, and being the captain of Ladder Company 3 meant that he got two green metal lockers. Pat's lockers were side by side. One of them opened up in the direction of a fire pole. Placed on top of the lockers was an assortment of running shoes. FDNY T-shirts hung over the edge of one; the other had a yoga mat draped over it. I reluctantly opened the door that was facing me. Pat's work shirts were hung up, and a box filled with fire department articles on rescues—most of which Pat had been involved in—was also in the locker. On the top shelf there was a grapefruit, his keys, about $40 and his ID. Opening the brown leather ID holder, I found his captain's badge, fire department picture ID and a very small yellow envelope. I looked inside this envelope and found a dental x-ray.

I wonder if he knew.

"Hey, Mike." It was Steve from inside the office. "Come on in, sit down."

The office did not look any better than the locker room. About 30 or 40 years ago, New York City must have had a surplus of olive green paint, because everything seemed to be painted with it— the office no exception. Steve was sitting at a small battered desk with an assortment of phones in front of him. He was in the middle of one of three conversations and motioned for me to sit in an old wooden chair in front of the desk. Different phones would ring and he would answer them all. He juggled the phones and the conversations as if he were a member of Cirque du Soleil. When I entered the room, it was obvious Steve was speaking to a family member and giving him or her an update on what was going on down at the site.

"Don't give up hope." He listened for a moment, then spoke softly into the phone. "No, that was really disappointing. I'll call you with any news as soon as I get it. Take care of the kids and don't give up hope."

Every time he would try to speak to me, another phone would ring. Other families were calling, and each conversation was almost identical. Steve looked beat up when the phones went silent for a moment.

He gazed at me from across the desk. "I know you have a thousand thoughts running through your head," he said. "There are a lot of things that you'll need to do. Take them one at a time and they'll all get done. Have you made any plans yet?"

"Plans," I repeated, not quite comprehending. *Have I made any plans.* At that time, it seemed that Steve Browne had the ability to see into the future. It turned out that what he was doing was looking at reality. It was a reality that I wasn't ready to accept yet, the reality that would be my future.

He continued. "You'll need to go to the family center and get a missing person's number. I'll take you there anytime you're ready. We're here to help you. Now, what do you need?"

What do I need? I need to be back in Vegas with Janet and our two dogs. I need to be back in the ER working. I need to be playing softball, worrying if I'll mortify myself by striking out, or playing golf and sending little white dimpled balls screaming through windows of the million-dollar homes that line the course. I need to find my brother alive. I need the clock to be turned back...

Steve knew what I needed. It was what we all needed.

"So what do you think, Steve? Is there any chance?"

His answer came without hesitation. I'm sure he'd given this statement too many times before when he was asked the same thing by families of the owners of the other lockers with the loose-leaf pages taped on them; family members who sat here in this same chair with bloodshot eyes fixed and breaths held. I'm sure that it was the same statement that floated around Steve's head before he tried to sleep and finally collapsed from exhaustion.

"Don't give up hope," he said. "There are reports of voids that someone could have survived in. We're waiting for that heavy crane to get set up. Don't give up hope." Steve then told me that "the job"—the term used to refer to the powers that be in the fire department—was asking all family members to gather DNA or dental records. "Just in case they need them," he said gently.

Without a word, I handed over the dental x-ray that my brother had left in his locker. It seemed that Pat might have also seen into the future.

Chapter 12

WHEN I MADE IT BACK downstairs, Bobby and Brendan were waiting. Bobby said, "Mike, you were up all night. When do you sleep?"

"What are you talking about? You haven't slept either."

Brendan cut in. "You need to get some rest."

I knew I looked like shit and that they were right.

"How you getting home?" Bobby asked.

"I'll take the train."

Brendan jumped in again. "No, we'll get someone to drive you home."

"Drive me home? I'll be fine taking the train."

"Then let me drive you to Penn Station," Brendan insisted.

I wanted to walk. The weather was perfect and the city was beautiful. It was a much different city than I remembered. Pat told me a few years ago that Mayor Giuliani had made New York once again a place where people actually liked to go. And after the effort it took to get here, I wasn't eager to leave Manhattan. It was Pat's city, and Pat was here.

"Are you sure you'll be all right getting home?" Bobby asked. "What about the Long Island Railroad schedule?"

My reply ended the discussion and put their minds at ease. "I put people back together for a living. I can figure out the Long Island Railroad."

So MAYBE I WAS out of practice. Penn Station wasn't as easy as I remembered. Everyone was rushing in different directions. There were announcements screaming out of cracked old speakers about what trains go where, at what time, from what platform, and where to change trains to arrive where you wanted to go. I stopped to read a wall full of train information and was run into by a woman who yelled, "What the hell are you stopping here for?!" There was also the ever present worry that if you got on the wrong train, you would end up in Amagansett or some other faraway town. At least the ticket booths were in the same place. I walked up to a window. Behind it was a gruff old man with an attitude as if he were serving out a sentence of eternal damnation by selling railroad tickets.

"One way—Westbury," I said when it was my turn at the window.

He looked at me as though he were about to tear my throat out. *Did I say something to offend him?*

I rephrased my request. "May I please have a one-way ticket to Westbury?"

He spit out the words as if they were one. "Peakoroffpeak!"

"Off-peak, please."

Now with ticket in hand, I pressed my luck with him. "And can you please tell me when the next train to Westbury is leaving?"

He shot out one long word (or were they several short words stuck together?) in a manner that I couldn't understand. After the third time of asking him to repeat himself—and him acting as if I'd asked him for fellatio—I finally understood what he was saying: "Track 19. Leaves in five minutes."

Chapter 13

LATER THAT DAY I took another trip to the rehab facility to see my father. He looked no better than he did the day before—in fact, maybe worse. I updated him on the progress of the rescue effort; he again brought up his will. More people were visiting him, but he was still extremely depressed. We both sat silently because there was nothing that needed to be said. Then I tried my best to encourage him to cooperate with his rehabilitation plan. He gave me a "screw it all—I just don't give a shit anymore" look, and I could understand his lack of motivation. The news programs were still showing, over and over again, the collapse of the towers where his son was buried. What could be tougher for a parent than losing a child? I knew that there were thousands of parents watching and going through the same torture.

I caught the train right back to Manhattan. During the next several days, the rescue efforts continued and so did the irrational hope. No matter how unreasonable it was, it was all we had. "We are still hoping to find voids" was repeated over and over. Janet was becoming anxious and couldn't take staying home any longer. She promised that if she came to New York, she would stay in Westbury; she said she understood that most of the time I would be in the city. And she assured me that she would have no problem with that.

There were still people continuing to drop by Ladder 3. It seemed that everyone in the city knew Pat. It also seemed natural that Bobby, Steve and I were becoming close friends. I was still stopped by Bobby's face and voice seeming so familiar, but I could not for the life of me figure out why. He was very protective of anything having to do with Pat, that was certain. And Steve was patiently allowing me to get used to my new reality.

One afternoon I had a meeting at Ladder 3 with Mike Currid from the FDNY officers' union. He knew Pat well and had asked to be assigned to his case. Our meeting mostly entailed going over paperwork—there was a lot of it. When I joined the fire department, the first two days were spent in an auditorium with 200 other men filling out forms, and now I knew why. We went through one form after another and Mike patiently explained each one. After our meeting, we walked outside and Mike gave me a fire department sweatshirt that he'd retrieved from the trunk of his car. On the front it said CAPTAIN BROWN, LADDER COMPANY 3. I thanked him, and he said, "I've known your brother for years. He is the best fireman this city has ever had, and if anyone could walk out of this, it would be Paddy."

Bobby was standing outside the firehouse. I threw the sweatshirt over my shoulder and the two of us quietly walked toward Third Avenue to find a place to have dinner. The city was still in shock and the restaurants were hurting badly. The fear of another attack on New York kept everyone from going out. I wasn't hungry and neither was Bobby, but he insisted on buying me dinner.

Third Avenue wasn't Third Avenue as I remembered it. It was as if we shooting a scene from a science-fiction movie where aliens had already killed off most of the human population. *The War of the Worlds*—we were walking on the set of an abandoned New York City street. Cue the attacking spaceships.

We found a restaurant where we could sit at a table under an awning right next to the sidewalk. I always liked to sit outside, and it would give me a great vantage point to view a flying saucer if one made a left down Third. I was taken aback by the sight of a tall Arab-looking guy striding toward us. When I realized he was our waiter, I felt completely foolish. But I'd been uneasy all day. We heard news reports earlier that members of an Arab community in New Jersey had been standing at the edge of the Hudson as the towers burned—and cheering. After a few moments, it was obvious that he was just a regular guy, a working man, courteous and very appreciative to have customers that night. He was like so many who were in the towers: all he wanted to do was make an honest buck and go home to his family. While we were ordering, two cops in a squad car spotted us, crossed all traffic lanes on Third Avenue and stopped in front of the restaurant. I guess they were suspicious of the only two Irish guys eating at a Middle Eastern restaurant. The police watched us for several minutes before driving away.

"So Bobby—how long have you known Pat?"

"We've been best friends for over 16 years." As he talked, I did my best to figure out how I knew him. I knew that I'd never met him before the day we ended up on the pile, but there was something in his voice. When he told a story about my brother, he did a striking imitation of Pat's voice and mannerisms. He actually had me laughing. *Laughing! Who was this guy?* Then it hit me like a brick right between the eyes. *Thinner.* Robert John Burke—the cursed lawyer from Stephen King's *Thinner.*

I knew that Pat had other close friends in the entertainment industry. There was actor James Remar, whom I'd met at one of the fire department's Medal Days. My brother also knew a jazz composer who lived in Hollywood and did arrangements for Bob Fosse. Pat used to date a movie producer; she'd taken him to the Academy Awards. One of the last times I saw my brother, I asked him how he'd come to meet and become close friends with all these Hollywood people. He shrugged. "Because I don't ask them for anything."

It was Medal Day, June 1988, when I first met James Remar. At that time, to receive a medal from the FDNY, you almost had to die in the performance of a heroic act. And here was Pat getting *two* medals. It was a big ceremony every year and took place on the steps of City Hall. That morning Pat Hyland, a good friend of mine from the Westbury Fire Department, presented Pat with a Police Harbor Patrol cap. This gift was significant because earlier that year, when Pat was a lieutenant in Rescue 1, they got a call that a helicopter had crashed in the East River. Rescue 1 arrived to find the helicopter capsized, its occupants trapped underwater. Pat and his men immediately went into action and removed the raft from the top of the rescue truck. They were just about to plunge into the water when they were stopped by a police officer: he wanted the police ESU—Emergency Services Unit—to perform the rescue. The police are in charge during these types of emergencies and they apparently needed the publicity. The only problem was that ESU had not yet arrived on the scene. Rescue 1 had their SCBA gear on and were in the raft. The guy in charge still would not allow them to proceed with the rescue. Depending on who tells you the story, Pat either had or was about to have a fistfight with this cop when ESU arrived just in time—to recover the dead.

Pat ended up on TV with the politically smooth police commissioner, who readily agreed with Pat that more cooperation was needed between New York's police and fire departments. Pat ended the news interview by pointing out an indisputable fact, in a very blunt and quite politically unwise manner: "The people in the helicopter are still dead."

So on that Medal Day, Pat proudly got his picture taken wearing the Harbor Patrol cap.

I'd graduated from Albany Medical College just the month before. Since I was still technically a member of FDNY, I wanted to go to Medal Day in my Class A dress uniform. One problem: I'd never gotten around to actually buying a dress uniform. So I borrowed one. I thought it was about two sizes too large, but the fireman who owned it assured me it fit perfectly. Never trust a fireman if he has a chance to bust your balls, and having my balls busted was exactly what happened—on the steps of City Hall.

"Kid, what are you doing wearing your father's uniform?"

"Don't worry, Mike, you'll grow into it!"

Then my brother arrived in his sharp, perfectly tailored Class A covered with medals, ribbons and commendations. The comments changed to "Hey, Mike—look at your brother! Where are all *your* medals?"

I did receive a company commendation from Engine 37, but since I never had the dress uniform to pin it on, I never bothered to pick it up. Pat said, "Yeah, that's right," and took a pin depicting a small bugle—an engine company commendation—from his uniform and pinned it on mine.

"Come on, Pat, that's yours."

Despite my protest, he pinned it to my uniform anyway. I was full of pride that day. My brother was covered with medals and was receiving two more. I

125

stood there proudly in my baggy uniform with a bugle on my chest.

Medal Day is a big deal in the FDNY, and there are always several parties to attend following the ceremony. Pat had quit drinking by that time, but Pat Hyland and I made up for that fact. We hit several parties, and at the end of the day found ourselves in a bar by Lincoln Center. Pat was flirting with a cute waitress who was on roller skates. I thought he needed a little brotherly competition. I walked over wearing my now rumpled, critically ill-fitting uniform and interrupted. Pat knew what I was doing and didn't say a word. She looked at me, then at him; then at me again, then at my bugle.

"What are you—in a band?"

Pat just grinned.

Chapter 14

THE DAYS PASSED; HOPES dwindled. Bobby and I were now close friends and would have dinner together frequently. There seemed to be so much to do, and it was good to have someone I trusted nearby. One night over dinner, he told me that I needed to get into Pat's apartment before anyone else did, and that he'd come with me if I needed. As always, Bobby was right. Pat had gained celebrity status, and people were starting to ask me for things of his. I'd already met about 10 people who assured me that they were Pat's "best friend," and a few ex-girlfriends who were "just about to get back together with him." And there was another thing that Bobby told me that night.

"Mike, there is something else you need to take care of. You don't have to do it right now. When you're ready, I'll tell you all about it."

"It" turned out to be a novel based on Pat's life.

My brother was too trusting. Over the years he'd gotten himself entangled in various business affairs; there were times when he'd invest in a nightclub or a bar and usually get ripped off to one degree or another. I know of one such deal in which he had one-twentieth interest in a club that became extremely popular, but, for some reason, Pat was told that the place never made a profit. I had already seen the woman who had written the novel on various TV shows. She assured everyone that Pat absolutely loved her book—he'd read it in galley form over the summer—and he was very proud that her troubled main character was based on him. According to Bobby, Pat was going to meet with an attorney to consider a lawsuit. Much more problematic for Pat than her portrayal of him: the supporting characters were clearly and recognizably based on his friends, family, other members of the FDNY. He felt betrayed. He wanted to ride to their defense. The book's publication date: September 11, 2001. Both author and publisher were now giving interviews, eager to tie Pat and the fire department to the tragedy.

After dinner, Bobby and I walked back to Ladder 3 and ran into Mike Moran, Tim Brady and a few other senior men getting off duty—as well as Chris Tighe, one of the younger members. They'd just spent another day on the pile digging through the heartbreak.

They were now finding body parts.

"Don't give up hope, Mike," said Tim Brady, but his red eyes told the truth.

They were on their way to a bar and asked if we wanted to join them. Why not, what else was I going to do? We went to Finnerty's, a tavern that called itself a pub. It was in a semi-basement with dirt on the windows older than I was, and a low ceiling that clung to cigarette smoke like a sponge. Even the firemen choked when that smell of stale smoke hit us. But the barmaid was pretty, friendly and appreciative of where these men had been just an hour before.

Finnerty's was perfect that night, and the beers as well as the stories were flowing. When Pat was transferred to Ladder 3, the rumors about him made it there well before he did. They heard that Pat was a hard-nosed ex-Marine, with a bad-ass attitude and ambitions to get medals and be on TV. They heard stories of his rescues, expected him to be six foot four and 250 pounds—and then he walked into their firehouse. They didn't expect someone more like five foot 10, 165 pounds, and with an unassuming, almost shy manner. Mike Moran said that Pat called a meeting, and within five minutes it was obvious that he was going to take good care of the men at 3 Truck. One of the first things Pat did was send the truck out for a retrofit to make it better equipped at fighting fires. With him as captain, the company really started to jell and feel like a team.

We closed Finnerty's that night…well, more precisely, Finnerty's closed around us. When we finally left, it was too late to catch the train back to

Long Island. I ended up comatose on the couch in Ladder 3's basement.

The next thing I remember was a hand gripping my ankle and shaking my leg.

"Mike, wake up." I rolled over not knowing where I was, what day it was, who I was, and why this weightlifter with a crew cut was madly jiggling my leg like the handle on a running toilet.

"Mike! Mike, wake up, Mike. I'm Vinny from Engine 69."

I still didn't know what was going on. He continued. "Mike, they called 69/28 looking for someone to take care of you."

"I don't need anybody to take care of me!"

"So Mike—what do you need?"

Slowly losing the haze of sleep and coming back to life, I told him that I appreciated what he was doing, but all I needed was a shower. And a few functioning brain cells. And to please let go of my ankle.

"Where you going today?" he asked. "I'll drive you!"

"I'm going to Westbury, but you don't have to drive me. I'll take the train."

"They told me you would say that. I have direct orders to drive you," he insisted.

"Then drive me to Penn Station and drop me off."

He beamed. "They *also* told me you were going to say that."

It appeared I had no choice but to cooperate, so I took a shower, put on a shirt from my brother's locker and got into Vinny's car. He noticed that the shirt was too small, so I told him where I got it and that I hoped my brother wouldn't mind.

"No, Mike, he wouldn't mind," Vinny said softly.

He drove me all the way to Westbury. As I was getting out of the car, I found out it was his daughter's 11th birthday, and that she was waiting for him at her mother's house.

IN WESTBURY, I CHANGED my clothes, visited and updated my father, ate lunch with my sister and was back in the city before I knew it. I met up with Steve Browne, and we went to the West Side pier to file a missing-persons report. He asked me if I wanted a hotel room in Manhattan. It was a generous offer, but I felt that as long as it didn't bother anyone that I was sleeping in the basement of the firehouse, I'd continue to do so. I felt comfortable on a couch in a firehouse basement. And if anything was going to happen, from someone being found alive at the site to a second terrorist attack, I was right there in the city. Janet at home in Las Vegas was the one sure and comforting thing that I had to hold on to, but her feelings of isolation and frustration continued to escalate. Our phone conversations were more heated. She was making plans to come, and that was that. She reiterated her promise to stay out in

Westbury, and she repeated—with just a trace of irritation—that yes, she fully understood that most of my time would be spent in Manhattan.

That understanding lasted about six hours. Our friend Lois, the ER nurse, was going to watch the dogs; Janet flew to New York. My brother-in-law Hector picked her up at Kennedy and drove her to Westbury. The next morning at about 3 a.m., while I was standing in front of the firehouse with Steve after a typically horrible day, my cell phone rang—it was Janet. She was hysterical. My sister and Hector were arguing; she was scared; she didn't want to stay another minute in that house. She wanted me to come out to Long Island and get her. She didn't want to hear that there were no trains at that time or that there was no way for me to get there, or be reminded that her whole family lived on Long Island so if she were that concerned, she should call someone from her family…This conversation went in circles until my phone's battery began to melt down, along with myself.

I turned to Steve. "You still have that hotel room?"

The next day—along with going back to the pier to complete more paperwork; meeting with three more of my brother's "closest friends"; discussing the Pat novel with Bobby and meeting with a lawyer about the same; speaking to Carolyn and worrying about her marriage; dealing with my father's still refusing to get out of bed; needing to supply the fire department with samples of Pat's DNA; having to get into his apartment before anyone else did and needing to read his will to find out his wishes because it was getting to the point that I had to make some decisions—Janet and I moved into the Hotel Delmonico at Park Avenue and 59th Street. Janet needed to be with me and had the right to be with her husband in this time of crisis, but nobody was thinking right at that time, including me. Especially me. I felt that Janet had manipulated the situation to get her way, and I knew that my mobility and independence were now lost, replaced by even more responsibility—and rising resentment.

It was early evening when I made it back to 3 Truck and was ready to tackle the emotions of going to Pat's apartment. Steve, with his uncanny ability to see into the future, warned me that it would be tough.

"Don't worry," I told him. "I'm a rock." Then I started to walk away.

"Ah, Mike, I'll wait for you here."

"Thanks, Steve—but you really don't have to." I waved goodbye over my shoulder and continued east on 13th.

My brother lived in Stuyvesant Town; he'd been there about 13 years. It's a huge complex on the East River, with courtyards, parks and tall trees between several 11-story buildings; it was about four blocks from 3 Truck. I sat on one of the park benches under a street lamp and unfolded Pat's will. I suddenly remembered that this was the same area where, a few years back, Janet and I were scolded by a lady for feeding peanuts to the squirrels. "You know—they're just rodents!" she'd yelled at us.

Pat's will was straightforward. But it was the two-page letter included with it that was more important. I'd already met a number of people who assured me that they were Pat's best friend and knew exactly what he would want. The only problem was that most of the time they contradicted one another. I was looking for clarity, and Pat's letter gave it to me:

10/29/00

Dear Mike,

I'll probably be around til 90, but I wanted to do this anyway. I'm giving you several friends' names. If something happens to me, let them help with decisions regarding: Funeral (St. Patrick's Cathedral if possible.) Cremate me + dump the ashes in Central Park. I marked a possible spot on the map where to do it. I like it there principally because I jog there and there's a beautiful view of the Manhattan skyline which looks really cool at night.

On the second page:

Friends
James Remar (Actor)
Bob Burke (Actor)
Rick Serrentino (Detective)
Terry Hatton (Fireman)
Tim Brown (Fireman)
Ralph Palmieri (Seido Karate)

A phone number followed each name. There they were—the people Pat trusted. I would do the same. I already knew that I could trust Bobby with my life. You can always trust a person who will accompany you to hell—in this case, the site—and back. I'd met Rick and Tim on the first day that I made it to Ladder 3. When they were told that I was at the firehouse, they both rushed up from the site to meet me. Tim Brown—no relation—was with the fire department but was currently assigned to the Mayor's Office of Special Operations. He was working with Rick Serrentino at the NYPD to help produce an antiterrorism plan for the city.

Rick said he first met Pat on the day of his graduation from the police academy. The following day, he was walking through Times Square and came upon an overturned car surrounded by a crowd. Rick forced his way through and was told that someone had already squeezed under the car to help. Moments later, the guy crawled out, covered in grime: It was Pat. When he spotted Rick, he exclaimed, "Hey, you're the guy from the academy!" Only a week later, Rick said, Pat was out for a run in his jogging shorts and FDNY T-shirt. He was on a path along the East River just near his apartment building when he saw, several yards ahead of him, a woman being mugged at knifepoint. Pat took off after the mugger, tackled him to the ground and easily disarmed him. A police car screamed up to them: It was Rick. He couldn't believe that here was Pat, again, this time holding down a mugger.

"Hey, Paddy—who are you, fucking Superman?" Rick had asked. They'd been close friends ever since.

Tim Brown was probably the last person alive to see Pat. He had been working the command post set up in the lobby of the North Tower. Tim told me that in the chaos of smoke, falling debris and crashing bodies, Pat and the men of 3 Truck powered through the shattered windows of the lobby more like a football team than a fire company. Tim gave him a warning. "Paddy, it looks real bad—don't go up there."

"What are you, nuts? We have a job to do!" was the last thing Pat said before he and his crew disappeared into the stairwell. Tim gave a similar warning to another close friend of theirs, Captain Terry Hatton, before Terry and Rescue 1 went into the same stairwell. If Tim hadn't been detailed to the Mayor's office, and therefore at the command post, there would have been one more name added to the list of missing firefighters.

A year and a half before, when the position of captain of Rescue 1 became available, both Pat and Terry Hatton actively pursued the prestigious post. Some firemen told me that Pat should have gotten the job, but Terry was chosen because he was more politically savvy.

More politically savvy? Yeah, I can see that. Terry never went on TV and told the police commissioner and his men that they were responsible for letting people drown in the East River.

Pat always wanted to be the captain of Rescue 1 and was very disappointed when he didn't get the assignment. Later, he told me that he was going for a spot in a downtown ladder company. It was much closer to his home than Harlem's Engine 69; I thought that was why he wanted it. That was part of it, but it wasn't the real reason. Ladder 3 was one of the best houses in the city. When I asked him if he was angry about not getting Rescue 1, he said no. He told me he was much better off in 3 Truck. I also later learned that Terry Hatton was a hell of a fireman—he didn't just walk into the position because of politics.

Just a few days earlier, someone in front of the firehouse told me that things would have been different for Paddy if only he'd gotten the Rescue 1 position. But I wasn't so sure. As Tim pointed out that night on the pile, when they finally found and dug out Ladder 3's rig, parked right next to it was Terry Hatton's Rescue 1.

I had briefly met Ralph Palmieri the day before, and he too asked me if I needed anything. He was very close to my brother and was responsible for getting Pat into teaching karate classes to the blind. It was a six-month commitment for one student from their karate organization, but nobody told Pat that there was an end date—so he just kept doing it, long after the six months were up. Bobby told me that Pat used to come out of those classes all beat up from getting hit by his blind students.

The only person from Pat's list that I hadn't spoken to in the past few days was James Remar. I punched in his number on my cell phone. I didn't expect him to remember that we'd met in 1988 at Medal Day, but he did. I thought he might be annoyed that I was calling him, but he was thrilled. James and I talked until my cell phone's battery was red-hot. He knew all about the book that Bobby was concerned about. He also told me not to worry about so many people insisting they were my brother's best friend. Pat had a unique ability to make everyone feel that way. After hanging up, I just sat there trying to get control of my thought processes. I looked to the sky.

One thing at a time.

My attention returned to Pat's letter, and something hit me.

Cremate! Pat wants to be cremated? And he wants me to "dump" his ashes in Central Park. How the hell could I do that?

My thoughts were starting to run away from me.

O.K., settle down. One thing at a time.

The one thing I needed to do at that moment was get into Pat's apartment. I hoped he'd understand.

Chapter 15

319 Avenue C, Apartment 11A

MAYBE IT WAS BECAUSE I felt I had no right to go through Pat's personal belongings; maybe it was because everything there was associated with Pat's being alive; or maybe it was just one more step in the process of giving up hope that made me halt at the entranceway to my brother's apartment building. I wanted to press the button next to his name. In the past, this action was always followed by his voice, then the buzzing sound from the main door being unlocked. I almost did it just to see if anything would happen. No, that would be silly. I had to keep going because Bobby was right, I needed to be the dog in the manger. I turned the key in the lock and stepped through the heavy metal doorway. The door slammed behind me, echoing throughout the empty lobby. Then silence. It was broken by the sound of my footsteps across the cold gray stone floor. I walked up a small set of stairs to a wall of mailboxes. The box for 11A was jammed with letters. *Shit, I forgot all about his mail*. I started to worry about how to take care of it. Should I bring it upstairs? When would it be proper to open his letters? Should I take them back to the hotel? *Stop, O.K., stop. One thing at a time*. I headed toward the elevators.

The feeling of gloom and the need to turn around grew stronger. This was not right. No, not right at all. I had no right to be there intruding into Pat's life.

I found myself in front of an old-fashioned type of elevator door—the kind that had to be opened manually, with a metal door that swings toward you into the hallway. The door was covered with notes, messages and cards. Most were concerning Pat, with almost all of them expressing the same hopes and asking for prayers. The elevator's arrival on the ground floor was announced by its descent, visible through a small window in the door, and the ceasing of the noisy motor. I stood there for several seconds until I realized that the door had to be pulled open. I got in and pressed the button for the 11th floor. The gate closed, and I was locked in—surrounded by more notes, fliers, pictures of my brother. The elevator rose and I was on final approach to his home.

The elevator stopped on 11—the top floor—and I stepped out into the hall, made two quick lefts, and there was Pat's apartment. His door was guarded by flowers. It also had cards and notes all over it, most along the lines of "Paddy, please call me as soon as you get this and tell me you're all right." Some of the flowers must have been there since the 11th because they were decaying, offering up a rancid odor. I stepped over them and tried the key, but the door wouldn't unlock. I spent several minutes trying different combinations of key positions, doorknob positions and door tension until finally, with a thump, the lock gave way to my manipulations. I was in.

Pat's apartment looked the same as I had remembered it, except for the addition of a baby grand piano tucked against one wall of the living room. He had told me that he was learning to play. *Why would he have such a big piano in a little apartment?* Then again, Pat never did anything halfway.

I'd always liked Pat's home. It was a sunny one-bedroom flat with a great view of the East River. Yes, the place looked about the same with one major exception—Pat wasn't there.

I felt that if I kept busy, I'd get through this. What I was looking for that day was anything that might be embarrassing or detrimental to Pat. The windows were open and the noise of the city crept in. On the piano bench was a photo of Pat, Marc and me taken the last time he was in Vegas. There were several other pictures left scattered around. There was one of him with Bobby's son Dylan at Dylan's baptism; Pat was his godfather. There were pictures of Tim, Rick, James; one of Pat holding another infant, who I later found out was Lisa Remar, James' daughter—and Pat's goddaughter. There were other pictures of people whom I didn't recognize. Strangely, there were no pictures of Pat's girlfriends. Bobby told me later that Pat never wanted to leave any evidence around.

On a shelf under his TV were lots of VHS tapes. Most contained footage of his rescues that had been aired on the local news. I found a few that didn't really fit in, like a *Good Morning America* clip about an FDNY captain that practiced yoga to relieve stress.

There was another tape from 1983 when he had a part in a soap opera. Through one of his actor friends— it may have been James—he found out that one of the long-running soap operas was auditioning actors to play a boxer. Pat got the part. For seven days, Paddy Brown the Fireman was Mad Dog Evans the Soap Star. I remember laughing about it with Pat in an FDNY hangout called Suspenders. He told me that the guys in his firehouse would replay the tape and cheer at his final scene when Mad Dog Evans is knocked out—by getting punched in the arms.

The walls of the hallway to Pat's bedroom were covered with plaques and commendations. There was a letter dated June 27, 1991, from President Bush, congratulating Pat on one of his rescues. The hallway closet was filled with similar awards that I guess couldn't fit on the walls. His bedroom was very neat. The bed was made, and lying on it were fire department work charts. I looked through the bedroom closet and found more awards, some yoga and karate stuff and a picture of Bobby and Pat on a beach, practicing karate. On his dresser was an open paperback, *The Road Less Traveled;* next to the book was his answering machine. It was full of messages. I pressed PLAY, and the voices of the people who loved him cried out. After each message, the machine would mechanically dictate the date and time—the messages had been recorded starting just after 9 a.m. on 9/11. Like me, every one of the callers knew where he was on that Tuesday morning, and as the digital voice ticked off the passing minutes, the voices became more and more desperate until they finally deteriorated into sobs. I turned away from the machine to continue working my way through the apartment. The frantic messages continued to fill the room.

Next to the bed was what seemed to be a small altar. About 18 inches high, it held religious objects unfamiliar to me; photos of firemen; a campaign-like button with the face of a young fireman on it; newspaper articles. I didn't recognize who these people were until I read the articles. One of them was John Drennan, and the year was 1994. John was the captain of Ladder 5. He and Pat knew and respected each other, both as firefighters and as men. While at a fire at a three-story building on Watts Street in SoHo, John and two of his men were caught in a flashover from the apartment burning just beneath them. One of them died at the scene; the other died the next day. Despite second- and third-degree burns over much of his body, John held on to life. Pat was temporarily transferred from Engine 69 and assigned to take care of the Drennan family. He said it was the toughest yet most rewarding assignment he'd ever had. Day after day was spent with John's family at the burn center. He called me almost daily with medical questions. I could explain the disease process, but he was on his own when it came to the family. John's condition slowly deteriorated to the point of multisystem failure: the damage from the extensive burns was overwhelming his body. Then, after 40 days and nights, Pat saw the will to live disappear from his friend's eyes.

"It's O.K., John, you can go," Pat had said to him gently, recalling that day in an NBC *Dateline* segment on Drennan. "Your family will be taken care of. It's O.K., you can go." And with that promise from Pat, exactly 40 days after receiving his injuries, John Drennan died.

Pat told me that after John's wife Vina and their children said their goodbyes, he brought two probationary firemen into the room. He placed their hands on John's chest and said, "If you ever prayed, pray now. You are touching a great man." He then charged the two firemen with guarding the door to John's room and told them, "No one gets in without my permission." Pat left with Vina and the four Drennan children.

Later, when the New York City fire commissioner tried to walk into John's room, the two probationary firemen stood in front of the door to block his entrance.

"I order you to let me in. I'm the goddamned fire commissioner!"

"Sorry, sir, can't do that," one of the young firemen said. "No one gets in without Paddy Brown's permission."

Realizing that he would never get anywhere with these probies, the commissioner asked, "Can you please contact Paddy Brown and ask him if I can go in?"

After a phone call to Pat, the commissioner was allowed to enter John's room.

THE PHOTO ON WHAT resembled a campaign button was of firefighter Pete McLaughlin. The article next to it, from October 1995, stated that he was killed in a Queens arson fire. I remembered that Pat became severely depressed after Pete's death. All these memories were starting to get to me. Worried, desperate voices were still coming from the answering machine. I needed to shut that damned thing off and get out of there.

As I left the apartment, my exit was blocked by the flowers in the hall. I brought them into Pat's small kitchen. I dumped the decaying stems into the sink as the air filled with the odor of thick rot. Trying not to breathe, I placed them in a plastic garbage bag. There was also a little stuffed bear dressed as a Marine out by the door. I brought it in, flopped down on the couch, and studied it. The sound of a clock measuring the passage of time became more prominent and almost drowned out the city noise 11 stories below floating up through the open windows. All over the country there were people just like me—lost in space and time. They could be rescue workers at the site; firemen at their stations; they could be wives, husbands, sons, daughters, brothers, sisters, fathers, mothers, cousins, aunts, uncles, all waiting by the phone; they could even be part of a list on a letter from a best friend. Everyone, everyone was cognizant that time was running out. Each tick of Pat's clock—the clock that had kept him on schedule—was now keeping time for no one. It had no function other than to point out to me that time was erasing my irrational hope, replacing it with despair. And finally, alone on his couch, holding the Marine bear and surrounded by the things Pat loved, I caught up to reality. I cried. But it didn't sound like it was coming from me. And it didn't even sound human. It sounded more like an animal caught in a trap in the woods, slowly dying of pain and loneliness.

Chapter 16

AFTER GOING THROUGH PAT'S apartment, I returned to Ladder 3 to find Steve Browne waiting for me.

"Ah, Mike—pretty tough, huh?"

He knew how hard it was going to be before I'd even started over there. Steve looked like hell. I think he'd just spent an hour or so getting yelled at by a wife in the anger-and-blame phase of grief. Whatever it was—Steve was never one to complain—he was as glad to see me as I was to see him. We stood outside the firehouse and spoke of funerals, wakes, memorials, sadness, lost firemen, their families, heroism and the frailty of life and spirit.

The word from the site was that the rescue operation was turning into a recovery operation—and not just the recovery of body parts. Buried somewhere under one of the towers was a large gold repository. The banks wanted to change course from the delicate, painstaking searches for anyone trapped in the rubble and have contractors hurry in, find the gold bars before anyone else did and bring them aboveground in armored trucks. Shifting the focus to this particular

148

recovery operation rather than searching for people did not sit well with the rescue workers. And tension was building between the cops and firefighters. It was one big turf battle.

Tension was also building between Janet and me. It didn't get any better when Marc made it to the city. He had a few days off from the pediatric ER, left his girlfriend back in Vegas and got a room at the Delmonico. The three of us had dinner together, and afterward Marc and I left Janet at the hotel, grabbed a cab and went to the FDNY hangout Suspenders. (It's gone through several name changes, but it will always be Suspenders to me. It's now known as the Bravest.) The inside of the bar was the same; the picture of Larry Fitzpatrick wearing his Ladder 26 helmet still hung on the wall. He was the owner of Suspenders when he was killed during a rope rescue in 1980. Larry was in the same firehouse as Pat and was a good friend and mentor to my brother. There were newspaper articles and more pictures throughout the bar, some of them featuring Paddy Brown.

It was about 11 p.m. when we got there. The place was relatively empty. There was a small group of people sitting at the near end of the bar who told us that they were ducking out of work. Two other people were seated at the far end and were apparently friends of the bartender. He was rough around the edges, and he was less than happy to make the Black and Tans that Marc and I ordered. The last time we had a Black and Tan,

Marc reminded me, was at Steve and Nikki's wedding in Rhode Island—just before the world changed.

Every time we waved the bartender over, he'd say, "Yeah? Whaddaya want?" and seemed to be directing the harsh looks at me in particular.

I finally got up enough nerve to ask, "Does Wanda still own this place?"

He immediately growled back at me. "Who wants to know?"

I reached my hand across the bar. "I'm Mike Brown . . ."

His eyes opened wide. "Paddy's brother! Your face has been *fucking* with me since you got here!"

The bartender's name was Danny. He was a retired fireman and had worked with Pat 20 years earlier when my brother was a bouncer at Suspenders.

"You know—his drinking days," he said.

That night Marc and I closed the bar again. Or more accurately, the bar closed around us, and we didn't leave until daybreak. Danny told stories about my brother the bouncer. It was a time when having a drink after work didn't make you a criminal, a time of young girls and heroes, a time of fire and beer. I told a story about a night when Pat was working there and a waitress invited me into the girls' bathroom to show me where someone had written Pat's name and phone number on the wall. Being the less serious brother and lacking any New York City sense, I followed her in. It quickly became apparent that there was something other than his name that she wanted to show me. Right then, I felt my brother dragging me out by the back of the collar. He started to yell at me, but soon stopped when he realized that his words were not penetrating. I stood there with a goofy smile, and Pat just shook his head and smiled back at me.

I was actually feeling a little better when Marc and I returned to the hotel. It could have been the memories from Suspenders, hanging out with Marc and Danny, or maybe I was just drunk; whatever the reason, I did feel better. Janet did not.

After a little bit of sleep, I was up, showered, and met Bobby in front of the hotel.

"Mike," he said, "I hope you don't mind that I got you a driver." Bobby knew that I was getting beat up and needed help. My two hours of sleep and Black-and-Tan brain, however, prevented me from showing appreciation.

"I spoke to Keith." He looked at me as if I should know who Keith was. "You know, Pete's brother." My blank look continued. "Keith—NYPD—Pete McLaughlin's brother?" Only then did it dawn on me who Keith was and the connection we had.

When a firefighter or police officer is killed in the line of duty, the city assigns a car and driver to family members to help them get around. New York City traffic is stressful enough when you're used to it. If you're not, and you add the stress of the sudden death of a loved one, it becomes impossible. Usually the vehicle supplied is a limo, a Lincoln Town Car or, at the very least, an undercover police car.

So there we were—standing outside the Delmonico on this cool, sunny, late September morning—waiting for my car and driver. The Delmonico is on the downtown side of Park Avenue, an area congested with traffic and noise. The street has three lanes in each direction with a wide, parklike median running down its center. Gridlock is everywhere, and to make it worse, the traffic lights aren't synchronized. I was told they're intentionally left unsynchronized to deter drivers from taking Park Avenue. In reality, it produced only more congestion, noise and exhaust.

Even though I was wearing my Harlem Hilton FD sweatshirt, I was still cold. As I held my arms tight to my body, Bobby said, "Keith was able to get your cousin as your driver."

"My cousin?"

Bobby's expression became worried, as if something were very wrong. "You do have a cousin that's a cop in Harlem?" I stared back uncomprehendingly. "You know, your cousin, Donny? The cop?"

I sure did have a cousin Don who worked as a cop in Harlem, but he'd retired—20 years ago. Bobby interpreted my blank look to mean that he must have inadvertently rekindled some kind of family feud, but no—I simply didn't know what the hell he was talking about. Our discussion was abruptly halted by a hair-raising screech coming from a brown 1983 Chevy Caprice that announced its arrival by scraping its bald, hubcap-less wheels against the curb. At least I think the car was brown, but it could have easily been any color before being bleached by the sun. The Delmonico doorman, in the street hailing a cab, jumped back to the sidewalk just in time.

The Caprice continued to bounce up and down long after it had come to a stop, common with city cars after their suspension gets beaten to death by potholes. The driver's door creaked as it opened, and a large, daunting figure emerged and headed directly toward us.

With more than a little stress in his voice Bobby asked, "Hey, Mike, you know this guy?"

"Sure—it's Donny." Bobby could not have looked more confused as Donny threw a bear hug around me. It was my second cousin Donny. I didn't know that he was doing the same thing his father did 20 years ago, in the same neighborhood. Donny was six foot three and 220 pounds of hard muscle and NYPD attitude. He had a heavy New York accent that spilled out of a mouth slightly skewed to one side as he spoke, as if he were controlling the path of sound waves. He referred to good-looking females as *tamaydas* and instantly gave me confidence that he was not going to let anyone fuck with me.

At that moment, Marc staggered out of the hotel. He and Bobby got into the back seat. I took shotgun and was still in the process of shutting my door when Donny pulled the car forward, still in the curbside lane, up to the traffic light. We needed to go uptown, which meant going two more blocks south to make a U-turn. Depending on traffic, this simple maneuver could take more than 20 minutes. We were stopped at the light, looking at one-way traffic moving from our right to the left, and I wondered how Donny was going to merge with the cars that packed the downtown lanes. The light was still red when the Caprice started to move forward, directly into the cross traffic. A shouting match broke out between Donny's mouth and the horns of all the cars we'd just cut off—and Donny's mouth won. As the rest of us scrambled for the virgin seatbelts, Donny casually made a left turn into the crosstown traffic, crossed the downtown lanes, and wound up in the uptown lanes of Park Avenue. He broke more traffic laws in 15 seconds that I'd broken in 10 years—and all the while Donny acted as though nothing were out of the ordinary.

Because we were at war, Donny explained, there weren't any official city cars available. So he had to borrow this one. His own car, a BMW, was totaled when his friend Freddy the Masturbator hit a tree with it. Donny was not upset when I asked about the BMW; he said he was just glad that Freddy wasn't hurt and could continue doing what made him famous.

We swayed in and out of traffic in unison with the other cars traveling uptown as if some invisible asphalt waves were causing this choreographed departure from a straight line. It was almost calming—except that we were going over 50 miles an hour. Every so often a pothole would send the old Caprice airborne, followed by a block or so of bouncing up and down and up until the springs were able to exhaust their potential energy. Donny's philosophy on how to utilize traffic lanes didn't help. Out of the right side of his mouth he explained, "Mike, you need to use the whole width, otherwise it goes to waste."

We were bouncing and swaying our way up to the Harlem Hilton—Engine 69, Ladder 28, Battalion 16. Bobby thought it was a good idea to stop by and meet with some of the men from Pat's previous firehouse.

Chapter 17

THE HARLEM HILTON IS a large three-story firehouse wedged in the middle of housing projects. Across the street is a schoolyard with a basketball court in use almost 24/7. Long ago I would occasionally be detailed from Engine 37 to work at Engine 69, Ladder 28 for the day, so once Donny found the firehouse, the territory was somewhat familiar. Donny parked in a fire zone. So he wouldn't be in the way of the fire trucks, he left half of the Caprice on the sidewalk. We walked up and banged on the large red steel door. While we waited, I again felt that we were intruding. A face appeared at the small window and the heavy door opened.

An expressionless fireman eyed us. "Can I help you?" Then he eyes opened wide as if he were staring at a ghost.

Nervously, I started to explain why we were there. I now felt that this might have not been a good idea. The fireman interrupted me midsentence.

"You're fucking Paddy Brown's brother!" The door flew open. He gave me an enormous hug and practically dragged us all into the firehouse. We walked back to the kitchen, where there was a picture of Pat on the wall, and I met the crew on duty that day. They made us feel welcome and invited us to eat with them. "Whatever you want!" they insisted, as they made lunch for us and told stories of Paddy Brown.

Jim Carney had been Pat's chauffeur—the driver of Engine 69—and he was obviously heartbroken. He told me that Pat never would have transferred to Ladder 3 if he had been around. The approval came through while Jim was on vacation. Like Pat, Jim was a Vietnam vet, and they'd become very close. He declared that Paddy never give a shit about what a chief would tell him and did everything he could for his men.

Jim backed this up with a story. During a fire, one of the men of Engine 69 was injured and needed to go to the burn center. The battalion chief refused to allow Pat to transport him. He wanted the fireman to be taken to a local Harlem hospital and then, if need be, the hospital could arrange a transfer to the burn center on Manhattan's Upper East Side. Jim and Pat got the fireman into the truck and Jim asked, "Where to, Paddy?"

Without hesitation Pat answered, "The burn center."

"So here we are," Jim says, "lights and sirens on, flying down the FDR Drive and *way* out of our district. I yell to your brother, 'Hey, Paddy—we can get into big trouble for this!' And he yells back at me, 'What are they going to do to us? Send us back to fucking Vietnam?!' "

With that, Pat and Jim started to laugh uncontrollably. The guys in the back of the rig had no idea what the hell was going on.

LATER THAT DAY I was to meet Steve Browne at Ladder 3. Donny took the FDR Drive back downtown. In my mind was a vivid picture of Pat and Jim Carney in Engine 69 racing down the same highway, laughing at the thought of getting in trouble for doing the right thing. I guess that's why we tell so many stories of our loved ones after they're gone. For those brief moments, we're back in time when they were still alive.

I needed to see Steve to give him samples of my brother's DNA. The rescuers at the site were recovering more bodies. Before this, they'd been finding parts of bodies—a hand with a wedding ring, a foot within a fire boot. They were scaling back the numbers of rescue workers at the site and had ordered most of the firefighters out of there, but there were some who refused to leave. No one from 3 Truck had been found yet. The bodies that were being recovered first were the people who'd fallen, jumped or were pushed in a panic from the top floors, as well as the people who'd been running from the building, so close to making it out alive.

As I handed over a small plastic bag with hair from Pat's brush, Steve said, "Ah, Mike, I was told that Paddy was heard over the radio just before the collapse. His transmission was very calm, and he reported that the evacuation was proceeding in an orderly fashion. He reported that there was some internal collapse. Then, with the same calm voice, he gave a mayday right before the tower came down."

As the days went on, more names of the missing firemen would be announced in department messages in every firehouse in the city. They were no longer missing. Each day a message would come over the speakers; people would stop and hold their breath, waiting to hear the names of friends, co-workers. It would start with a loud tone, followed by *"Stand by for a department message…"*

IT WAS THE END of September. Janet and Marc wanted to go down to the site, so Donny picked us up in the Caprice and took us there. We sliced through the three layers of security without anyone questioning his authority. We made it to the front of the quarters of Engine 10, Ladder 10—the firehouse built years ago to service the World Trade Center. The pile was still several stories high, most of the fires were out, the street in front was clear, but the rescuers looked the same. There was an Irish setter rescue dog resting next to the curb. He was exhausted. When I bent down to pet him, the dog looked at me with the saddest eyes I'd ever seen. We stood there and watched the rescue efforts, wishing they would find a body, some "closure" for another family. After about an hour of hopelessness, we returned to the car in silence.

THERE WAS A VERY good chance that many of the missing 343 firefighters would never be found. Firemen who were recovered had funerals; the missing had memorials. The members of Ladder 3 were looking at 12 memorials—12 wakes, 12 memorials, 12 devastated families and their friends. I still don't know how the surviving men of 3 Truck did it. There was all that planning, preparation and pain. Janet, Bobby, Donny, Marc and I went to the ones we could, and they were just heartbreaking. Since there were so many each day, the fire department turnout was thin and the ranks were filled with visiting fireman from all over the country—and the world.

The first 3 Truck memorial we attended was on Staten Island. We arrived in the Caprice to find two fire trucks parked in the middle of the street outside a small church. There were about a hundred firefighters lined up in front of the building as people walked past them and into the church. We could hear the music from the organ through the open windows. The five of us decided to stay outside. We agreed that we didn't want to take up seats. We didn't want to be reminded that soon it would be our turn. During the eulogy, an unmarked police car came flying up to us and out rushed four plainclothes cops.

Alarmed, Bobby asked, "Donny, what's going on?"

"Just watch, you'll see," was Donny's reply.

At that, two more cars came roaring up to the curb, and Mayor Rudy Giuliani got out of one of them. He was quickly escorted into a side door of the church. A few moments later, we could hear him giving a second eulogy. After he was done, he was escorted back to his car and the small motorcade sped away.

Donny turned to us. "He has 11 more to go to today."

New York City's mayor tried to attend every one of the rescuers' memorials and funerals, and there were times when the number reached nearly 20 for one day. No one likes to go to funerals, but knowing how important it is for the families to have the mayor speak, Giuliani did it. And by the time it was all over, he'd probably done it more than 400 times.

Shortly after the mayor's entourage sped away, a fireman walked over and tapped me on the shoulder.

"Someone told me you're a doctor," he whispered. "Can you come with me? We need your help."

In a small room off the church vestibule, one of the retired firemen was having chest pain and refusing to go to the hospital. He was dressed in his Class A uniform and didn't want to leave. My advice to him was short and to the point.

"We don't need anymore funerals to go to," I told him. He reluctantly agreed, someone called an ambulance, and he was on his way.

I returned to my group outside the church just as the firemen were lining up. The bagpipes played *Amazing Grace* and the procession came out into the sun. One fireman was carrying a helmet in his outstretched arms—there was no casket, only a helmet. He was followed by a tearful young widow with two toddlers by her side. There was no way anyone could hold back tears. I turned to Janet and muttered, "This really sucks."

Chapter 18

MARC FLEW HOME TO Las Vegas a few days later.

As for Donny, he was planning to attend a double funeral at St. Patrick's for two brothers. They were uncles of a good friend, and Donny had known them for most of his life. The brothers had worked together in the South Tower. Their bodies were found right next to each other.

Donny was also planning what he'd be doing after the funerals. He was going to a crosstown bar. Not only was one of the bartenders there a real *tamayda,* he assured me, but she was also in love with him. He told me to give him a call and we would meet up that night.

Also on my agenda for the evening: dinner with a friend of Pat's who was anxious to meet with me. He'd insisted it be just the two of us. I thought this was a little strange, but then I recalled having met him years before. Even back then, David was a little odd. I called him; he wanted to meet at Paddy's favorite diner on 90th Street. So my plan for the day was simple enough: Janet and I were going to spend some much-needed time together; then I'd have dinner with David; and afterward meet Donny in that crosstown bar.

The New York City morning started as it did every other day. Janet and I were awakened at 6 a.m. by the sweet sounds and smells of garbage trucks. You'd figure that after one of those monsters finished gobbling up the trash on the street below that it would gladly move on and wake up other New Yorkers. But no. Just when you thought that maybe you could get one more hour of sleep, a new truck joined its brother, now having seconds below our hotel window.

"How much garbage can there be on this block?" Janet wondered aloud.

The noise from the trucks was frequently drowned out by the blaring horns of impatient drivers stuck behind them. But it didn't matter that much to me. Sleep was a waste of time.

While Janet tried to get a little more rest, I made my morning calls: Bobby, Steve Browne, Ladder 3, a few friends of Pat's who wanted to know if there was any progress, my sister, Donny's father to check on my father, my father to try to motivate him, Paul Fischer— my boss—to make sure I still had a job, and Lois to check on the dogs. Bobby reminded me once more that Janet and I needed to spend time together before there was no longer a Janet and I.

The garbage-truck parade ended and Janet finally got some sleep, so our day was starting a bit late. Our plans were to walk around, find a place to eat, then go to the Central Park Zoo. Once on the street we passed several carts selling pretzels and monkey meat. Growing up, I'd always loved New York pretzels— heated and covered with some secret ingredient that fell from the city sky, but that's what gives them their distinctive flavor. Most vendors had signs saying that the pretzels cost a dollar each. I walked up to one vendor and handed him a buck.

"Dollar fifty," he spat out.

"What do you mean? It's a dollar," I corrected him.

"Dollar fifty! Dollar fifty!"

"I passed about a *hundred* of you guys and they all have signs…" I noticed this guy didn't have a sign, so I reluctantly forked over $1.50 and walked off. It turned out to be the worse pretzel I'd ever tasted. I tried to feed it to what Donny called the "flying rats." As the pretzel crumbled in my hands, I threw the pieces in a grassy area at the entrance of Central Park. At first there were maybe two or three pigeons; then 10; then 40. Soon the whole area was covered with pigeons. One of the street vendors, who looked as though he were selling stuff he'd pulled from someone else's garbage, started to scream at us for feeding these creatures so close to his place of business. I didn't blame him. The pigeons were walking all over his merchandise.

Janet and I walked briskly into Central Park and got lost looking for the zoo. It was late afternoon when we finally found the entrance. The sign said that the zoo closed at 4:30 p.m. and ticket sales stopped at 4 p.m. We got there at 3:45—but no one was in the admission booth. There was a security guard at the exit and he was letting people in.

"Excuse me, Sir, do you think we can get in?"

"NO!" he barked. "You need a ticket!"

"I would buy a ticket if someone were there to sell me one," I responded.

He tried to stare me down, then said, "You need a ticket. Whaddaya think—it's free?"

"No, I don't think it's free. What about the people you just let in?"

"They had tickets."

I was beginning to get a bit...overheated. "No, they didn't. Where the hell did they get the tickets—from the empty ticket booth?"

Janet interrupted. "Come on, Mike. Let's go. MIKE!" So that was as close as we got to the zoo—and was the end of our day alone.

THAT NIGHT I MET with David, a balding, slightly overweight middle-aged man that I instantly recognized when I spotted him pacing back and forth in front of Paddy's favorite diner. But the years had not been kind. Or maybe it was just the weeks since 9/11 taking their toll. David looked much older than I thought he'd look. He was choking back tears when we shook hands, and I was not any better. But it was obvious that there was something on his mind. We sat in Paddy's usual booth and ordered.

"It's on me, Mike. Whatever you want."

I wanted the meatloaf.

"No, that's not good here."

I tried again. "Pasta?"

"Nope. Not a good choice."

This went on until he ordered for me. Then David cut to the chase. He wanted a few things from Pat's apartment to remember him by. He also told me, a least five times, that he was in Pat's previous five wills—until this last one. I started to get a little suspicious since as far as I knew, the copy of the will I had was Pat's first. David went on and on about the piano, but had the location of it in the apartment wrong. He talked on about how he and Pat were best friends, and that he knew best when it came to what Pat wanted. I knew they'd been friendly years ago, but there was something that just wasn't sitting right with me.

Then he made this enlightening statement. "You know, your brother and Terry Hatton hated each other."

That was it—time to go and continue on my journey. David was not on the list of names that I could trust in Pat's letter, but Terry Hatton, captain of Rescue 1, Pat's close friend—and great rival too, but certainly his friend—definitely was on the list. I jumped into a cab and was glad to be on my way to hook up with my little cousin Donny.

The bar where I was to meet him was a typical crosstown tavern. It had a narrow storefront entrance and a bar area warmly lit and stretching deep into the rear of the building. The bartender was a typical Donny *tamayda:* attractive, slender, with a long, soft body. Donny's friends—the nephews of the deceased brothers—seemed to have gone directly from St. Pat's to the bar. Like Donny, they were in their late 20s or early 30s, good-looking, nicely dressed, friendly and understanding of what I was going through, for they too were now in the Club. I met the owner of the Caprice, Freddie the Masturbator, as well as the two girls who told me why they'd given him that nickname.

Everyone has their breaking point, and that night even Donny Brown found his. Donny was not a heavy drinker, so it was unusual to see him tossing back shots of some kind of sweet alcoholic concoction. I was not involved in most of the conversations, but that was fine with me. At that time, what this group of friends needed most was one another. Freddie brought over several shots of alcohol and wanted me to take one. The last thing I needed was a faster way to get drunk, so I retreated to a vacant seat at the bar. The bartender, Donny's *tamayda,* approached me. She had a smile that welcomed conversation and a city wit that made the conversation interesting. She wanted to know why these well-dressed young professionals were getting stinking drunk. After my one-sentence explanation, she understood completely. Donny was full of life and must have been telling a funny story because he had everyone's attention. Referring to the lively group, she asked me, "So how do you fit in?"

Using my beer to gesture toward Donny, I said, "You see that big guy there?"

"Yeah."

"Well, that's Donny. He's my driver."

"Your *driver?*" She shot me a "Yeah, right" look and went to another part of the bar to serve another customer. Donny approached with one of his female friends. She was about 25, in great shape, and a total looker—another real *tamayda.* The bartender returned and Donny tried again to get me to do a shot.

"No, no, no, not me. No shots. I'm happy with my beer."

Donny leaned over the bar, ordered two shots and, even though I had a full one, bought me another beer. He intensely studied the bartender as she walked away. Then, referring to his female friend who had walked over with him, he said to me, "She looks good, don't she?"

With an approving smile I said, "Yes, she does."

She was also smiling when Donny said, "You know she works out." He had her do a pirouette for me.

"Yes, apparently she does," I enthusiastically agreed.

The bartender returned with the drinks, just in time to overhear Donny explaining to his female friend, "He would know because he's a doctor."

The bartender handed the shots over and said flatly, "He's no doctor."

She was kind of correct. With the exception of that one fireman with the chest pain, I'd done little in the time I was in New York to be called a doctor.

Smiling as she set the beer down in front of me, she said, "And *he* ain't your damn driver."

Now I needed to correct her. "Not only is Donny my driver, he's my bodyguard and he is also my little cousin."

She had that same "Yeah, right" look as she turned and walked away. Watching her depart, I was able to appreciate Donny's fondness for *tamaydas*. Donny commented, "Hey, Cuz, do you think she works out?"

"Yes, I think she does."

Donny and his cute athletic friend downed the thick red liquor that filled the shot glasses, and then, for no apparent reason, she gave me a sticky kiss on the cheek. While both of us watched her walk back to the group, Donny asked, "So, Mike, what's the plan for tomorrow?"
His question brought me back to reality.

"There's a 3 Truck memorial in the morning. Think you can take us?"

"Sure, whatever you want," Donny said. "Just tell me what time to pick you up." I got the impression he was talking about the bartender, who was looking at him. "You know what, Mike? She wants to fuck me."

Turning back to look at her over my shoulder, I noted that her smile didn't reflect lust. *Contempt* was more the word. "Yeah, she wants to fuck you, all right."

With that Donny Brown confidence, he replied, "No, you're wrong. She's obviously just overwhelmed by my good looks and exceptional intelligence." He directed his crooked, irresistible smile at her and repeated to me, out of the side of his mouth, "No, Mike—you're wrong."

I thought I was right, but the only thing we agreed upon over the next hour was our increasing degree of intoxication. Someone in the group demonstrated exceptional intelligence by getting us all to leave the bar. Before walking out, and to my utter disbelief, Donny did get the bartender's phone number. Freddie the Masturbator, the *tamayda* with the sticky kiss and rest of us poured out of the bar and onto the sidewalk.

Outside in the damp night air, Donny declared, "We all need to go to another bar!" Everyone thought he was nuts. Well, everyone, that was, except me. I thought that Donny indeed had exceptional wisdom for coming up with the idea. The group was trying to say its goodbyes, but we all ended up making fun of one another for a while. I had an unfair advantage because no one really knew who I was until one of Donny's friends asked him, "Who is this guy?"

"That's my cousin Mike. He—"

I interrupted, reaching my arms skyward to proclaim, "I am the Master of the Universe!"

This gave them the needed ammo to respond to the good-natured abuse that I'd been handing out, and from that moment on, Donny's friends knew me as nothing less than the Master of the Universe.

We were all still laughing when Donny hailed a cab and he and I got in. Little Cousin Donny and the Master of the Universe were on our way.

"Seventh and someplace," Donny yelled to the driver. "Don't turn your meter on and I'll give you eight bucks for the ride."

To my amazement, the driver didn't start the meter and we drove off. Wow, Donny could break the law even from the back seat!

We made it almost a full block when Donny yelled, "Oh, shit! I'm gonna be sick. Hey, pull over here! I don't wanna get sick in your cab. Yo, pull over!"

The cab driver made a left on Sixth Avenue, a one-way street heading uptown, and pulled over to the left curb. Donny made a hasty exit just before all that red, sticky liquor that must have been so tasty going down exploded from his mouth. This was followed by multiple eruptions from Mount Emesis.

I leaned forward to talk to the driver; he would not make eye contact with me. He was wearing a baseball cap down over his eyes. "I'll give you $20 if you wait here until he's done and take us to my hotel," I offered.

I looked at Donny, who was still outside the cab vomiting into the street. I turned back to the driver who had his hands cupped together and was shaking them, so that's where I dropped the $20. I turned back to see Donny slump down to the sidewalk and flatten out on his back as if he'd been shot.

"Oh, *shit.*" I leaned back over the front seat toward the driver. "Give me ten back and we'll call it even."

The driver handed me a ten and I scrambled out of the back seat, but the cabbie did not pull away. I turned toward him to see what the problem was. He got ten bucks for driving one block, for Chrissakes! Without saying a word, the driver cupped his hands together again and started to shake them. What the hell was going on? I looked at Donny on the sidewalk like a sniper victim and this driver, who wouldn't even look at me, kept shaking his hands. I'd reached my limit. Even the Master of the Universe gets to a point when being rational is no longer rational.

The words shot out from me. "Are you fucking kidding me!?!"

The cabbie remained silent and kept gesturing with cupped hands. He slowly raised his head and, like two wild dogs about to fight to the death, we made eye contact. I was searching for that last bit of inner restraint—the restraint required to survive in the ER and that I've used every professional day of my life. There was that time in the ER, for instance, when a psychotic six-foot-four Native American in full war paint and Indian dress jumped on my back and started to hit me in the head. Once I got free I had the opportunity to hurt him bad, but I didn't because I'm a professional. And this situation was no different. I wasn't going to let this no-eyed mute New York City cab driver get to me. I needed to take care of my comatose cousin, and that's what I was going to do. This was my plan until, while shaking his hands, the cab driver raised his head one more time and we again made eye contact.

"Fuck it!" I started slapping the brim of his hat down on his face.

And he just kept doing it—shaking his hands, looking at me, not getting out of the cab. If this great battle to the death between a cab driver and a New Yorker who has been abused by cab drivers all his life was to take place, I needed him out of the goddamned cab. My next step was to start kicking the door and, for the good of both of us, he finally drove away.

Here was my little cousin, passed out in his $500 suit on the corner of 23rd and Sixth. It was 2 a.m. and I hadn't a clue what to do. I tried to wake him, but he would only groan, his eyes would flicker a bit, and then he proceeded to curl himself into a more comfortable position on the sidewalk.

"O.K., Donny," I said slowly, "I am going to get us a cab, and you are going to stand up."

But cabs stayed far away. Cars stayed far away. People walking on the sidewalk would cross the street before getting close to us. Even police cars wouldn't stop. So I sat down on the sidewalk, put Donny's head on my leg using his suit jacket as a pillow, and watched the world go by. I could have been in worse places and certainly in worse company, so it wasn't that bad.

But soon enough it was 3 a.m. I was getting cold, and I didn't want to wait for sunrise.

I started to shake him. I shook him harder. No response. "Donny! WAKE UP!" This went on for several minutes until he slowly opened his eyes.

"Water."

"What?!"

He repeated. "Water. Mike, get me water."

"Get you water? What, are you crazy? Come on, come on, stand up. We'll get a cab and I'll get you all the water you want."

He moaned. "No, leave me here, get me water."

"Leave you? I'm not going to leave you."

"No, Mike. Leave me here and get me water."

I attempted to pick him up, but he was dead weight.

So here I was. My brother, buried under millions of pounds of steel and pulverized concrete with little chance of any part of him being found; my father, with major depression and intractable pain imprisoned in God's waiting room; my sister, going through the same shit as I was and now having heated arguments with her husband; a failed day with Janet, with the same heated arguments; Pat's novel and the lawyer meetings, his "best" friends who wanted to get into Pat's apartment and into his will, the baseball-capped cabbie and my brief trip to the other side of the looking glass, and now—now, at 3 a.m., stranded in the cold on a New York City sidewalk with my 220-pound little cousin, who refuses to move unless I get him some FUCKING WATER.

I needed help, but I didn't know which number to dial. I ran a long list of names through my head, but with each name was a reason I couldn't call. I knew this much: if I called Janet, she would just yell at me. I felt that could wait. Then it hit me. I took out my cell phone and dialed the number that I'd depended on since the beginning of this whole horror. The phone rang several times until a half-asleep and half-angry voice that I didn't recognize answered.

"Hello, Ladder Company 3, Firefighter McCain."

I didn't recognize the name.

"Ah, ah...this is Mike Brown. Ah, ah...I'm Captain Patrick Brown's brother and I'm stuck on 23rd and Sixth with my driver, who I can't get up off the sidewalk."

The now *really* pissed off voice said, "You must be fucking kidding me! You're *who?* Hang on."

He left to wake up the lieutenant and was transferring my call. It didn't sound like he was going to help me. A minute or two later, I heard a drowsy voice on the other end of the line.

"Hello, this is the lieutenant. You're whose brother? Where are you? Your cousin is where and wants what? Don't move."

I sat back down, put Donny's head back on my leg and draped his suit jacket over him. Before this night, I worried how I was ever going to repay Donny for what he'd done for us.

He opened his eyes and croaked, "Mike—water."

Now I didn't have to worry.

Just then the white noise from the traffic was cut by two blasts from 3 Truck's air horn. I stood up; the massive fire truck pulled in front of us with its crew on board. A company can't leave the firehouse without all its men in case there's a call. So in response to my plea for help, they turned out the whole ladder company to rescue us. I didn't recognize anyone from Ladder 3, and there was a good reason—our rescuing ladder company was not Ladder 3. They were from Ladder 113 in Brooklyn. Ladder 3 had been relieved of duty to attend a wake the night before and a memorial service later that morning. I'm sure the covering men from Flatbush were not very pleased to be awakened at 3 a.m. to pick up two drunks off the sidewalk, but they never showed it. They acted as if it were business as usual. Two big guys hoisted Donny like a sack of potatoes, then gently placed him in the back of the rig. I got into the front seat. We were saved.

I woke up back on my couch in the basement of 3 Truck a few hours later. I went upstairs to find Donny, still quite comatose on another couch.

"Donny. Wake up!"

Donny bolted upright. "Where the hell are we?! How did I get here?"

"Come on, Donny, we need to go to a funeral. Hey—you want that water?"

Chapter 19

BY THE END OF September the cold air had made its way in. Wherever I went or whatever I did in New York, there was someone who was a close friend of Pat's and needed to share a Paddy Brown story. The stories were powerful, made me very proud, made me feel that Pat was superhuman and just couldn't be dead—and some even made me laugh. But all the stories made me miss him more and wish I'd made a point to spend more time with him. The phone would ring, and it would be someone who needed to meet with me. I would go to these meetings, over a beer or coffee or on a street corner, and each time the person I met was devastated. They would tell stories of great heroism, or insist that their lives had been forever changed having known Paddy Brown. They were really telling me how much they missed him too. It was all becoming overwhelming.

I'd replaced eating and sleeping with drinking. It wasn't as though I would wake up and down a bottle of rum. Most of the people I was meeting were firemen who were hurting just like me and, at some point during the evening, we would end up in a bar after a wake or after a funeral or after a memorial or during dinner or after dinner or at a meeting or after a meeting or while waiting for a wake, funeral, memorial, dinner or meeting. Day after day—New York had become a massive, perpetual Irish wake. It was time for me to make my way back to the desert, back to the ER, back to my life. I needed to go home.

Janet planned to leave for Vegas the next day and was going to have dinner with her family. She thought it was selfish of me not to go with her and preferring to be alone. She headed out to Queens; I headed downtown. Bobby told me that Bleecker Street in the Village would have live music, so I was off to be alone in a crowd. I was in no hurry. It didn't really matter if I made it to Bleecker or not.

It was good just to walk, and I did eventually make it. There were several clubs, each with its own unique personality, and music flowing into the street. There was a heavy-metal club with healthy, good-looking New Yorkers outside doing their best to look ugly and unhealthy, and the rap club with these kids who seemed, for some reason, to all have exceptionally long limbs, a grand time swinging their arms around to the music, making signs, grabbing their genitals. It was as if I were walking past a deaf-mute camp during a scabies outbreak. There was a club playing that awful electric loop music, the type that plays a set of notes or a rhythmic pattern over and over until you're so sick of it that you consider the composer a genius when a new pattern is added to the mix. (There was no one outside this place.) It was way too early for the X people to start partying. I felt a certain calmness watching all these animated, vibrant people refusing to allow the threat of terrorism to get in the way of their lives.

It was also good not to be drinking. If I did find a club, I planned to have one, maybe two beers at the most, stop at 3 Truck, and make it back to the hotel before Janet. Well, I made it to a bar called the Red Lion. The band was playing some good acoustic rock/blues, so I walked up to the bouncer in front collecting money and asked, "How much?"

"Five." He did a double take. "Hey, don't I know you?"

Getting my wallet out to pay, I said, "No, don't think so."

He was staring at me. "Sure I do. You live around here?"

"No, I'm sorry, it's not me. I live in Vegas," I said, handing him a ten.

His face lit up. "Vegas! You're Paddy Brown's brother! Put your money away!"

Does Pat know everyone in New York? Aren't there, like, 12 million people in this city?

I was escorted in. Not only the bouncer but also a bartender and most of the staff knew Pat too. My plans for an early night turned into an early morning. The Irish wake continued, and somewhere in the back of my mind I was concerned that I'd never go home or get my life back.

By the time I got out of the Red Lion, it was too late to stop at 3 Truck. In truth, I was embarrassed to be intoxicated again. I took a cab back to the hotel without incident or unplanned gutter stops. Janet wasn't happy when I got in, but at least she was all packed to go home. She had a late-afternoon flight and wanted to go to the site one more time before she left. For me it was a nap, shower, shave and a new day.

DONNY PICKED US UP and drove us to the Metropolitan, the restaurant that his father had owned for years. It was across the street from One Police Plaza—NYPD headquarters—and around the block from City Hall. We arrived to find concrete barricades blocking access to the streets; police and National Guardsmen were brandishing automatic weapons. This made it almost impossible to get to the once thriving restaurant and reminded us that we were at war. The mood was as heavy as the air drifting due east from the Trade Center.

At the time, a federal fund was being set up to help local businesses that were suffering because of the tight security in lower Manhattan. The problem: almost all the available money went to the lawyers and other businesses that didn't depend on foot traffic and weren't terribly affected by the barriers and roadblocks—but knew how to get money out of the government. Unfortunately this was all new for Don Brown. He lacked that special skill. He'd never asked for such assistance in his life. His Metropolitan was slowing bleeding to death.

My cousin's place is a traditional New York restaurant/bar. The front door leads into the bar area, which is separated from a moderate-size dining room. Everything is wood, giving the place a warm, relaxed atmosphere. There are old photos on the walls in the bar area that had been there for years. Since the Metropolitan is located across from police headquarters, the pictures initially were of policemen like Don and his father, who had also been a cop. But as time passed, as Pat was awarded more and more medals and had newspaper articles written about him, so stories and photos of Pat were slowly taking over the walls. There was even a picture of me from the 1988 Medal Day. There I was with Donny's sister Stacy, wearing my ill-fitting uniform with the bugle proudly pinned on my chest.

A new picture had made it up on one wall. It was of a fireman named Kevin Bracken. Kevin was from Engine 40, which shared quarters with Ladder 35 on the Upper West Side near Lincoln Center. I'd read that on 9/11 they headed toward the Trade Center like the cavalry turning their horses toward the sound of gunfire. Along with Kevin, 11 others were missing from Engine 40, Ladder 35.

We were at the Metropolitan to have lunch with a part of my family that I'd met maybe once or twice in my life. Don Brown had a brother Jim, also my first cousin; Jim had been killed in an automobile accident about 30 years before. He was survived by his wife Mary and their two sons, Jimmy and Greg—my second cousins. We all sat at a long table by the bar. Jimmy's wife Kathy sat next to me; across from us, Kathy's brother Bill and their dad Hugh. No one really ate. We all just kind of picked at our food, and there was some talk about various experiences since 9/11. There was no rush to fill in the silent breaks in conversation because the silence was not uneasy. We all belonged to the Club—that special organization where the members had an instant bond. It is a club that no one would ever want to join or even knew existed until they were a member. Kevin Bracken was Kathy and Bill's brother; he was Hugh's youngest child.

Hugh Bracken looked up from his plate of untouched burger and fries. "Mike, do you think you can get us into Ground Zero?"

Bill spoke up. "Someone had offered to take us down there a week or so ago, but at the time it was just too much for us to handle," he said. "Now my father and I realize that we need to see for ourselves. Can you get us in?"

I was taken aback by the question, not because they said they needed to be there—that part I understood—and not because it was the same question that I'd asked Dan Browne. I was taken aback because unlike Captain Dan Browne, I had no authority. Regardless, I answered immediately. "Sure, come with us. We're going down right after lunch."

Authority? Who needs stinking authority— when you have a brown Caprice and a driver who can do anything?

After finishing my third Coke, I assured them, "Don't worry, Donny can get us in anywhere."

My cell phone rang and I went outside to answer it. The caller was John L. Smith, a columnist from the *Las Vegas Review–Journal.* Someone from the hospital told him of my situation, gave him my name and number, and now he wanted an interview. I sat on one of those concrete barriers and answered his questions. The interview ended with the final thought—that if I were the one buried in the collapse, my brother would be doing just what I was doing now. I said, "It's what brothers do."

I hung up and just sat there. I guess I lost track of time because Don Sr. came out to get me. We both sat there—it was chilly despite the afternoon sun—with the smell of concrete and broken hearts coming from the site so close, and the guards with their automatic weapons all around us. Both of us were appreciating the value of family and the little time we have here on this earth.

"Mike," he said, "I remember when my brother Jim was killed—I thought about him every day. I know exactly how you feel. I walked around with this painful void inside me. But then one day, 20 years after his death, I was driving to the city, and the void just...closed." He paused, as if still surprised by it. "I remember clearly when it happened. Oh, I still think of him every day, but I no longer have that awful hole inside me." He gave me a gentle warning: "Don't expect anything to change for a long time."

DONNY, AS EXPECTED, GOT us to Ground Zero. We walked down a hill past construction workers, people from FEMA, police, firemen and the National Guard, ending up in front of Engine 10, Ladder 10's firehouse. Janet, Donny and the Brackens and I stood together and watched the men climb, dig and search in hopes of finding a body. I searched the great hole in the sky for Pat's spirit, but this time he was no longer there. Janet had to go, so we said our goodbyes and Donny drove her to the airport.

Bill and his father Hugh took several minutes before they could hold their hearts together well enough to carry on a conversation. Overwhelmed, Bill finally said to me, "It looks different from all the pictures I've seen."

I agreed. "Yeah, it's like the Grand Canyon, you need to be there to appreciate its depth."

We stood and watched someone carry out a fire boot; his expression told us it wasn't empty. Hugh Bracken took pictures of one of the steel hills and, after some time, was ready to leave.

"Do you want to see the North Tower?" I asked them.

"Do you think it's all right?"

"Sure, come on."

We started to walk through the site, stepping over fire hoses and across steel plates that were covering holes. I said, "Just look like you're supposed to be here, and watch those trucks. They'll run you over."

No one bothered us. Perhaps they recognized that we were members of the Club.

Chapter 20

THAT NIGHT OVER DINNER, which Bobby again paid for, he and I started to plan the inevitable. We discussed locations, dates and times for Pat's memorial. The more we talked, the more obvious it became that we were going to need several people to help put it all together. To do what Pat wished and deserved was going to be a major production. I remember years ago reading an interview with Andrew Carnegie on how he'd become so successful. He said that he surrounded himself with people who were smarter than he was. It was my turn to do the same.

It made sense that I would discuss every decision with Bobby. He knew Pat even better than I did. It was as though I had another brother in Bobby that I never knew existed. Steve Browne had become a great friend. He had also become something that he never wanted or ever expected: an expert on fire department wakes and funerals. I also valued his ability to see into the future. Then there was Donny and his family, the guys from

Pat's list, 3 Truck and 69/28 in Harlem. Most of the Inner Circle was already together—all I had to do was open my eyes.

Bobby agreed that the later the date for Pat's memorial, the better. The advantages: more people could attend; my father would be stronger. There was also the chance that Pat's body would be found before that time. My feeling about finding his body was that right now, he was with some of the most courageous people who had ever lived—maybe that's where he belonged. On a deeper level, I just didn't want to have to make the decision about cremation.

During dinner, my cell phone rang. It was Donny wanting to know if we had plans for later that night. Bobby had to go home.

But me, what was I going to do? Sleep?

AT 11 P.M., DONNY and I were in Times Square looking for something to do. Drinking was not high on the list. Donny seemed to know every cop in the city and got a suggestion from one of the officers who patrolled the area. We found out that a Times Square bar was hosting a benefit for a local firehouse. A bar, yeah!—that's different. We walked in and paid $20 each, only to find the place empty. We sat at the bar looking around until we realized the benefit was on the second floor. Holding our almost untouched beers, we made it upstairs. The room was packed. There was a great band playing, with a kick-ass guitarist. Donny yelled over the music. "Mike, can you play as good as this guy?"

I laughed. "Sure, they're only notes."

Then I really started to listen. The style of the guitarist was unique. It hit me—the guitarist was George Benson, and he was playing with some of the members from the *Saturday Night Live* house band.

I shook my head. "Donny, I'm wrong. I can't play like this guy."

An intoxicated man wearing an FDNY sweatshirt stopped in front of me and yelled into my ear. "You're Paddy Brown's brother! I was his best friend!"

The music was excellent, and all I wanted to do was sip my beer and listen to one of my guitar heroes, but the fireman continued to yell over the music. "I want to give your brother's eulogy!"

Bobby and I hadn't even discussed eulogies, so I told him truthfully, "I haven't decided, but I'll keep you in mind."

The band had a fantastic Chicago blues thing going on and it was cranking. Again, he yelled over the music. "I'm serious! I want to give your brother's eulogy! You know, at St. Pat's—" The music stopped.

"I'll consider it," I said dismissively.

Benson started to play *On Broadway*—and the fireman kept talking. There were a few other well-

known musicians there, and I looked over to see
Paul Shaffer, band leader for David Letterman,
about to pass in front of us.

"Shit, Donny—that's Paul Shaffer!"

I put out my hand to him and he shook it. "Mr.
Shaffer, I'm a big fan of yours and appreciate what
you do."

His handshake was not the firmest in the world.
He moved to Donny, who said, while shaking his
hand, "Paul, you're a great musician."

Then the fireman who wanted to give Pat's
eulogy shook Paul Shaffer's hand. He yelled,
"Come on, Paul, shake my hand like a man!"

Donny broke the uneasy silence that followed
by saying diplomatically, "He's a musician—he
has to protect his hands."

I didn't choose that fireman to eulogize my
brother.

THE NEXT DAY I checked out of the Delmonico, said
goodbye to the staff—who all knew me by then—
and met Donny on the sidewalk.

"Donny, where's my limo?"

"I couldn't get it. My brother Jimmy lent me
his truck."

Jimmy—also a cop—is Donny's fraternal
twin. Not possible they could be identical: I
couldn't imagine two Donny Browns on the same
planet. Jimmy's truck, a gleaming black diesel
Dodge Ram, is not what you'd want to drive in the

city. But I relaxed. Because of its massive size, I was sure there was no way Donny could maneuver this thing like a maniac. I settled back for a less stressful ride out to Long Island to see my father before going to the airport.

I was wrong. With people screaming and horns blaring at us, we ripped through the streets of Manhattan. And Queens. And Nassau County. Traffic regulations, lights, signs, barricades—not even police cars concerned my little cousin.

Chapter 21

GOD'S WAITING ROOM WAS as cheery as ever. When Donny and I walked into the building, the staff looked happy to see other people who were actually alive. The girl behind the desk greeted us and spoke to me as she looked up through her lashes at Donny.

"Hello, Dr. Brown," she murmured. "Your father is still refusing to get out of bed."

Donny and I walked down the hall to my father's room. He turned to me and said, "See that? She wants me."

"Get outta here. She was just being nice."

"No, Mike—she wants me. She noticed how incredibly good-looking I am. She wants to sleep with me."

I groaned. "Donny, do you ever listen to yourself talk?"

"You just don't understand," he said with a shrug.

In the doorway of my father's room, we could see the shadow of the man once so strong and proud. My father was lying motionless in bed, fixated on the TV. *"We are continuing our coverage of the World Trade*

Center" boomed out of the set. When he saw us, his heavy, dull eyes came to life.

"Mike! Mike! Donny! Look at this!" Then, "What are you doing here?"

We both gave him a hug and sat on chairs next to the bed. Donny and I gave him a full update on what was going on. He looked at me and said, "What do I have to do?" He was obviously referring to Pat's funeral arrangements.

"Dad, I'm taking care of everything. You just have to get yourself out of here."

"But Mike, I'm in too much pain."

"I know you're in pain." I paused, then gave him a dose of cold reality. "If you don't get out of here, you will never forgive yourself. Do you understand?"

"Yes, but I'm in so much pain."

Soon it was time for us to go. "Come on, Uncle John," Donny ordered. "Get in the wheelchair—we'll walk with you to the elevator."

"No, Donny. It hurts too much."

As I knew by then, you can't tell Donny no. It was like a freaking miracle. Despite all my father's objections and pleas for help, Donny managed to get him out of bed and into his wheelchair by himself. He wanted us to push him, but we refused. So he came out with us past the girl at the desk. As we passed her, Donny, from the corner of his mouth, directed his voice waves directly at her. "Sweetheart, I'll see you soon." She returned the comment with a look directly back at him—one of those sulky pre-bedroom smiles, the type that comes mostly from the eyes. Like a master ventriloquist, he effortlessly redirected the sound waves toward me as only Donny could. "See, Mike? I told you she wants me."

The three of us made our way to the elevator. I was about to say goodbye to my father when he continued into the elevator with us. He escorted Donny and me out of the building to Jimmy's truck—which, of course, was parked right out front. Illegally.

In a much stronger voice, my father asked, "Mike, where are you going now?"

"We're going to get something to eat, then Donny's dropping me off at the airport."

He surprised us by saying, "Well, let me come with you!"

Donny said, "Uncle John, we can't do that. You're a hospital patient. You need to stay here and get better."

Donny and I made sure he could get himself back into the building, then climbed into Jimmy's truck. But before we drove away, we watched my father—just for a moment—sitting up in his wheelchair, breathing in the fresh air, a slight smile on his face. At that moment in time, John P. Brown rejoined the living.

At that moment in time, the right choice would have been to take him to dinner.

Chapter 22

AFTER MY PLANE LANDED in Las Vegas, I noticed that the baggage-claim area at McCarran Airport was very different than at any other time I could remember. The two huge video screens at each end of the enormous space were still streaming out ads proclaiming the very best restaurants, the very best slot machines and the very best shows to the very few travelers who had no intention of visiting the Strip. If they were like me, they lived in Southern Nevada and just wanted to get home. The luggage conveyer belts were relatively empty, and I waited by one of them with a few other ex–New Yorkers. We all idly watched one piece of lost luggage perpetually circling the racetrack pattern waiting for its owner, who was probably too frightened to board the flight. True, the terrorists had everyone on edge; yet in many ways they'd also resurrected the American spirit. But what they did to Vegas? They'd rendered it insignificant. It had lost its purpose. It was a hollowed-out shell. As hollow as this airport baggage-claim area. As hollow as I was.

"Mike." It was Janet's voice coming from behind me.

I turned and there she was, with a sad welcome-home look on her face. We embraced for a long time, and just for that moment, I no longer felt hollow.

When we made it back home, our two old dogs were so happy to see us both that they ran around the house and the yard like puppies. And that night, for the first time in several nights, back in my own bed, I was able to sleep.

The hotels and casinos may have been empty, but the Las Vegas emergency rooms were overflowing. A large number of casino workers had lost their jobs along with their benefits, and had nowhere else to go for medical care. It was also the beginning of the malpractice crisis that would take its toll on Nevada, resulting in a mass exodus of physicians from the state. I was nervous about going back to work and didn't know if I could handle it. Even worse, I didn't know how my coworkers and friends were going to handle *me.* One thing I did know—the ER was going to be busy as shit.

MY FIRST DAY BACK, the ER was severely bound up. My best clinical analogy: like a pound of cheese in the bowels of a 90-year-old. The ambulance entrance was choked by a long parade of paramedics who were stuck because there was no place to put their patients. I knew most of the paramedics; I played softball with a few of them, and over the years some became my friends.

They were good people. I've always felt that Las Vegas has the best paramedics in the country. Now I worried that they too were going to make an exodus out of Nevada. Everyone passing by in the halls welcomed me home. Katie was there and gave me a big hug. "Welcome back, Doc! You doing O.K.?"

"Yeah. Thanks, Katie." As we stopped to talk, I also received a surprisingly warm welcome home from her patient—he spit a river of blood at me.

Katie's patient was an intoxicated, busted-up, belligerent bastard whose face looked like hamburger. (By the way, it is written in the ancient Emergency Medicine Physician Tablets that you are allowed to refer to anyone who spits blood at you as a bastard.) He was also spitting profanities and pronouncements on why someone had busted him up in the first place, and in doing so, he seemed to be requesting that the beating resume.

We all had an interesting dance with this gentleman as we secured the appropriate hardware to prevent him from hurting himself or anyone else. As this waltz was going on, a patient in the hall who had been brought to the hospital because he was too drunk to stand up decided to stand up and—*bang!*—fell into the wall. He then sat back in his chair. His diagnosis went from "too intoxicated to ambulate" to "too intoxicated to ambulate with a facial laceration."

Back at the dance, I held the blood-spitting hamburger meathead still. Katie placed a surgical mask over his face, muffling that old familiar song,

"Fuck you all! You have no fucking right! Get me my fucking lawyer!" Holding him down, I spoke into his right ear.

"Your fucking lawyer is not going to put your fucking face back together—I AM. So if you don't want to look like fucking Frankenstein, you'll fucking cooperate."

This stopped him for about 30 seconds before he resumed his tirade about all the people he was going to sue.

"Katie, I'll see you inside," I said.

I walked past one more patient before going into the main department of the ER. She was in her 70s, frail, pale, lying on an ambulance stretcher and stuck in the busy hallway waiting for an ER bed to open. There was panic in her eyes, worry that her cancer had returned or her heart was giving out, or maybe she had pneumonia, or perhaps her body had finally betrayed her and was just simply giving out. Here, surrounded by the violence and arrogance of other patients, this gentle, frightened soul—truly someone who needed emergency medical care—was forced to lie on a stretcher in a hallway. She waited silently, her face filled with fear and uncertainty. For patients like this little old lady, a good paramedic needs compassion just as much as skill; for patients like Hamburger Face, all you need are restraints. Otherwise the ambulance crew would have dropped off that lovely individual in the middle of the desert and not at an emergency room.

It was time to get back into the game. Because all idle thoughts were spent on what was happening in New York, I was not as efficient or as fast as I once was. The other doc on duty was picking up the slack. There was certainly enough to do and, as the day went on, the patient build-up was getting worse. Only the sick as shit were getting in: intracranial bleeds, sepsis, respiratory failure, stroke, MI—myocardial infarction, a blockage that can lead to a heart attack—stuff like that. We had to move a "rule out MI" patient to make room for a cardiac arrest, a 36-year-old male found "down." The paramedic's magic failed and so did ours. He came in dead and was still dead.

When do you stop working a code? There are no textbook answers; only experience and judgment to rely on, and we probably worked this one too long. The obvious reason for extending the effort this time was his age, and that he was healthy—well, healthy until his heart stopped beating. There was also a subconscious, maybe even selfish reason that I kept the resuscitation attempt going. It was my first day back, and I didn't think that I could face his family.

After working on him for almost an hour, during which time we had tried, failed, and exhausted all efforts of resuscitation, the charge nurse said, "Dr. Brown, his wife is in the quiet room."

I asked, "Does she know how sick he was?"

"I don't think so. Are you ready to go in? I'll go with you."

There was no way out. It was the cold reality of life, and I had no idea how she would react to the horrible news. I had no idea how *I* was going to react when I gave her the horrible news. We walked in to find the patient's wife: about 30 years old, scared as shit.

"Mrs. Davis? Please sit down," was all I needed to say. She read my eyes and broke down.

"What happened?" she asked through her tears.

"I think he had a massive heart attack." I went on as she wept. "The paramedics found him not breathing and without a heartbeat. They did everything they could and so did we, but nothing was going to bring him back. Can you tell me, did he have any heart problems?"

"No, but—" She took a ragged breath. "He was having chest pain all week; I told him to go to the doctor, but he refused." Tears of guilt were added to her tears of grief. "I should have *forced* him to go! He kept refusing. I knew something bad was going to happen, but he wouldn't listen."

Taking her hand in mine and in my best Steve Browne voice I told her, "No, you can't blame yourself. He was his own man and made his own decisions. What could you have done—knocked him out and dragged him in?"

She gave me a sad smile. I continued to channel Steve. "You have a lot of thoughts racing though your head," I said softly. "Take them one at a time, and you'll get through it."

THANK GOD IT WAS near the end of my shift—because I was starting to feel useless. My plan was to clean up what I was working on and not get involved with any other difficult cases. I picked up the chart of a 50-year-old man visiting from out of state. His complaint was a black sore on his forehead. He said he'd noticed it a few days earlier, and it was getting bigger. Sure enough, that's what he had—a big, black, necrotic skin lesion smack in the middle of his forehead, and no idea how it got there. Strange.

I was very tired, but my brain immediately launched into search mode. *The differential diagnosis in a person with this presentation is limited and includes a brown recluse spider bite—but also includes anthrax.* Neither I nor anyone else I know had ever seen a case of anthrax. Got to be a spider bite. *Such a strange place for a recluse spider bite.* At that time there was one suspected case of anthrax in Florida, but it was an isolated case, not considered to be a biological attack. I discharged him with wound-care instructions, then added a prescription for Cipromycin. Anthrax was impossible—but then again, I'd just returned from the impossible.

I HAD THE FOLLOWING day off and planned to discuss Pat's memorial arrangements with Bobby. I turned on the news to see what was happening at the WTC site and there it was—anthrax in Washington.

Oh, shit!

In a second I was off the couch and back in the ER. I tried to contact my patient, but he was flying home. I finally got through to his job and left a message to call me as soon as he got in. Then I called the FBI.

"Hello, my name is Michael Brown. I'm an emergency medicine physician and I need to report a possible case of anthrax."

After being transferred to several FBI departments and being placed on hold over and over again, I was transferred to the cell phone of the special agent that was assigned to biological terrorism in Las Vegas. Finally. At least I would be able to speak with someone who would be interested. I quickly explained the situation to her. Long pause. "I'm driving in my car," she replied. "I have nothing to write with to take down your information."

I couldn't believe what I was hearing. This information was coming from an ER doc, not from someone who'd noticed some white powder next to a damned coffee pot. She also said that she didn't think driving in to Sunrise Hospital to interview me would do any good. At that point I fully agreed. I thanked her and hung up.

LATER THAT DAY I got back to my yard, dogs and phones. I started to make calls. I spoke to Bobby for over an hour, and we discussed everything from white powder next to a coffee pot to Pat's final wishes. I didn't bring up the possibility of cremation or my now stupid, irrational hope that Pat was still alive under the pile. I hung up and the phone rang almost immediately. It was Steve Browne giving me updates on the activity at Ground Zero and at the firehouse. We also spoke for about an hour. These calls reminded me of how much I needed to do back in New York.

The phone rang again. This time it was Ellin Martens, a reporter for *Time* magazine. A few years back, she'd done reporting for a cover story about adrenaline junkies. The focus was on different kinds of daredevil activity that gave the participant a rush of adrenaline that each truly craved. Pat was one of the people she'd interviewed and, as he pointed out to me when the story appeared, just about the only one in that article who was saving lives. Afterward she and Pat dated for a while, broke up, but always remained friends.

She told me to expect a call from *GQ* magazine because they'd selected Pat as the GQ/Discover Card Man of the Year. On impulse she'd written a contest essay about him, sent it in just before 9/11, and they chose Pat as their winner—before they knew if he'd survived. She spoke to Bobby before she called me. When she gave him the news, the phone went silent. She thought he was going to cry, but his voice came back and he said, "Jesus Christ, the guy is gone and they're *still* giving him awards!" Discover Card wanted to make a donation in his name. Even though her name was not on the list, Ellin belonged in the Inner Circle.

I hung up and the phone rang yet again. This time it was James Remar. I don't know if he knew it at the time, but he was already part of the Inner Circle. As we talked, I was reminded of Pat's visit in October last year. James had a part in a television series called *The Huntress*. During Pat's visit, he didn't care what we did—with the exception of watching *The Huntress*. In the middle of the program, Pat picked up the phone and called James. I was impressed. I watched my brother have an enthusiastic conversation with one of the main characters of the show. I sat there and listened as they discussed the plot, other characters and performances. Before that, the last time I heard Pat so excited was when he told me about one of his rescues.

It was easy to talk with James. He was still as crushed as I was and frustrated that he couldn't be more involved in the planning. He had commitments in L.A., but he assured me he would not miss his best friend's memorial.

I hung up and the phone rang again, but this time it was a local call. I heard the voice of my friend Ernie on the other end of the line. "Hey!" he said. "I'm coming over to take you out for wings and beer."

Ernie and I had a lot in common, from electronics to medicine. He was an ER nurse and wanted to be a doctor. We both flew airplanes. I took flying lessons and earned a license; Ernie built an ultralight and flew it until it scared the shit out of him. Then there was our interest in music. Ernie was a drummer; I played guitar. We also had similar tastes in music, weird stuff like

Tom Waits—and not a lot of people understood Tom Waits. We had the computer connection: I wanted to digitally record music, so Ernie built me a supercomputer for super money that was super time-consuming. The only thing this supercomputer could *not* do was record, which was a real frustration both of us. The greatest thing we had in common: a mutual love of good conversation—about medicine, flying, music, computers and life—especially over wings and beer.

That night at the bar, despite my dull affect and my sadness, Ernie asked me to be in his wedding party. *How cool is that?* I was very happy for him and Lisa. Since we both had to be at work the next day, we couldn't pull a New York thing and have the bar close down around us. But Ernie and Lisa's upcoming wedding deserved one more beer before we called it a night.

THE NEXT DAY I was back in the ER and back in the shit. The hospital must have been given a cathartic because the patients were moving again. We were all running around doing that ER thing when I received a call from my sister telling me that my father was not doing well. I had to hang up because the paramedics rushed in a 24-year-old female in cardiopulmonary arrest. The report was that she'd just flown in from North Carolina for her wedding; her fiancé lived here in Vegas. She was found "down and dead." Her fiancé was now in the quiet room. The firemen and the paramedics feverishly tried to reverse her condition, and they all had a look of sheer desperation. They transferred her to us and we took over her care—and their desperation.

Prior to this, she'd been very healthy: no medical history, good physical condition, took care of herself, and was young—way too young to just up and die. Everyone from the firemen to the paramedics to the nurses to the radiology techs to the pulmonary tech to the pharmacist to the radiologist to the on-call cardiologist to the ER clerk to the charge nurse to housekeeping to me used our knowledge, hearts and prayers, but nothing was going to change the fact that she was dead. We worked the code for far too long before I finally had to make the decision to stop. All of us on the ER team who had been involved in the resuscitation effort were left sweating, exhausted, shaken up and bitterly disappointed. As everyone went back to doing whatever ER thing they were doing before she arrived, I thought how proud I was to work with such fine people. It reminded me that this was the reason I wouldn't want to work anywhere else.

"Dr. Brown, Dr. Brown!" It was the social worker. "Dr. Brown, you need to tell the family. If you want, I'll come with you."

We slowly made our way to the quiet room. We stood in front of the closed door to gather some composure, took a deep breath, and opened it. Standing at the end of the small room was the patient's 24-year-old fiancé. He was my height, with eyes full of tears and panic. He ran up to me as soon as I opened the door.

"How is she doing? Is she going to be all right?!"

In a calm voice, I said, "Why don't we sit down?"

He yelled into my face, "Don't tell me to sit down! Is she is going to be all right?!"

"I'm sorry. She—"

"You're *sorry?* What's wrong with her?"

I understood his desperation. I continued, using a calm voice. "When the paramedics found her, she didn't have a heartbeat. We all did the best—"

"Are you telling me she's *dead?*" I thought he was about to deck me.

"I'm sorry. We did the best—"

"No, NO! You get back in there and *do* something! What kind of fucking doctor *are* you? There must be something more that can be done! Get the *fuck* back *in there!*"

He yelled at me for what seemed like an eternity. It was obvious he didn't want to understand that his future with her would never happen. He was becoming violent. I needed to leave.

After that, I couldn't go right back to the ER; in fact, I thought that I never wanted to go back to the ER. I escaped into the doctor's locker room. There was plenty for me to do in there—CT scans to be checked, blood-work interpretation, all that other doctor stuff. But right now no one was dying, so it could all wait. I sat at a small round table tucked into the corner of the small room and tried to make sense of things, tried to regain control, tried to follow Steve Browne's advice: one thought at a time. I slowly looked up and saw my locker with the label MICHAEL E. BROWN, M.D. MASTER OF THE UNIVERSE. *Master of the Universe, yeah, right—what a joke.* At that moment, I didn't even feel like a doctor.

I think I would have hid there forever if it weren't for the voice that exploded from the PA speaker: *"We need a doctor to Room 4. Full cardiac arrest, two minutes out."*

I stood up, took a deep breath, and spoke aloud to the empty locker room—and to my brother. "Doesn't anyone ever die at home anymore?"

There we were, part of the same crew that had just coded that 24-year-old girl, wondering what we'd be facing this time. The ER doors flew open and a crew of paramedics came through with an 85-year-old man from a rehab hospital. There was a fireman riding the side rail of the stretcher doing chest compressions. This man had lung cancer. Just a few days ago he'd been considering DNR status, which means, "Please, just let me die." Well, he never did sign those papers to make it legal, so we performed our ER magic. I saw his cardiac rhythm change on the monitor. Over the commotion I yelled, "Hold CPR and check for pulses!"

Holding her hand on the patient's carotid artery, Cheryl, one of our nurses, looked at me as though we'd just committed a sin. "I have a pulse."

The pulse didn't last long before his cardiac rhythm changed again, and it was back to CPR, back to our black magic. The rhythm of his heartbeat changed, and once more, we had pulses. This scenario kept repeating until we went through every algorithm from the Advance Cardiac Life Support, plus a few we made up on our own. Everyone knew it was useless and the patient was going to die, either now or in one to two days. This poor guy was clinically dead at least six times, but with our ER magic, we wouldn't let him go.

"Restart chest compressions, give another epi. Shit!—V-fib. Let's shock him again. Any pulses?"

"None," said Joe, another nurse who was part of the team.

I was puzzled as I glanced once again at the monitor. "Check again. This is the same rhythm he had before, and he should have pulses."

Cheryl answered, "No."

Joe confirmed. "I have none. What do you want to do now, Doc Brown?"

"Someone get a Doppler."

Giving me a "you must be kidding me" look, Cheryl went and returned with the handheld Doppler machine. She placed the probe over the femoral artery, and we heard a wild swishing noise with banging and clicking. It was far beyond the normal sound of blood flowing through the femoral artery. This cacophony was in sync with the cardiac monitor. Referring to all the noise from the Doppler, Cheryl asked, "Hey, Mike—what the hell is that?"

"That's the sound of this man's soul trying to escape," I responded. "What do you say we let it?"

Everyone agreed.

IT WAS OBVIOUS THAT I couldn't do this anymore. It was far from taking care of one thing at a time. On my way out after my shift, I passed a new parade of paramedics with their patients awaiting an ER bed. I crossed the parking lot to Dr. Paul Fischer's office. I was both physically and spiritually a mess when I flopped in the chair across from him. His melodic South African accent was soothing.

"Michael, was it busy over there today?"

I was exhausted. "No," I said. "Not really. About normal." I paused, then blurted, "Paul, I need to go back to New York."

With total understanding he replied, "Yes, Michael, I know. We'll cover you. Take all the time you need and give me a call when you're ready to come back."

JANET AND I HAD another argument that night when I told her I was going back to New York and she needed to stay in Vegas. She was back in school at UNLV and needed to take care of our home and the dogs. Simple, right? No. She didn't care. She was coming. We spent an angry hour in one of those stupid conversations that was totally irrational. The words made no sense, but there was an underlying meaning—and it had nothing to do with the dogs, the house or school. In New York there was a month's worth of work that I had to do and

210

only days to do it in. I needed the freedom to go anywhere, at anytime, and not worry about eating or sleeping. And truthfully, what I needed most was to go to some shithole bars with a bunch of firemen who were going through the same shit I was. I knew that if Janet came, no matter what she said, there would be no way I could do it all. She was also angry at the fact that Marc might be going back with me and couldn't understand why I would agree to *his* going but not *her*. I told her that it didn't matter if Marc went or not because he wouldn't slow me down—and *he* didn't *mind* going to shithole bars.

This was not a good thing to say. It set off another hour of nonsensical arguments.

By the time Janet dropped me off at the airport, that wall between us was back. I was running from one set of problems and smack into another, but I was headed right where I needed to be—New York City.

Chapter 23

COLD AIR AND A blazing early morning sun greeted me as I made my way out of the JFK terminal. After 10 years in the desert I'd adapted to the heat, so I was attracted to a small sunny patch in the passenger pickup area like a cold lizard to a warm flat rock. There must have been an easterly breeze because the smell of the Trade Center site was evident even out here in Queens—an instant reminder of why I was here. I never liked flying the redeye, but it sure beat the hell out of driving 46 hours. I had my cell phone and a small notebook, which now was full of phone numbers, directions and notes on what needed to be done. I had spoken with Bobby before leaving Vegas; he would not hear of it when I told him I'd cab it into the city. He was going to pick me up. No arguments. I didn't protest; nor did I point out to him that he didn't own a car. After a short wait, Bobby came rolling up just as he'd promised. He was in a dark sedan—an official fire department car—and Jim Carney from Harlem's Engine 69 was at the wheel. I shoved my suitcase in the trunk and got in the back seat. As Jim pulled away from the curb, he and Bobby brought me up to date on what was really going on at the site. Still no one from 3 Truck had been found.

During my last trip to New York I'd asked Donny to stay at Pat's apartment, just to keep an eye on things. Bobby told me that Keith McLaughlin was trying to get the NYPD to reassign Donny as my driver. My cell phone interrupted our conversation. It was a representative from *GQ* magazine. This was the phone call that Ellin Martens had told me to expect, informing me that they'd chosen Pat as Man of the Year in September. The woman recalled their shock and sorrow when they found out that he was one of the missing. Co-sponsor Discover Card wanted to donate $25,000 in Pat's name—and me to pick the charity.

"Let me think about it for a while," I told her. I opened my small notebook and wrote *Discover Card $25,000 donation???*

With undeserved guilt, Jim Carney looked at me in the rear-view mirror and repeated what he'd told me in the kitchen at the Harlem Hilton. "You know, Paddy would have never transferred downtown if I hadn't been on vacation. I *know* I would have talked him out of it." The unspoken implication that was torturing Jim: if Pat had been working in Harlem that morning, way uptown on 143rd Street, he would have been late to the scene—and alive today.

I don't remember, nor does it matter, what Bobby's or my response was. They were calling it survivor's guilt, and it seemed that every fireman had some degree of it. *If I hadn't changed shifts. If I didn't take that early relief. If I hadn't been on vacation. If my kid hadn't gotten sick. If I hadn't been stuck in traffic. If I didn't get detailed to another firehouse.* Survivor's guilt is one of those tidy terms we use so we don't have to visit the horror of the feelings they represent.

As we approached Manhattan, the conversation returned to the elephant in the living room, that big hole in the sky that used to be the World Trade Center. My feeling then was, and still is, that it shouldn't be rebuilt. "They would never think of raising the *Arizona,*" I said.

Jim said, "To keep it from becoming a target, the top floors should be a prison—"

"If you want it completely safe," Bobby interrupted him, "put CIA headquarters on the top floors."

"Just leave it alone," I said. "Leave a big hole in Manhattan—a void in New York's spirit."

When they dropped me off in front of the W hotel that cold morning, I felt as though I were home.

Steve Browne seemed to be able to do anything, and when he heard that I was coming in, he set me up at the W at Union Square. I'd never heard of the W and had no idea it was so high-class.

The hotel is about four blocks from Ladder 3 and across the street from Union Square; it has a great bar and a seating area with huge windows that overlook Park Avenue South—the perfect place to sit in a controlled environment and watch people contend with the uncontrolled environment outside. From the first time I saw the bar, I christened it the Fish Bowl. It seemed so appropriate that I never could remember its real name.

My original plan was to sleep in the basement of 3 Truck on what had come to be known as "my couch," but my couch was booked. Ladder 3's basement was now the temporary home of firemen from Chicago. In an arrangement happening across the city, thousands of firefighters from all over the world were bunking in city firehouses so they could attend memorials and funerals. That's what firemen do: they were dropping everything to come to New York to show respect and solidarity for their fallen brothers. These men in their Class As did a great job filling the thinned ranks at the services. For this, I had no problem giving up my couch—and admittedly no problem dealing with the luxury of the W. When I checked in that day wearing my Capt. Brown sweatshirt, and from that point on, everyone from the doorman to the waitress called me Captain Brown. I never corrected them. It was easier than explaining why I was wearing it; but I think they knew anyway. I was always proud to have been a fireman and now a doctor, and for this brief moment in time after the attack on the towers, being a fireman was more prestigious. September 11 had pressed the world's reset button. Nothing was soft or fuzzy. It was either right or it was wrong.

AFTER LEAVING MY BAGS in the room, I headed for 3 Truck. Manhattan was slowly coming back to life, but it was far from New York City normal—people were still being nice to one another. Walking out the door of the W, I saw the pictures and candles in Union Square, but now the people stopping to look were tourists with cameras. On the next corner was a grubby-looking guy with a shopping cart full of stuff. As I approached, I recalled how Pat would try to help the homeless by giving them sandwiches or money. I found a few singles in my back pocket and gave them to him. I didn't even realize that I'd paused briefly for a show of gratitude; I shook myself and moved on. He yelled after me, "Hey, thanks for the money—but you could've given me fucking twenty!" *What?* It brought me up short. *Maybe he knew my brother? He knew Pat would always give him a twenty?* I didn't want to get involved in this conversation. As I walked on, it suddenly struck me that Pat never would have paused to expect a thank you. And wasn't that what he had told me, when I asked him how he'd befriended all those Hollywood people? They knew he never expected anything from them.

Finally I was back in front of Ladder 3's firehouse, where I left the inanity of the city outside for the overwhelming sadness inside. Steve Browne, the unwilling authority on fire department memorials, was happy to see me.

The plans for Pat's memorial were becoming very complex, and the only way to get a handle on it was to have a meeting. Steve was able to get the W to donate a conference room. Initially, because Ladder 3 had so many other memorials to plan, 69/28 were going to take care of Pat's arrangements; they were more than motivated to do it for the man who had been their captain for eight years. My decision to delay the services until November seemed to change the dynamics of that plan, and I could only imagine the discussions that went on between those two firehouses. By delaying the date, everyone thought I was hoping Pat would be found. Not so. I was trying to allow more time for my father to recover, but the main reason was to give Pat what he'd wanted and deserved: a line-of-duty fire department funeral, body or not. There were still up to 15 funerals and memorials a day, and there would be no way that everyone who wanted to attend Pat's could do so.

"Mike," Steve asked, "what are you going to do if they find him?"

"I'll deal with that if it happens," I told him.

Steve Browne wanted to introduce me to another fireman, Steve Gonzalez, better known as

Gonzo. The guy was a little intimidating as he approached: taller than me, well built, with a dark frown as he gave me that wary "Now who the fuck is *this* guy?" fireman look. But when he heard my name, his face broke into a wide smile. And as I would soon find out, Gonzo had a heart of pure gold. Steve Browne declared that Gonzo was the man to go to if you needed something, anything done.

From the get-go, for some reason, Gonzo called me Mikey. "So Mikey, have you thought about the gathering after the service?"

"What gathering?"

I never knew what to call it, that event following a funeral when you have close friends and family back to the house. You sure couldn't call it a party; but it many respects it was a celebration. In the FDNY, it came to be known as the collation. There was no house that would be large enough to hold all of Pat's closest friends for his collation. Gonzo said he'd immediately get to work securing a ballroom at the Hilton New York, walking distance from St. Patrick's.

A loud tone went off on the firehouse's PA. It was the citywide message alert announcing the names of firemen whose bodies had been identified. Everyone froze as they listened for the names of men they knew. The list went on for several minutes. There was no more talk of voids in the firehouse. Only a handful of people had been found alive in the rubble, and they were rescued not long after the towers collapsed.

"Ah, Mike," Steve said, breaking the silence, "If they find your brother, I want to be the one to tell you. Is that all right with you?"

"Steve, that's perfect."

"Mikey, what are you doing later on?" Gonzo asked.

"Well, this afternoon I have to meet with some lawyers."

Steve broke in. "Not that book thing! Your brother told me about it. He agreed to one thing, and they completely turned it around. If you need anyone to testify, call me. I would love to tell those people what I think of them."

THE ATTORNEY THAT I had been working with on this most unwelcome and unneeded situation was Wilder Knight. That day we were going to sit down with all the players. Several years earlier, my brother had briefly dated a woman who was a freelance writer. He'd trusted her, introduced her to his circle of friends, even to widows of firefighters whom he'd known. She befriended them all, telling them she would like to use their stories "on background" for a novel that she was writing about firemen. Her main character, she said, would be based on Pat. He enthusiastically supported her, and the friends—out of deference to Pat— supported her too.

She finally delivered a galley proof to him in June 2001. When he read it, he erupted in anger. Sure, the main character was a Vietnam vet and a New York City firefighter. Yes, there were parallels to our family life in Queens and Westbury. But truths were twisted to the point where readers wouldn't know where reality ended and the novel began. Worse, the people whom Pat had introduced her to were so thinly disguised—the physical descriptions were dead-on—that anyone with a glancing knowledge of the FDNY would recognize them. And her imagination had embellished their lives as well.

Pat said he didn't mind his life story being twisted; although, he observed, he could probably live without looking like a total wacko. What made him incensed was how friends and acquaintances—people who had come to trust her, letting her read personal letters, even journal entries—would be so exposed when the book came out. As with Pat's life story, a reader wouldn't know where these people's life stories ended and the fiction took flight. He was especially upset with the fictional treatment of my parents. The last days of Pat's life were spent in discussion with Bobby and others on how to handle the novel when it hit bookstores on Tuesday, September 11.

Wilder met with me before the meeting and introduced me to David Ross. Wilder was a negotiator; if the issue couldn't be resolved by negotiation, then David Ross, the litigator, would be the one to take it to court. The three of us walked into the meeting room and were introduced to the players: Glen, the publisher; his lawyer, Root Thomas; and Crystal, the writer. Outfitted in an expensive dark suit and sporting a pompous attitude, Root was a typical lawyer trying not to show weakness. Crystal did not look like a bookworm. She was young, in great shape, wearing a low-cut blouse that revealed breasts too large for her frame. They made a swishing noise when she moved. Playing with her long, soft blonde hair and using her come-and-screw-me blue eyes, she would silently try to flirt with whoever was talking on our side of the table.

I sat next to Wilder; David sat next to him. Glen assured me that Paddy was thrilled with the novel, and that his small publishing house would never, ever try to cash in on the occurrences of 9/11. Crystal reinforced each statement with a smile and a swish over the table toward us. She wasn't very effective, but she was beautiful and fun to look at. As with most meetings, it was only a matter of time before the bullshit started to flow, like melena out of a GI bleeder's butt—and what we had here was one major gastroenterological hemorrhage. They explained all the benefits of publication, including a lot about money and Hollywood producers. And then, on cue, Crystal got up and settled herself into the empty chair next to me. She said that I was cute and, with a purr, promised that I would be "oh so well taken care of" after she sold the movie rights to a major studio.

Wilder abruptly stopped the meeting when he saw my expression change into that of a serial killer. Anxiously he said, "O.K., O.K., let's take a break."

The room emptied. Wilder, David and I discussed our nonexistent case in Wilder's spacious office. What we had going for us: The wishes of my family to protect Pat's name and their fear of court costs. On their side: Any publicity would be to their benefit and that, once Pat was dead, he no longer had any rights. Fortunately, Wilder pointed out, Pat had not yet been declared legally dead. And my father—not a public figure, and so easily recognizable in the book—was still very much alive.

We returned to the meeting room and I took the chair next to David. By doing so, my team indicated we were ready for court. Crystal started to move in my direction.

"Don't you come near me," I warned.

Glen told her to stay where she was. The negotiations continued. Everything was discussed, including money. An hour later, the discussion was coming to an end when everyone seated at the table turned to me.

Wilder asked, "Mike, what do you want?"

Locking eyes with Glen, shoving the book back across the table at him, I said, "Just change the fucking city."

Chapter 24

THE NEXT MORNING: OCTOBER 24, 2001. Bobby met me at the W for breakfast. For a few eggs and coffee, the bill came to $57 without the tip.

"Bobby, let me get this one."

He grabbed the check and changed the subject. "There's a producer for *Dateline NBC* who wants to interview you."

"What do you mean, interview me? Like on camera? *Ahhh!*"

"Come on, Mike. It'll be fun!"

"Fun? I'd rather kiss a light socket."

Bobby was surprised and puzzled. "Your brother *loved* being on camera."

"Well, not me."

Bobby asked me to consider it at least, and the conversation turned to our plans for the day. But I couldn't get the request for a TV interview out of my mind. My brother was a natural on camera; I was not. It had never bothered me until now. One of my favorite Dirty Harry quotes is "A man's got to know his limitations," and I knew public speaking was mine. So I steered clear of all such opportunities. And speaking in front of a camera? Forget about it.

I'd always had a little trouble verbalizing; when I was a kid, I barely said a word until the fourth grade. The nuns told my parents to think about putting me in Special Ed. Even as a teenager, I generally kept mum. I suddenly flashed back to a car ride with my father when I was 16. For some reason I was talking a blue streak—the words were just tumbling out. I can't recall what I was talking about, but I clearly remember we were stopped at a red light and my dad turned to stare at me in shocked amazement. He finally said, "Mike, if you ever master the English language, you will rule the world."

After a while I said, "So, Bobby, what do you think? Should I do that interview?"

He said nothing at first; then replied softly, "Your brother would want you to do it."

"Can this producer be trusted? You know, being part of the media and all that?"

Bobby assured me. "He and your brother were friends. Pat was the one who allowed him to do that story about John Drennan. He ended up winning an Emmy for it. No way would he do anything to disrespect you or your brother."

Cautiously I said, "Well, O.K. then. I guess I can talk to him."

Bobby took out his cell phone.

"Bobby, wait. I'll do it under two conditions. One, if he asks about that stupid book situation, I'm standing up and walking away. Two: He has to promise that he won't make me look like an asshole."

Bobby smiled. "If he does, I'll kick his ass."

He made the call.

THAT MORNING THERE WAS a memorial in Brooklyn for Jimmy Coyle, a fireman from Ladder 3. I'd met his parents at the firehouse in September. They were about my age. With their hearts torn out of them and through the unbelievable grief of losing their boy, they finished each other's sentences to tell me, "Jimmy was thrilled when he was assigned to Ladder 3. He just loved your brother and was so proud to work with him. When he came home from work, he acted as if he were the luckiest man alive." Neither mentioned what Steve later told me: that Pat had played a major role in getting their son assigned to 3 Truck; and that Pat was Jimmy Coyle's godfather.

Pat's memorial-planning meeting was scheduled for later in the day. That meant that I'd have to fit the *Dateline* interview, which was to be at Pat's apartment, between Jimmy Coyle's memorial Mass and the meeting. I called Janet and gave her an update. Everything was fine until I inadvertently told her that Marc was coming to the city for a few days.

"What?!" she angrily exclaimed. "Where is he staying?"

"I don't know…"

"Well, he's not staying with *you!*"

"Ummm, O.K."

She continued, anger rising, "What I want to know is, How come he gets to be with you while I'm stuck here?"

Here we go again. I fired back: "He's upstate visiting his mother and he's going to drive down to the city. What was I supposed to say?"

During this intellectual exchange with Janet, Bobby went outside to wait for Donny, who was to pick us up for Jimmy Coyle's memorial. After I hung up, I joined Bobby on the sidewalk in front of the Fish Bowl. Nothing was or needed to be said about my phone conversation.

Bobby remarked, "You know, Donny couldn't get his friend's car today."

Shaking off my anger from the phone call like a chill, I said, "Oh, no, I liked the Caprice. What do you think? Maybe he got a Lincoln this time?"

Bobby answered with a you-must-be-kidding-me look. Then I saw a vehicle approaching us with Donny at the wheel. It was my brother's old Honda Civic, which Pat had always referred to as "the car worth its weight in gold." As it pulled up in front of us, the grinding noise from the rear brakes was so loud it could be heard over the city traffic. It seems that both Bobby and Donny were using Pat's car to get around.

"Bobby," I said, "don't you think this car could use new brakes?"

"Nahh, don't worry about it. They just need to be warmed up."

We took off for Brooklyn, but not in the direction that the car was facing, of course. Donny was driving. Instead of going forward and around the block, with the Civic's brakes snarling, he backed up through three lanes of northbound traffic and made a right turn. There we were, swaying through traffic while Donny talked out of the side of his mouth in typical Donny fashion, Bobby in the back seat holding the right rear door so it didn't fly open during left turns, and all of us feeling as if we'd known one another all our lives. Here we were on that sad, cold October morning doing exactly what Paddy Brown would have been doing—traveling in the car that was worth its weight in gold, on the way to one of his men's memorials.

Chapter 25

BOBBY, DONNY AND I were driving back from Jimmy Coyle's memorial, but instead of our usual banter, there was little conversation in the Honda. The scenes of the past few hours remained all too vivid and the pain too real. I remained stone-cold silent and tried to make sense of it all. It seemed that wherever we went there was sadness and death; we were ill-equipped to deal with it.

Most of us don't take time to contemplate the inevitable; those who do tend to become very religious. Death is never easy. Maybe it's meant to be painful and slow. When death takes months, even years, the dying person carries the greatest agony. You start out healthy, alive, with unlimited potential and a fighting spirit. Then one at a time, or sometimes all at once, the organs fail. You can go from charging up a tall hill on a fresh fall morning, for no other reason than to breathe in the cool air, to lying in a hospital bed just trying to breathe. It is that person who, 24 hours a day, bears the agony of the death process. No matter how much we hurt for them, we can choose to get away—if only physically. But when death comes suddenly, unexpectedly, it's the survivors who carry the agony night and day.

"Mike!" Bobby called from the back seat, clutching the armrest of the door to keep it from swinging open. "Mike—we're going to be late."

I turned around. By the puzzled look on my face he knew that I wasn't even in the same time zone as he was. I had completely forgotten about the interview with this *Dateline* guy. Bobby pulled out his cell phone and called him to say we might be late.

Directing the sound waves over his right shoulder and out the side of his mouth, Donny said, "You know, they're putting a new roof on Paddy's apartment building. It's as loud as crap and I don't think they'll be able to film anything there."

"Sounds O.K. to me," I said in a hopeful voice. "Maybe we'll have to cancel!"

Bobby replied, "You can't back out now. He's already there with a crew, waiting for us."

And so they were. In front of 319 Avenue C were Steve McCarthy, a cameraman and a soundman. McCarthy was not what I expected. He was calm and disarming. It was evident that he and Pat were close friends; he was hurting like the rest of us. And, like me, he was wearing cowboy boots. *How bad could he be?*

We squeezed ourselves and all the film equipment into the small old elevator, and it slowly started its ascent to the 11th floor. As we approached the third floor, the clunking of the elevator was drowned out by pounding and scraping from the roof. By the time we were on the 11th floor, it sounded as if the workers were going to fall through the ceiling. McCarthy had to shout over the noise. "Does this go on all the time?"

"It's constant," Donny complained. "It's impossible for me to sleep during the day."

"How are you going to film with this racket going on?" I asked reasonably. Maybe we should just forget about it."

McCarthy was not impressed with my wise suggestion, nor was he discouraged. "Let's set up and see what we have."

So on we went to apartment 11A. Since Donny didn't do anything other than sleep in the apartment, it was exactly as Pat had left it. It was Pat's home, and we were all—well, I was—hoping for a miracle that Pat would return to it. McCarthy sat me down in a chair at the end of a small table. I realized why it was important for him to film me there. It was the exact spot were he'd interviewed Pat and Vina Drennan for the *Dateline* story about Captain Drennan.

Someone dabbed me with makeup and pointed bright lights in my face, almost blinding me to everything except a big, black, ominous camera lens that seemed to be silently sucking the remaining essence out of me. This was not for me. I wanted to do my best for this producer who was my brother's friend, but it felt wrong. This was my brother's home, and here I was allowing all these strangers with their cameras and equipment in. Everyone assured me that my story was interesting, and by interviewing me and others who knew Pat, we were actually telling my brother's story. But it was not a good idea for me to be interviewed. I was a mess. These feelings of uncertainty and discomfort plus the anguish of just coming back from this young kid's memorial equaled one unstable interview subject.

Steve McCarthy was not having an easy time getting me to say much of anything. When something of interest finally passed my lips, it was drowned out by the banging that came from the roof. At one point, he had me relive the moment in the ER when I watched the North Tower collapse and knew my brother was dead. I sat there with the camera lens tugging my soul out of me and tried to explain how I felt at that particular minute. As I attempted to do this, I fell apart.

The soundman interrupted. "No good, have to do it again," he said. "I couldn't hear him."

McCarthy responded with annoyance. "Did you get anything?"

"Nope, just a bunch of banging."

The tears were still running down my face. McCarthy said, "Mike, you're going to have to do that again."

My brains were like scrambled eggs, but even I could see the logic. This was the most powerful section of the interview, and it had to be done right. I composed myself as we waited for a break in the noise. Then I told it all over again and broke down again—as if on cue. Like the shot before, it was raw and emotional. Unlike the shot before, this time I felt like a fraud.

The banging resumed, and McCarthy turned to Donny and Bobby. "Do you think you can ask them to take a break?"

Donny got up from the couch where he'd been observing the interview. "Come on, Bobby," he growled. "We'll get them to stop."

A few minutes after they left the apartment, there was silence. I found out later that Bobby and Donny told the workers they were FBI agents. I can see why the crew believed them. At the time, Bobby was playing the part of an FBI agent on the HBO series *Oz* and truly looked the part with his short hair and in-charge demeanor. Bobby asked the foreman if they could work on a different section of the roof because the FBI needed to search an apartment and were using sensitive listening devices. The foreman refused—until Donny got in his face and told him that if he didn't cooperate, the whole fucking roof-renovation project would be shut down for the day.

And so there was silence.

After dredging my soul for the interview, McCarthy wanted to film Pat's apartment. This was O.K. with me—until he requested that I go through it with him and the cameraman to explain what everything was. How was I supposed to know what everything was? I did my best. I let him listen to the messages from 9/11 on Pat's answering machine, and he asked me for a copy. He asked me to go through my brother's closet. This was really weird. Here I was, going through his shirts like I was his grieving widow or something. This is not what brothers do. Distraught, I stopped several times, but Steve encouraged me to continue. He assured me that anything I didn't like would not be included in the film. That black camera lens was relentlessly following my every fraudulent move as self-loathing filled my empty gut.

Then, from out of nowhere, my brother saved me.

The sounds of fire trucks and police cars screaming far below past Pat's apartment halted the torture. They were racing north on the FDR Drive, and we all watched from the windows as one after another flew by. We all feared the worst—another terrorist attack on New York.

"Something bad happened," I said quietly. "That's Rescue 2 that just went past. They're out of

Brooklyn. For them to come to Manhattan, it has to be big."

What followed was a comical routine of six smart, technically savvy men trying to get Pat's police scanner to work. The TV news had nothing about it, but it was Steve McCarthy, after placing a phone call to NBC, who finally found out what was going on.

"A scaffold collapsed at the W Hotel in Union Square," he announced.

"Let's go," I said. "Steve, that's where the meeting about Pat's memorial is. Do you want to come?"

Chapter 26

IT WAS GETTING DARK as we packed the equipment into the camera crew's SUV. Then the four of us jumped into Pat's Civic with Donny at the wheel. Steve, experiencing Donny's driving for the first time, was visibly nervous. It didn't help that he almost fell out of the car during a left turn when his door flew open.

"Oh, Steve," Bobby said. "Sorry, forgot to tell you—you gotta hold that door shut on left turns."

We parked at Ladder 3 and walked the four blocks north past Union Square. Fire and rescue trucks surrounded the W. Bobby and Donny were the first to reach the police lines obstructing our way to the hotel. They casually pulled up the yellow police tape and started to walk beneath it, but three police officers immediately converged on them.

Steve and I were a short distance behind. "I don't think they're going to let us through," he said to me.

"Don't worry," I reassured him. "We have Donny with us."

By the time Steve and I made it to the police line, the three officers were holding up the yellow tape for us to walk under.

Steve pointed at Donny and asked incredulously, "Who *is* that guy?"

I shrugged. "Oh, he's my little cousin."

THE FIRE TRUCKS WERE putting on that old familiar light show and using their radio calls as a musical score. Even the rig from Ladder 40, my old Harlem firehouse, was right there in front of the hotel. We continued into the W as if we were with the Mayor's office, and I scanned the area for anyone I knew. Steve Browne was waiting in the Fish Bowl. He informed us that scaffolding on a building at the rear of the W had collapsed, trapping some of the workers. So far, three construction workers were dead. The fire department had all the help they needed, so we headed to the meeting.

In the lobby, a very attractive woman was waiting for an elevator. She was tall with long, straight red hair and beautiful eyes. Donny positioned himself next to her, quite confident that it was only a matter of time before she noticed how incredibly good-looking he was and started talking to him. She peeked out from behind Donny like a child hiding behind a large tree, gave me a warm smile and said, "You must be Pat's brother. I'm Ellin Martens."

Donny moved aside and she shook my hand. After introductions, the elevator opened and we all got in. Ellin wanted to know if Pat had ever told me about her. It took a few seconds to realize that yes, in fact, he did tell me about this reporter he knew at *Time* magazine. Over the years my brother had dated a lot of different women, but he only told me about a few. By the time the elevator door opened on the third floor, those memories of what Pat had said and my recent phone calls with this stranger melded into one.

"Yes, Ellin—he did tell me about you."

THE MEETING ROOM WAS relatively small and contained one long rectangular table—it reminded me of the Last Supper. The windows were letting in a muted version of the fire-truck light show, a constant reminder of the drama unfolding outside. The setting was perfect for the planning of Paddy Brown's memorial, and the rest of the members of the Paddy Brown Memorial Coordination Team were already present and chatting softly as I entered the room. There was Jim Ellson, the retired fire captain whom I'd met on the first day I arrived at 3 Truck, and Tim Brown, FDNY, who was still assigned to the Mayor's Office of Special Operations.

I finally met Keith McLaughlin face to face; in many ways he reminded me of Donny. They were about the same height and build, and both had the

238

same New York City cop attitude. Keith had been transferred from NYPD Highway Patrol to the Office of the Mayor to serve as driver for Giuliani's secretary. New York City was in crisis; City Hall must have been the same. But Beth Hatton was also dealing with a personal crisis: her husband was Pat's good friend Terry Hatton, the captain of Rescue 1. We knew Ladder 3's and Rescue 1's rigs were parked adjacent at the World Trade Center; we all speculated that Pat and Terry must have been very near each other in the North Tower when it collapsed.

Giuliani must have known that by tapping Keith as Beth's driver, he was also assigning her a guardian angel: Beth had just learned she was pregnant with her and Terry's first child. She was due in May.

Jim Carney from Engine 69 could not attend; he had been reassigned to FDNY headquarters to oversee the planning and implementation of the 300-plus memorial and funeral services. He personally knew many of the firefighters who had perished, and I could only imagine how difficult a job he'd been given. Steve "Gonzo" Gonzales, Jerry Brenkert, Rob Burmeister and Ray Trinkle, all from Ladder 3, were there in full uniform. They too had been at Jimmy Coyle's memorial that morning and had been through too many memorials already, but were ready to step up to do it one more time for their captain. Steve McCarthy fit right in;

and, of course, Steve Browne and Bobby were ready for anything.

I took a seat in the middle on one side of the long table. In front of me was a large pile of photos of Pat. Immediately the questions started coming at me, fast and furious.

Steve Browne: "Ah, Mike, you're definite on the date?"

"Yeah, November 9," I said. "It's Pat's birthday. And I like thinking of 11/9 as the reverse of 9/11. Good vs. evil. But there's a problem."

"What problem?" Keith asked.

"Well, that date lands on a Friday. I was thinking of the traffic backup it will cause. So maybe we should have it on Saturday, November 10?"

This brought about a general consensus to screw the traffic. Tim Brown said it best: "Your brother gave a lot to this city. The city can put up with a little inconvenience."

Gonzo inquired, "How many people do you think will be at the collation, Mikey?"

"I don't know. How many people does St. Patrick's Cathedral hold?"

"Three thousand," answered Steve.

"Three thousand!" exclaimed Gonzo. He was doing caterer math in his head. He looked worried. "Do you think they'll all go to the Hilton?"

"That's three thousand *inside* the church," said Keith. "What do we do about the people standing outside the church?"

"Maybe the church won't even fill," Rob offered. "Nobody knows what's going to be happening at that time."

"Oh, it'll fill," Bobby replied. "Paddy knew half the people in New York. Even if the fire department personnel can't be there, the civilians will."

Jim Ellson agreed. "When he was covering in Rescue 1, people would come up to me every day and ask if Paddy Brown was working. It was like he knew everybody."

The meeting continued and we discussed the cathedral-seating plan. It was decided that there would be a reserved section for the family, dignitaries and Ladder 3. I added a section for Engine 69, Ladder 28. And I wanted to make sure the members of the Westbury FD got into the church too.

My father was still wheelchair-bound, so I felt that the best way to navigate the steps in front of St. Pat's would be to have four firemen carry him in his wheelchair up and down the stairs. I made a note to ask Jim Carney if Engine 69, Ladder 28 could do it.

Ellin asked, "Mike, have you thought about what music you want?"

"Music?"

Everyone was talking at once.

"Yeah, what about a singer?"

"How about that blind opera singer?"

"You mean Bocelli?"

Gonzo shook his head. "No good. We already inquired, and his manager wants us to pay for a private jet to fly him from Italy. And a suite at the Ritz too."

After a pause, I asked, "What about that cop who's been singing at the Yankees games?"

"Yeah, Danny Rodriguez," Keith responded. "I spoke to him already. He said, 'Sure, I'm a cop. I'll do anything for a day off!'"

Ellin asked me if it was all right for her to invite the American Boychoir to sing. I shrugged. "Sure, that sounds good," I said. It was one of the many decisions made that at the time seemed trivial, but turned out to have overwhelming importance—like Bobby's suggestion to have Dueling Taps played by two buglers outside the cathedral after the Mass.

Ray asked if I would like the eagle that flies out at the start of the Yankees games. He left to make a few calls; when he returned, he looked disappointed. He told us, "The eagle is already booked that day."

Since Pat was a Marine, we wanted a flyover.

Ellin said, "I spoke to the captain of the aircraft carrier that's been sitting just off the New York coast. He said that he would love to do it but—"

I interrupted her. "You talked to an aircraft carrier?"

She looked at me as if it were no big deal. "Unfortunately, he said he couldn't do it. The jets would scare the hell out of everyone in New York. You know, flying down Fifth Avenue."

Keith and Tim had a short conversation. Keith said, "We'll see if we can get police helicopters."

Steve Browne signaled for my attention. "Mike, you need to pick a picture of your brother for the prayer card."

"A picture for what?"

Steve explained that instead of having a picture of a saint on one side and the prayer on the other, as is customary, other families had been putting a picture of the deceased fireman on the front.

"Go ahead and pick one," Bobby encouraged me.

Hesitantly I got up from my chair, leaned over the pile of pictures, and slowly went through them. There were pictures of Pat fighting fires, giving mouth-to-mouth resuscitation to a severely burned young woman, holding one of Bobby's infant sons, wearing his Class A uniform with Governor Mario Cuomo. Then there was the *Time* magazine photo of him in full uniform standing on a railing along an East River walkway, framed by the Chrysler and Empire State buildings. Paddy Brown pictures—a whole table full of them.

With a chuckle Jim Ellson declared, "There was never a camera that Paddy didn't like."

Everyone watched, but no one helped. It would be my choice alone. I didn't want to do it. It was too much responsibility; there were so many pictures. Which one would capture Pat's essence and personality? Which one did I want people to take and carry with them to remember the man my brother was?

I was about halfway through the pile when I saw it. I picked it up. Examining it, I stated, "This is the one." It was as if Pat had picked it out himself. "Yeah, I'm sure of it." It was a picture of the rope rescue. Pat was leaning over a parapet 14 stories above Midtown Manhattan, holding on to the rope that was holding firefighter Kevin Shea 13 stories above 48th Street. The building was on fire; the heat and flames had forced one man out a window and onto the ledge on the 12th floor. From behind him, you could see the fire blasting from the window. He had no place to go but down.

Jim Ellson took the picture from me, passed it around, and said, "There may have been only one or two other officers in the fire department with the experience and the guts to pull that off."

Steve Browne studied the photo. "That's Paddy all right. It was an impossible rescue, and then they turned around and did it *again*—using the same rope! They turned right around and rescued a second guy ready to jump from the other side of the building. That's Paddy all right."

Gonzo suggested that we set up a giant TV screen at the Hilton to run a continuous slide show featuring photos of Pat. Steve McCarthy asked if he could make a short video of the highlights of Pat's career. Keith told him that he had just the music to accompany it.

Multiple questions with important consequences were shot at me with an increasing rate of fire.

"Mike, your brother would want this."

"I think *this* would be a good idea."

"What about a priest? Sharon—you know, one of Paddy's ex-girlfriends—said that Paddy would want a Buddhist monk."

I laid my head on the table.

The meeting was moving backward. Decisions already made were starting to unravel. I needed to regain control of the meeting—and myself. I raised my head and said, to no one in particular, "A Buddhist monk? In St. Patrick's Cathedral?"

It felt as if we were producing a Hollywood epic. But by the end of the meeting, we'd all developed respect and trust for one another. It was getting late, and with the lights from the fire trucks still flashing around us, I brought up one final idea. It was a potential solution to a problem that was tormenting me daily: Pat's request that his body be cremated and his ashes dumped in Central Park.

After hours of roaming around and getting lost there, I had the idea of placing a small plaque, with Pat's name and a few words engraved on it, in an appropriate area of the park along a road less traveled. The plaque could be placed in a way that it would appear to have always been there.

The plan: Do it on the night of Saturday, November 10. Attendance at the clandestine event would have to be restricted to a very few firemen and the Inner Circle—the people who had been working so hard on planning Pat's memorial. We would steal into the park late at night, set the plaque, say a few words and leave. It would mark the end of what we had to do. No more memorials to plan. It would be the day to start rebuilding our own lives. When I brought this up, I was surprised that it was immediately hailed as a great idea. The discussion became livelier and more enthusiastic, with other suggestions being lobbed back and forth across the table.

Jerry Brenkert said something to Rob, then announced, "I'll get a tree to plant."

A new wave of excitement hit the group as everyone discussed what type of tree would be best. *A tree? O.K., sounds good, but how the hell do you walk into Central Park in the middle of the night and plant a tree?*

We adjourned and were moving downstairs to the Fish Bowl just as a hotel employee came by to ask Steve Browne for help. Because of the ongoing rescue operations, there was no access to the hotel unless you were a fireman, a cop, a reporter for *Time* magazine—or if you happened to be with Donny Brown. Steve was able to negotiate with the cops in charge of securing the building and arranged permission for the hotel to use one doorway to let guests, visitors and employees in and out. The W's management was truly grateful.

Instead of the usual view of pedestrians streaming past the large windows of the Fish Bowl, rescue trucks surrounded the hotel. The operation had already gone from rescue to recovery, and we all knew too well what that meant. The talk in the bar was that, so far, five were found dead and twice as many were injured. Another tragedy. It seemed we were all living a tragedy. New York City was one big tragedy. Could we do anything? We were assured there was plenty of help—and grief—outside already.

We ordered beer. Bobby came over to me. "Did you eat today?"

"Yeah—breakfast with you, remember?"

"That's all? For the whole day?" He shook his head and left to order a bunch of appetizers.

When he returned I reminded him, "Hey, Bobby, you didn't eat either. You were with me all day." The food appeared at the same time that two firemen from my old firehouse walked through the revolving door and into the bar.

Steve Browne turned to me. "You remember these guys from your days at 37?"

I hadn't seen them in more than 13 years, but it felt as if I'd never left Harlem. They were on a break, so they took off their helmets and turnout coats, carefully laid them with their tools under the high tables where we were sitting, and ate with us. We talked about Chucky the Trucky, a former member of Ladder 40 who was also lost at the Trade Center. I glanced around. There is a dress code at the Fish Bowl, but that night it seemed natural to have firefighters in bunker gear sitting at the tables.

The bill never arrived. Gonzo told us that a man who had been sitting at the end of the bar paid it in full, then left without saying a word. The staff said he didn't want them to give out his name; all we knew was that he was from South Beach, Miami. The tab for all of us had to have been substantial—nothing is cheap at the Fish Bowl. It was another one of those random acts of kindness that had been happening since 9/11.

We closed the Fish Bowl, then went off to close a few more bars around Union Square. The rest of the night's details are a little blurry. It ended with Gonzo and I having a beer with the bartender in a pub way past closing time. I remember the sun slicing through the closed shutters of the bar and into my consciousness.

"Gonzo, what time is it?"

"You've been drinking all night, and now all of a sudden the time becomes important? Where do you have to be?"

"I'm meeting Steve Browne at 8 a.m."

"The only thing you're meeting is your pillow," Gonzo said, laughing.

"GonzoIgottago," I slurred as I got up off the barstool. I needed to concentrate on my balance as I walked to the door. The door wouldn't open and, frustrated, I pushed harder and harder on it.

The bartender yelled, "It's locked!"

After sliding the obvious deadbolt, the door still wouldn't open until I gave it a shoulder shove, and— *bang!*—it gave. Reality blasted into my brain along with the glaring New York City morning sun. I had no idea where I was; I looked up to the sky for my bearings. The Twin Towers were still gone, my brother was still buried under them, the smell of entropy was still in the air, and drinking all night long didn't change a damn thing except one: No sleep for me today.

WHEN I FINALLY MADE it to 3 Truck, I was showered, red-eyed, and had a bit of a headache. But no one else looked that healthy either. Steve Browne came out from the kitchen.

"Ah, Mike, you O.K.? You know, we can do this some other day." We had to go back to the pier to fill out still more paperwork.

"No, this is the only time I have." I rubbed my eyes and asked, "What time did you leave last night?"

"I said goodbye to you. Don't you remember?"

"Yeah, yeah, that's right. You left from the W. You were smart."

"By the looks of you, I guess I was smart to leave when I did," he laughed. Changing the subject, he asked, "So is your driver coming today?"

"I just called him. He mumbled something about catching up with us. I think he may have picked himself a tomato."

"No problem—I'll drive. Get yourself some coffee."

I went back to the kitchen, poured myself a cup and received my fair share of abuse from the guys there about my obviously hungover state. Then I went outside and sat alone on Pat's bench to wait for Steve. Another loud garbage truck was slowly making its way down 13th Street, eating the mounds of trash thrown into its mouth by the handlers. People were rushing past me on the sidewalk, going to work or school or wherever else people go; horns were blasting; taxi drivers with twisted turbans were slowing down, I thought, to give me a bad look; and I was just sitting there peacefully contemplating the importance of breathing.

A well-dressed woman approached and sat next to me on the bench. In a serious voice she said, "You're Paddy's brother."

She told me her name—which, of course, I don't remember. I stared at her curiously, wondering if I'd met her before. Had Pat described her to me? She saw what I was trying to do.

"No, you don't know me." She continued. "Very few people are aware of this, but your brother saved me."

"Which fire were you—"

Shaking her head, she cut me off. "You see…" She hesitated, then started again. "You see, about 15 years ago, I was walking home late one night when out of nowhere, a man jumped out in front of me. I turned to run, but there were three more of them. They grabbed me and started to drag me into an alley. I was kicking and screaming until one of them put a knife to my neck. They started to…"

A tear rolled down her cheek as her voice started to break.

"They were raping me just when Paddy was walking by. He told me later that he didn't like what he heard coming from that alley. Even though they all had knives, they were no match for Paddy's rage. He beat the hell out of all of them."

The memory of the terror from this woman's ordeal forced her to stop for a moment before she continued. "Then he picked me up and carried me out of that awful place. Paddy and I have been friends ever since."

She started to cry, got up and walked west toward Fourth Avenue. I never saw her again.

Chapter 27

Donny made it to 3 Truck but ended up falling asleep on a couch in the break room. He promised me that he was never going to drink again—then headed back to Pat's apartment to sleep it off. Steve watched Donny walk away.

"Well, Mike," he said, "You definitely don't have a driver today." So we set off for the West Side pier with Steve at the wheel, discussing the memorial plans made the night before. "I have to warn you," he said seriously. "There are some people who will try to make you change your mind about what you decided. Stick to what you believe in."

Later that afternoon, I took the subway uptown to Campbell's Funeral Home. Having the wake at Campbell's on the Upper East Side had been thoroughly discussed at the meeting. This is where they wake celebrities and dignitaries, and it was the appropriate place for Paddy Brown. The management knows how to conduct a dignified, respectful event. Waiting for me outside the building in the cold—well, what I consider cold—were Keith, Tim, Ricky and Bobby. We all walked in and looked around the warmly lit, comfortable foyer while waiting for Dominic Carella, Campbell's director. He was a large man, friendly, with an engaging manner—he immediately put me at ease. Our group was led into his office.

As soon as we all took seats, he hit me with another barrage of questions. It was a great help to have the other guys there. The planning went on, and I asked Dominic if he knew where I could have a small plaque made for our Central Park event.

"Wait a minute," he said warily. "You plan to go into Central Park, plant a tree and place a plaque? Do you have a permit?"

Keith answered, "We don't need no stinking permit."

"That's why we're doing it in the middle of the night," I explained helpfully.

Dominic was smiling now. "I'll have your plaque made. What you end up doing with it, I don't want to know." He picked up a pen. "So what do you want it to say, Mike?"

I didn't have a clue. "I'll need a little time," I said. "I'll call and let you know, if that's O.K."

Dominic suggested a stone instead of a plaque, and I yielded to the man with the greater experience. The matter of prayer cards came up. I handed Dominic the 8-by-10 photo of the rope rescue. As if on cue, Keith and Tim exchanged glances and moved their chairs closer to mine.

"Mike, the rope-rescue picture is a great photo, but you can't use it for the prayer card," Keith said.

I was surprised and confused. "What do you mean I can't use it?"

Leaning closer to me, Tim explained, "You need to pick a picture with Paddy's face on it."

Keith pulled a prayer card out of his wallet and handed it to me. "Here, look at this," he said. "This is my brother's prayer card. It's always with me." The card had the same picture that Pat had on his altar of Peter McLaughlin's young, handsome face.

Ricky joined the discussion. "People will want to know what Pat looked like. You need a different picture—one where you can see his face."

I knew then what Steve Browne had warned me about. I hid my face in my hands and wondered how I was going to do all that I had to do, especially with the multitude of opinions that were being thrown my way. I slowly raised my head and looked at Dominic.

"Let's go see your rooms upstairs where the gathering will take place and I'll think about this."

After making what seemed like a hundred more decisions, I sat back down in my chair in Dominic's office. Then it came to me—a jolt that hit me just as the New York sun had that morning.

"O.K.," I declared. "We'll use a full-face picture of Pat in his Class A on the front and put the rope rescue on the back."

"Wait—what about the prayer?" Keith asked.

My answer was immediate and definitive.

"The rope rescue is a prayer."

After another lively discussion, we decided to have a few words under the rope-rescue photo. But what words? I didn't care that much; as I saw it, the card was perfect with the two pictures alone.

Keith spoke up. "I know a saying that your brother lived by. 'To thine own self be true.' "

Perfect.

Dominic asked, "How many do you need?"

"Oh, maybe 7,000."

He was surprised at the high number until Bobby said, "Yup. That seems about right."

I FLEW HOME TO Vegas the next day with most of the arrangements set. The viewing, for lack of a better word, was going to be at Campbell's on November 7 and 8 and the Mass would be on Pat's birthday, November 9, at St. Patrick's Cathedral on Fifth Avenue. More important was that we had a team that ran more like an organization. If there was a problem, I knew which person to call. Now if they found Pat's body beforehand, these plans would have to be changed somewhat. But I'd deal with that if and when I had to.

Janet was waiting for me in the baggage-claim area at McCarran. As I approached her, I could see that she'd been crying. Panic swelled up inside me. Was it my sister? My father? She shook her head no. She put her arms around me and in a sobbing voice said, "It's Lisa."

"Which Lisa?" I asked. "Take a deep breath, then tell me what happened."

Between sobs she managed to tell me the terrible news.

"Ernie's Lisa…She was killed…He wants you to call him."

THAT NIGHT, IN THE same loud place where Ernie had asked me to be in his wedding party, we drank at the bar all alone in the crowd. His wedding plans had been replaced by Lisa's funeral plans. In the past several weeks, I'd learned all too well what one says to a grieving friend. This time there was no need to do that. There was no need for comforting phrases, no need for sad clichés. There was no need for me to speak at all. Ernie was now in the Club— the club that no one ever wants to be a member of, but one that the actions of evil people force you to join. We only picked at the chicken wings that we'd ordered but really didn't want. Ernie was drinking heavily, even more than I was—which at the time was a tough thing to do.

"It's the only way I can sleep," he explained.

I understood perfectly, and my heart broke as Ernie told me of the drama that had unfolded in Lisa's home a few days before. As he did, I watched his mood shift from uneasiness, grief and absolute despair to anger and vile hatred.

I've heard that true love comes to a person once, maybe twice in a lifetime—and that's if you're lucky. Lisa was Ernie's true love. Since she was a doctor, Lisa's mother expected her daughter to financially support both her and her unemployed boyfriend. The two were living with Lisa in Lisa's home. This arrangement was working out well enough until Ernie came along. Ernie always had a strong work ethic. He would routinely hold down two full-time jobs and had no patience for anyone who refused to go to work. To say the very least, Ernie didn't get along with his future mother-in-law or her lazy boyfriend. Previously Lisa's mother had been very successful in destroying her daughter's romantic relationships and, in doing so, maintained these living arrangements—but not this time. Everything her mother would try failed miserably when it came up against the strength of Lisa and Ernie's love. The woman hated her daughter's resolve to marry Ernie.

But lately, Ernie said, things seemed to be at peace. In fact, on the night that Lisa was writing out their wedding invitations, her mother helped address and stamp the envelopes. When it was time for bed, Lisa said goodnight and went into the bathroom to brush her teeth. Her mother followed her in, pointed a gun at her only child, and shot Lisa in the back of the head.

Chapter 28

EVERYTHING WAS PRETTY MUCH set by the time Janet and I flew back to New York in early November. Well, almost. Donny's twin Jimmy, with Bobby along, picked us up at JFK. I hadn't seen Jimmy in more than 20 years, but this much I'd learned ahead of time: he was nothing like Donny. Even in looks. True, Jimmy was as big as his twin and had a Marine-type haircut, so he looked the part of the tough cop; but he was well-spoken, well-mannered, concerned for our well-being. He kissed Janet hello and greeted me with, "What do you need, Cousin?"

For now I needed to get to Manhattan, and with a sigh of relief I saw Jimmy actually obeyed traffic regulations. As we headed toward the city, I consulted my small spiral notebook on last-minute details. This was like planning a state funeral.

POSTER BOARDS. Around the corner from 3 Truck is a store called the Village Copier. The owner had donated his resources to the fire department and had been copying and enlarging photos of the missing fireman for the families to display at the viewings.

When Ladder 3 dropped off the large pile of Pat's pictures to be copied, the staff just about shit—but still refused to take any money. Gonzo had framed some of the photos, and Steve McCarthy's wife Kathleen mounted others on poster board. We needed to bring them to Campbell's for the viewing. Some would also be on display at the cathedral and the collation.

EULOGIES. Bobby and I had spent a great deal of time deciding who was going to speak at the service, and we thought the lineup was perfect. Mayor Giuliani would speak first, followed by former New York State Governor Hugh Carey, then Fire Commissioner Tom Von Essen. Next to speak would be Michael Daly. He and Pat were good friends. Mike, a columnist for the New York *Daily News,* had been a finalist for the Pulitzer Prize. Donny would say a few words. Then Mike Moran would speak, representing the men of 3 Truck. Mike did a powerful job eulogizing his older brother John back in September. Next: Jim Ellson, the highly decorated retired captain who had known and worked with Pat for many years; they were close friends. And after all these magnificent speakers, it would be my turn. This was perfect, all right, except that I had no idea what I was going to say.

Jimmy and Bobby dropped Janet and me off at our hotel. For this final trip, Steve Browne arranged for us to stay at the Hotel Delmonico again on Park at 59th. The staff there generously upgraded us to a large suite.

Janet wanted to go over some details of the memorial, but my cell phone would not allow that.

Whenever we began to talk, the phone started to vibrate across the tabletop. Janet finally gave up and retreated to the bedroom. My phone went off almost immediately.

It was McCarthy. "Mike, this is Steve. Listen, I'm not going to make it to Paddy's viewing. I'm very sorry."

The tone of his voice told me something was wrong.

"What happened?"

Steve softly responded, "My father died."

So the next day, in the car worth its weight in gold, with Donny driving and Janet in the back seat holding the door closed, we headed to Brooklyn.

The wake for Steve's father was a simple, classy send-off for a retired New York City police officer. Steve said his father loved being a cop. He'd chosen to be buried in his uniform. Putting his own grief aside for a moment, Steve asked me how I was holding up. He then told me that in his car were the poster boards of Pat's photos, which his wife had assembled. And Kathleen did all this while consumed with her own family's grief. We were deeply touched. After paying our respects, we loaded the boards into the Honda and, with the car's brakes still not warmed up, headed back to the city.

THE CELL PHONE WAS continuously vibrating now as members of the coordination team checked in. But by that evening, all calls abruptly ceased. All the questions and final details had been decided. It was actually a little unsettling. *Wow! Was it true? Could everything finally be done?*

Ellin had given Janet and two of her sisters tickets to the Broadway show *Rent*. They left me, my cross-country driving partner Eddie and my other brother-in-law John in Carmine's restaurant to have dinner. As usual, the popular place to meet and greet before a Broadway show was packed. We never got farther than the bar. And of course, the three of us were just heartbroken about being stuck at the bar. Eddie and I gave John the details of the journey from Las Vegas to New York and actually laughed about our stop in Joseph, Utah. Everything was in place for Pat's wake the next day, and the cell phone confirmed this by not interrupting my evening. It truly was done. There was nothing more I could do—what was going to happen was beyond my control. I was no longer carrying the ball. I finally started to relax.

Then, once again, that goddamned cell phone vibrated. I left the comfort and safety of my brothers-in-law and the warmth of Carmine's to go outside, away from the noise of the restaurant. It was a freezing cold November night. I shivered out there among the half-frozen cigarette smokers as I listened to the fireman on the other end of the line. I'd met him before and knew he was a friend of Pat's.

"You don't know this, but Paddy hated Von Essen."

He went on and gave me all the reasons why the fire commissioner should not be allowed to speak at St.

Patrick's Cathedral. Whatever heat I had left in me turned to ice when he said, "Mike, you need to call Von Essen now and tell him that the family does not want him there."

Politics had reared its ugly head. Now what do I do? I looked down at my hand and realized that I was holding the ball again. *O.K., this goes under the heading of fire department decisions. Simple enough— call Steve Browne.*

I got Steve on the phone, and he told me that Pat and Von Essen had a very strong mutual respect.

"Paddy always did what he thought was right and didn't care what anyone would tell him," Steve said. "Von Essen and Paddy would argue at times about fire department policies and procedures, but neither would ever dream of talking bad about the other in public. Ah, Mike, I actually think that they were good friends. In fact, I'm sure of it."

As the conversation continued, Steve became increasingly angry that someone would tell me something like this the day before my brother's wake. He wanted to know who had called me so he could kick the shit out of him. Gratefully, I looked down at my hand and realized it was empty. The ball was gone. I went back into the restaurant, where Eddie and John had a cold, fresh beer waiting for me at the bar.

ON NOVEMBER 7, 2001, Campbell's didn't seem to be a funeral home as Dominic gave Donny, Bobby, Steve Browne, Janet and me a tour of the viewing area. It had been converted into Paddy Brown's personal museum. There were pictures, newspaper articles, medals and awards everywhere. Atop a table where visitors first entered sat a new black FDNY helmet, heavy-duty plastic, with a Ladder 3 captain's face piece on it. On either side of the table were very large poster-size photos of Pat. One was of him standing in front of Ladder 3's firehouse; the other was a side/rear night shot of him standing in front of a fire scene. With the fire out, he stood there with all his equipment on, dirty, exhausted, serious and alone. It was a younger picture of him when he was at Ladder 26, and it was a perfect representation of a firefighter, the perfect representation of being human.

At the right side of the room was Pat's altar, set up just as we'd found it in his apartment. It had been such an important part of Pat's life that I thought it necessary to have the place where he prayed and meditated here. On the altar were the pictures of Pete McLaughlin and John Drennan along with a few corresponding newspaper articles. The display also included his small metal religious statues and a few other artifacts. I took the dirty, sooty Engine 69 and Ladder 28 helmets that I'd found under his altar and placed them on the table on either side of the new Ladder 3 helmet. They made that 3 Truck helmet look like a toy.

Bobby, Steve, Donny and I took a step back and surveyed the large room. The flower arrangements were magnificent. Any pictures that had been previously hanging on the wall were replaced by pictures of Pat; the ones that Kathleen McCarthy mounted on boards told the story of one hell of a firefighter's life. The only thing that wasn't Paddy

Brown's in that room, actually on the entire second floor of Campbell's, was that smooth plastic helmet. It was a cold reminder that Pat's helmet was probably still on his head and buried under tons of rubble in downtown Manhattan.

Steve Browne turned to me. "Ah, Mike, are we missing something?"

"It's that helmet," I said, frowning. "It looks like it doesn't belong."

"I know what you mean," said Bobby.

Out of the side of Donny's mouth came, "Pat has an old helmet in the trunk of the Honda. Want me to get it?"

Donny disappeared, and in a moment came into the room holding the helmet. It was made of leather—warped, dried-out, charcoal black. Deep black soot was baked into the surface, remnants of fires fought by my brother long ago with his typical passion and skill. The face piece was missing. Steve attached the Ladder 3 faceplate, and we placed it between the other two helmets. Janet, noticing what we were doing, joined the group and pronounced, "Now *that's* Paddy Brown."

The three fire helmets formed a trilogy, and I wondered what company that old beat-up helmet had come from. Could he have worn it during the fire that occurred in Harlem when a crack lab exploded? On that call, he charged up 26 Truck's ladder and dove through a window under the fire. He reappeared a minute later and, through the smoke and flames, handed an unconscious child to a fireman standing in the bucket of a tower ladder. Then he crawled back into the burning room, only to appear at another window with another child. Word was that their mother was still trapped in the apartment, so Pat and another fireman crawled back in under the flames. They found her in another room, barely alive, and dragged her back to the fireman waiting in the bucket. All three victims survived. Yes, that could explain the wear on the helmet.

Or maybe it was from the time he had to confront the red devil to save a fire company stranded on the roof of an inferno. By charging through the flames to get to the trapped men, Pat's airway was burned severely. Almost immediately the hot, noxious fumes produced tracheal edema—his airway swelled shut. He almost died of asphyxia. He spent several days in the burn unit at Cornell before I was sure he was going to be O.K. Yeah, a helmet worn during that episode would surely look like that one on the table. Or it could have been from any or all of the hundreds of fires that he was in from the Bronx to Manhattan to Brooklyn. The helmets from Ladder 28 and Engine 69 didn't look much better. What a trilogy: Ladder 28, Engine 69 and Ladder 3. Wherever he wore these helmets, it was obvious that they—and therefore he—had taken one hell of a beating.

A thought came to me: this helmet that Donny found in Pat's car might not even be his. It could have been Pete McLaughlin's, or John Drennan's, and he was keeping it close to him when he would report to duty. There was really no way to know. Wherever it came from, for the next two days it would hold a position of supreme honor.

DOMINIC BROUGHT US TO see the Central Park stone. In its own small viewing room down the hall from the main room, the stone had been placed on a long raised table. I guessed that at a more standard viewing, the casket would have been placed there. The stone, black granite, obviously weighed well over 100 pounds and was surrounded with lush green grass and beautiful flowers. The effect was breathtaking. These words had been carved into its polished surface:

**CAPTAIN PATRICK J. BROWN, FDNY
WHO DEDICATED HIMSELF TO SAVING
THE LIVES OF THE PEOPLE OF NEW YORK
CITY
AND LOST HIS LIFE THAT DAY
ALONG WITH SO MANY OF THE OTHER
TRUE HEROES OF THE WORLD
NOVEMBER 9, 1952 – SEPTEMBER 11, 2001
WE WILL NEVER FORGET**

FOR TWO DAYS, TWICE a day, an army of people marched through the Paddy Brown Museum. Firefighters from all over the world came to pay tribute; they mixed with family and friends, some of whom we hadn't seen in years. Then there were all the people whom we'd never met, the ones who told us how their lives had been touched by Pat in one way or another. It was overwhelming. My father sat in a large upholstered chair, and Carolyn, Janet and I stood around him at the head of the reception line. People would tour the Paddy Brown Museum, then get on the seemingly endless line to offer their condolences. By the time we shook their hands and accepted their kind words, even the visitors who had never met Pat were overwhelmed. They were struck not only by the sadness of the heroic death of a legendary fireman, but also by the senseless loss of a great man. One after another, we would shake hands and have a 20-second conversation before we had to turn to the next person in line.

Everyone wanted to be there for us, wanted to share his or her stories about Pat, just wanted to spend a little time in conversation with us. Then there were Pat's friends, who wanted to do something to honor him, like Vinny and Ellen McLaughlin—Pete and Keith's parents—who were very close friends of Pat's. They'd all helped one another through the worst time of their lives: Pete's death, his funeral and the trial of the arsonist who had set the fire. Ellen told me that she was trying to get a park named for Paddy. Before I could discuss this with her, a fireman pulled me away. He told me how he'd helped Paddy with his eye test to get on the department. Then there were Jimmy Coyle's parents, wanting to know how we were holding up. Vina Drennan said that Paddy would have loved all this—and that was all she had time to say before I was called away again. The man who ran the FDNY Explorers group that Pat had joined when he was a kid wanted to meet me. I was again interrupted: the members of the Westbury FD had arrived, and I was happy to see them. After being consumed by my brother's life, it was nice, just for a moment, to be brought back to my own. Pat Hyland, that good man and great friend with whom I'd served on the WFD for many years, grabbed my hand both of his. I was able to tell him where the WFD members should be on November 9 to make sure they got into St. Patrick's. Then I was pulled away again. It was another fireman who told me that *he* had helped Paddy with his eye test to get him on the fire department. *Pat must have had*

*worse eyesight than I thought to need all this help
passing his eye exam.*

Then there were the people who wouldn't be alive
if Paddy had not been in the right place at the right
time. He had quite a knack for that. These folks were
with members of their families. Some I'd already met,
and all of them wanted to do something more. They
would tell me of special prayers, poetry, songs, stories,
music, even a Buddhist meditation; they all wanted
their offerings to be presented at the Mass at St.
Patrick's. One of the men who was saved during the
rope rescue had composed a musical piece that he
wanted to perform during the Mass. *How the hell do I
say no to these people?* We were to be guests at
perhaps the most famous cathedral in the Western
Hemisphere, and after all the work that everyone had
already done, there was no way I could ask to have
things changed. And as far as I was concerned, I did
not want the ball back in my hand. It was bad enough
that we were violating St. Pat's policy of limiting
eulogies to four; we had double that number. If the
Cardinal suddenly chose to enforce that rule, I would
be the first to volunteer not to speak.

I needed to get away for a few moments and
sought refuge in the room that housed the stone. There
was a line of out-of-state firefighters there as well; two
at a time, they walked up to Pat's stone and crisply
saluted it. Meanwhile, unbeknownst to me, Donny was
out in the main room telling everyone what we planned
to do with the stone. When I returned from my private

vigil, I found myself suddenly surrounded by everyone—even people who had never even met Paddy Brown—pleading to come with us to Central Park. Those hundreds of 20-second condolence talks turned into explanations of why they couldn't come bury the stone: we had to do it in the middle of the night; we had neither an official permit nor unofficial permission to do it; it was illegal; it would be impossible to do with a large group; it was illegal; it was restricted to the small group who had helped plan the memorial; it was not going to be a ceremony. And it was illegal. It was supposed to be a kind of fun, adventurous thing to do, but now it had become an event, a much more important and symbolic one than I had time to realize. When I told someone that he or she couldn't come, even after enumerating all the reasons why, the feelings of hurt and rejection were obvious. Some people were not shy about informing me of this fact. Janet almost took my head off when I told her she couldn't be there.

"What do you mean, I can't come?!" she demanded. "You've got some nerve! I'm hurting as much as anybody, and Pat was my brother-in-law. You have to let me go!"

Oh, boy. I sure didn't need all this. I must have rejected 200 requests.

Then James Remar approached. "Mike, I want to come with you to plant the tree."

Without thinking, I said no—and instantly realized that not only had I made James feel rejected,

I'd also destroyed whatever spirit he had left in his soul. No reversal of the decision or number of words could repair the emotional bank account that I'd depleted with one word. I broke away from the 20-second conversations to find Bobby.

"Hey, this thing with the stone is getting out of hand," I told him.

"Yeah, Mike, I've heard."

I continued, "You agree with keeping it to just the people that were involved with the planning?"

"What?"

"You know, what we discussed. It's for us, right? The Inner Circle, right?"

"Mike," Bobby said cautiously, "what did you do?"

"Well, James asked me if he could come, and I told him—"

Bobby stopped me with a look that cut like a laser.

"You did what?! You told James that he couldn't go? Your brother's best friend! You can't tell him no! He was the first name on Paddy's list!"

I realized that I'd made some mistakes before, but this—this was a major fuck-up. The damage was done. A wide gap had now opened in James' and my developing friendship that was never going to close. And not only that, Bobby was furious with me. I couldn't handle much more of this.

IT WAS THE NIGHT before the Mass, and Janet and I

273

returned to the Delmonico. The gap between us was also widening. The only words that passed between us were for the sake of utility, along with her occasional repeated outburst: "I can't believe you're not letting me come plant the tree!" I tuned her out because I had other words to worry about—my eulogy. Janet retreated to the bedroom; I sat on the couch looking out onto Park Avenue.

Where does someone start to express the importance of a brother? I wrote, crossed out the insufficient words, stopped, then started again. I tried to write stories from our childhood and make it funny and cute, but there was nothing funny or cute about any of this. I tried to write what people expected from a doctor, that didn't work; a former firefighter, no; a brother from Vegas, no good. It turned out that I was writing nothing but pages and pages of contrived bullshit. What did I expect? I wasn't a writer. And I sure as hell wasn't a speechmaker. I didn't even like talking all that much.

I'm going to look like a retard tomorrow.

We had a lineup of great speakers. Then there would be me, the retard. What was I, nuts? Then it hit me smack in the face—not the inspiration that was so desperately needed, but the morning sun. God's alarm clock was ringing. *It's November 9. Time's up, buddy.* The garbage trucks were making their way along 59th Street consuming their morning meals. This woke Janet, who, yawning, came out of the bedroom.

"You've been up all night?" She noticed the writing tablet in my hand. "So, what have you got?" she asked.

My eyes were bloodshot. "Nothing."

Janet put her arms around me. "Don't worry," she said. "You'll come up with something. I *know* you, Mike. You'll do fine."

Chapter 29

ON THE MORNING OF November 9, a very large group of our family and friends—maybe 50 or 60—gathered at Campbell's. When everyone had arrived, we all loaded into the vehicles that would take us the 30 blocks south to St. Patrick's Cathedral. A fire department pumper would carry Pat's helmet displayed on an American flag made of flowers. There were two firemen on the back step, guarding and honoring the helmet. Steve Browne would ride in 3 Truck, which would immediately follow the pumper. The next vehicle in the procession would be the limo carrying my father, my sister Carolyn, her husband Hector, my father's close friend Roslyn, and Roslyn's grandson. Janet and I would ride in a second limo accompanied by Donny, the *News'* Michael Daly, and Bobby and his wife Blair. At first there was some confusion over who would ride in our limo, but just like everything else, we got it right. Jim Carney had arranged for a tour bus to transport the large number of people who were close to Pat. The bus fell in line as, one by one, the vehicles slowly pulled away from the curb.

The procession made its way slowly down Fifth Avenue that autumn morning. We had a police escort that blocked each intersection, allowing us to proceed unimpeded. An errant car pulled in front of us and stopped; Donny almost jumped out of the limo to take the driver's head off. After a few New York words were exchanged, we started up again. The group inside our limo talked about all the time and effort that had gone into the planning of the day's events and wondered how it was going to work out. We were all concerned about the number of people who would show up. About two weeks before, I'd considered asking my fellow volunteer firemen from Long Island to help fill the ranks, but I never got around to it.

We stopped on Fifth Avenue three blocks north of the cathedral and I noticed there was something missing—something so obvious, but so foreign to New York City that it was not immediately apparent to us. It was the quiet. Midtown Manhattan on a Friday was quiet.

The motorcade briefly stopped and we saw Steve Browne jump out of Ladder 3 and run up to our limo. He frantically banged on the window, not even waiting for Donny to open it fully before he began speaking.

"There are thousands. *Thousands.* It's packed!"

From his vantage point two vehicles ahead of us, he could see the crowd in front of St. Patrick's. His eyes shone with delight and relief. He then told us he'd just received word that HBO was doing a special and wanted permission to film in the cathedral. Another decision! Steve McCarthy was still doing his story about Pat for NBC and I didn't want to steal his thunder, so I called him. He told me that the more people who knew about Paddy, the better.

I told Steve Browne, "HBO or anyone else can place their cameras anywhere they want."

Cell phone to his ear, Steve rushed back to his seat in Ladder 3. It was a major relief that Pat would have the turnout he deserved. But I still had a major problem—I didn't know what I was going to say. And now HBO cameras would be rolling, catching every unrehearsed word.

Once Steve left, the deafening quiet returned for just a moment before it was broken by the gut-wrenching dirge crying out of the bagpipes. The wail was accompanied by the sound of a bass drum that kept time as the FDNY's Emerald Society Pipes and Drums slowly led the procession to its ultimate destination. The mournful sound sent shivers up my spine and tears to my eyes. Three tremendous horses carrying mounted police officers closely followed. Like archangels, they guarded the fire truck carrying Pat's helmet to the steps leading into St. Patrick's Cathedral. The limo started to move again, and as we got closer to the church, the magnitude of the event became apparent. On the right were firefighters from all over the world lined up seven deep for several blocks; on the left were the civilians—hundreds and hundreds of them huddled in the chill, standing silent and still, paying their respects to a real New York hero. Paddy Brown's best friends, his Inner Circle, did this for him. They closed down the biggest city in the world on a Friday afternoon.

Bobby and I were breathless. Paddy would not have had it any other way. *He is loving this. I can almost hear him saying, 'Good job, little brother.'* I found myself wishing that Pat's body had been found so this could be a funeral and not a memorial. He was still buried at the site or was part of the dust in the air that we were breathing, but his body was not here in the procession. All we had left was an old helmet and the spirit of fucking New York City.

Donny interrupted my thoughts. "Mike," Donny said. "Have the driver stop. I've got to find a bathroom."

We were all shocked by Donny's request. We'd been caught up in the midst of this magnificent display of selflessness, grief, love and spirituality—humanity at its best—when we were brought back to reality by Donny's bodily functions.

"Tell him to stop. I have to urinate."

"Urinate?" I repeated in disbelief. "Donny, if you leave this car now, you will never get into the church."

Donny briefly gave me a look that said, *Did you forget who you're talking to?* We stopped and Donny jumped out, disappearing into the crowd. The lead vehicles had reached St. Patrick's Cathedral. The men of 3 Truck carefully took down the floral American flag with the helmet resting on top. We waited for our turn to pull up at the curb. The bus parked and its passengers were escorted to a special area on the steps of the church. Just then the door of our limo flew open and Donny jumped back in.

"I don't believe it! Did you know that there's no place to pee on Fifth Avenue? I'll have to hit the bathroom in the church." Janet and I looked at each other. We didn't know whether to laugh or cry. Or lean over and strangle him. This had to be Pat, playing a joke on us at the expense of my little cousin's bladder. I could almost hear that Paddy Brown laugh.

We'd finally reached our destination and we all stepped out of the limo. The dignitaries silently greeted us: Mayor Giuliani, former New York Governor Carey and Fire Commissioner Von Essen were all standing in the cold waiting for us. *This is class, Pat. This is for you.* Across Fifth Avenue, two ladder trucks had their ladders extended high with a huge American flag hanging between them. It was an awesome sight. The four men from Ladder 3, carrying the flag of flowers with Pat's helmet atop it, slowly started making their way into the cathedral. Four men from Engine 69, Ladder 28, each at a corner of my father's wheelchair, gently lifted and carried him with respect and dignity up the wide stone steps. We joined the procession. Janet was on my right; Steve Browne escorted us on my left. We were all very much relieved when Donny suddenly joined us; he'd apparently found a cathedral bathroom. He walked alongside Janet as we walked past the massive bronze doors at the front entrance and into the church.

I had never been in St. Patrick's Cathedral before, but I immediately saw the reason Pat wanted his funeral held there. Upon entering the huge church, I was reminded of the wedding scene in *The Sound of Music*. This wasn't a wedding celebration, but we'd make today a celebration of a life well lived. More than 3,000 people were already packed into the pews. There was a large section up front for the blind—Pat's former karate students. There were homeless folks present, whom Pat had helped out on a regular basis with money, food, kind words. There were people from every part of his life.

We were just a few steps into the cathedral when the music began. The tones from the majestic organ rang out deep and full. The American Boychoir was singing *Amazing Grace* from above in the choir loft like voices of angels raining from heaven. It was breathtaking.

We sat in the first row on the right. I needed the aisle seat because I would be getting up to go to the altar and say whatever the hell I was going to say. Instead of a casket, to my immediate left in the center aisle was Pat's helmet. My father was seated next to me in the pew, with Janet next to him. During the Mass my dad remained seated; the pain he experienced when trying to stand or kneel was obvious.

The celebrant, Father George Rutler, spoke with the smoothness of a Broadway actor, and in a slow, deliberate cadence that reminded me for some strange reason of Alfred Hitchcock. Father Rutler had been down at the World Trade Center on September 11, granting absolution to a steady stream of firefighters who ran up to him, bowed their helmets and made the Sign of the Cross just before running up the stairs. With the power of a Shakespearean actor whose heart was broken, Bobby did the first reading. Don Sr. did the second reading, and as he spoke, I remembered the conversation the two of us had on that cold sunny day outside his restaurant—when he'd talked about losing his brother, and the void that remained inside him for so long. Officer Rodriguez sang *Ave Maria* with beauty, honesty and emotion far beyond what any professional opera singer we'd considered could have done. But maybe that was an unfair comparison. Rodriguez was hurting like the rest of us and sang from his soul.

One of the priests introduced Mayor Giuliani—it was time for the eulogies. By that time, I think I had my opening line and knew what I wanted to say. There was a line that I remembered from the movie *The Right Stuff*—there are some pooches you can't screw. For me, this was one of them. No matter how bad I might be, or how dumb I might look, those people in St. Pat's would forgive me.

Giuliani was, well—Giuliani. Here was a man who had turned New York around and made it a fine city again. And when his city was under attack, he held it together. He kept it from imploding. In fact, he held the entire country together. After 9/11, as New York went, so went the nation.

The Mayor had given hundreds of eulogies before this one, but he took pains to make each unique and personal. It was evident that he was sharing our sadness that day as he stated how lucky New York was that Paddy Brown chose to be a firefighter. He went on to say that before he came to the church, he'd attended a ceremony to celebrate the birthday of the Marine Corps. He'd been presented with two plaques. One had the famous picture of the Marines raising the Stars and Stripes at Iwo Jima. Mounted in the same frame, alongside this photo, was what had become an equally famous picture of the three firemen raising the flag at Ground Zero. The two photos were eerily similar. He read the inscription:

*Presented to the
Mayor of the City of
New York,
For the selfless
sacrifice of Marines
past and present who
honorably served and
continue to serve this
great city.
Once a Marine—*

Always a Marine.
Semper Fidelis.

The Mayor declared that Paddy Brown had died as a firefighter in the greatest rescue effort in the history of our country; one that had saved more people than had ever been saved during one disaster. He connected Pat's firefighting duties at the World Trade Center to his military service, saying that Pat had also died a Marine, protecting our country while it was under attack. Then Giuliani picked up the second plaque and showed it to us all as he read from it:

Marine Fighter
Attack Squadron—
251 "Thunderbolts"
First Launch,
"Operation Enduring
Freedom."

Turning the plaque over, he read aloud the description attached to the back:

> *The aircraft in this photo is the first Marine Corps F/A-18 launched from the* U.S.S. Theodore Roosevelt *to conduct air strikes against the Bin Laden terrorist network in Afghanistan. The United States Flag, raised by firefighters on 11 September amidst the ruins of the World Trade*

*Center and commonly published in papers across the country on the 12th, is aboard the plane with the pilot. This has been captured symbolically by super-imposing the flag over the upper right-hand corner of the photo. When the pilot dropped his bombs, his call across the radio was **"This one's for you, New York."***

Giuliani met our eyes in the front pew. He said that he didn't deserve the plaques—the Brown family did. He left the podium and gave both of these incredible and meaningful plaques to my father. There was thunderous applause and a standing ovation as the Mayor returned to his pew.

Fire Commissioner Von Essen was next to speak. Not only did he lose a great firefighter that day, he said, but when Paddy Brown's name came to be among the 343 deaths that day, he knew he'd lost a good friend as well. He went on to say that, while every rescue worker who responded to the Trade Center was a hero, there were only a small few who were warriors. Paddy Brown, he said, was a warrior.

As the commissioner was speaking, his eyes filled with pain, my thoughts flashed back to that night outside Carmine's restaurant when I was told not to allow Von Essen to speak. Had I listened to that firefighter, it would have been a great disservice to my brother, the commissioner and everyone else in St. Patrick's. Steve Browne set things straight on that night, and I had to wonder how many other things I might have screwed up if it hadn't been for Pat's Inner Circle.

Former Governor Hugh Carey got up next and read a letter from the current Governor of New York, George Pataki. He then put the letter down and gave an extemporaneous, rousing and emotional speech.

The increasing amount of acid in my stomach was a reminder of time passing. I could not ignore that my eulogy was soon to come.

Donny, Michael Daly and Mike Moran were escorted to the side of the altar to wait their turn to speak. Donny took the podium and read from a framed quote he'd seen hanging in Pat's apartment. It was an excerpt from a speech given by Theodore Roosevelt in 1910, *The Man in the Arena*. Donny spoke with confidence and grace. Speaking to such a large crowd didn't faze him at all. It was as if he were talking to me, with one exception: up there on that huge altar, he was speaking out of the front of his mouth. I didn't think that was possible! I was impressed with how well he did, but couldn't ignore what felt like a heart attack thinking about the impression I would make at my brother's memorial.

Donny ended his short address by telling the congregation that he too—Donny was also a Marine— had been at City Hall that morning to attend the anniversary ceremony for the Marine Corps. With another anniversary of sorts in mind, he finished by saying, "Today is Paddy's birthday. Happy birthday,

Paddy." We all stood and clapped to honor what would have been Pat's 49th birthday.

Watching Mike Daly step up to the lectern brought me back to a discussion I'd had with Bobby weeks before. After the meeting at the W, we agreed we needed one more great speaker, perhaps the President, maybe the Commandant of the Marine Corps...Bobby and I went over the pros and cons of each possibility and then, out of nowhere, as if Pat had placed the thought in my head, I said, "How about Mike Daly? Do you think he'll do it?"

Bobby looked at me as if I'd just parted the Red Sea. And as Mike began to speak, I realized why he was the perfect choice. His voice was soft at first, but the words—powerful. They echoed off the walls of the great cathedral. It was the supreme eulogy for a dear friend:

Happy Birthday, Paddy Brown
Son...Brother...Friend...Student...
Teacher...Sensei...Marine.
Gallant captain of the New York City Fire
Department.
First in, last out. Even now.

Much better men than I can tell you about
Paddy Brown in a fire, how he was ever
calm, ever steady, always thinking one
step ahead, so uncommonly brave that the
department   was   sometimes   unsure

whether to give him a medal or charges.

The picture of the rope rescue on the back of his holy card truly is a holy picture.

I can tell you how gently Paddy Brown stroked John Drennan's hair in the emergency room that night in 1994 when his friend was terribly burned fighting a fire on Watt Street.

Being a firefighter, Drennan's first concern was for the others. Paddy did not have the heart to tell him that James Young was dead, and Christopher Seidenberg seemed sure to follow. Drennan's condition did not seem much better. 'How bad is it?' Drennan asked. 'It's bad, John, real bad,' Paddy said. Drennan then bestowed on Paddy an honor that meant more to him than all the medals in the world. 'I want you to take my spot until I come back.'

Paddy pledged to himself that he would also look after Drennan's family. Paddy spoke his first words to Drennan's wife, Vina. 'I don't talk much, but I've been assigned to you.'

John Drennan was taken up to the burn unit, where Paddy had himself twice been a patient. The memory of those ordeals came rushing back as Paddy stepped off the elevator, and he nearly began his angel guardianship by passing out in front of Vina. 'One thing you really don't want to do when you're a captain is faint,' Paddy said.

Paddy described the days that followed as being tougher than anything he had experienced in Vietnam. He stayed at the Drennans' side through it all, saying just the right words to Vina and the kids, whispering assurances in their father's ear. On the 14th day, Paddy and Vina went down to Battery Park City at the base of the World Trade Center. He thought to throw a coin into the river to wish for his friend's recovery. That didn't seem enough, and he threw a whole pocketful of change into the rushing water.

But not even the entire city's prayers could save John Drennan. Paddy knelt at his friend's bedside and whispered, 'Look, John, if you want to go, it's O.K. It's O.K., John, you can go. We'll take care of your family.' A tear rolled down Drennan's cheek, and Paddy oh so tenderly wiped it away.

After a biblical 40 days, John Drennan's struggle ended. Paddy stood with Vina in the room. 'Just me and her,' Paddy said afterward. 'We cried over his body and stuff. It was kinda beautiful, you know?'

At the funeral, Paddy sat right here in the cathedral with Vina. Father Mychal Judge said the Mass, and I am thankful none of us possessed the gift of prophecy. Paddy remained the Drennans' guardian angel. In Vina's words, 'When it was over, when it got lonely, when it got quiet, when it got scary, Paddy was there for us still.'

Men would come up to Vina and take her hand and look into her eyes and say, 'Vina, how are you? How are the children?' Women would come up, take her hand, look into her eyes and ask, 'Vina, what's Paddy Brown like?' If I recall correctly, there were at that time 17,846 women whose hearts leapt at the mention of Captain Patrick Brown. That was just below 14th Street. And of course the number grew each time he bounded out the door. I do not need to tell you who all the girls stared at during our monthly dinners at Zino's restaurant.

I can still hear Paddy's laugh as we sat in that happy circle. Peter McLaughlin and Terry Hatton and Dennis Mojica and Tim Brown and Ricky Serrentino and Father Mychal Judge and a newspaper guy who felt a scribe of old who had been accorded the undeserved honor of a seat with the Knights of the Round Table. I can still see Peter McLaughlin, shining with life and goodness and charm. It just did not seem possible when he died in a fire. Nobody was more heartbroken than Paddy Brown. But Paddy was not one aching heartbeat slower in responding to a fire. If anything, he was even more determined when he faced the red devil who had taken his friend. He continued to show that being a firefighter is an even higher calling than knighthood.

Firefighters are armored only by their courage and nobility. Nobody astride a steed was ever so brave as a firefighter crawling on his hands and knees into the blinding smoke and flames. The only instance on record when Patrick Brown showed fear was when he was given a baby to hold. 'What do I do? What do I do?'

Like Sir Lancelot, Paddy never married. He did find a true home at the firehouse on 13th Street. After all the years of antagonizing bosses and then wondering why they did not give him Rescue 1, Paddy decided that he could have been in no better place than 3 Truck. He put a teak bench outside and declared that he was exactly where he wanted to be. 'Everything kind of worked out, you know?'

There was no secret to his happiness: he loved his men and they loved him. They discovered that a true hero arrives at his command on a bicycle wearing Spandex shorts and unrolls a purple mat on the apparatus floor for a little yoga. He might even get the likes of big Mike Moran to attempt a Dancing Shiva. For a firehouse dinner, a true hero preferred grilled chicken Caesar salad. He naturally asked for the balsamic vinegar.

Paddy's friends outside the firehouse

already knew that a true hero lives in an apartment with a red rug that would make Martha Stewart one woman who had no use for Patrick Brown. And, that when a true hero goes to Bed, Bath and Beyond, he buys red towels to match that rug. A true hero also has a Mickey Mouse phone. A true hero may have made it a point to learn how to turn off the fuel if the President's helicopter ever crashes, but he cannot work a Mr. Coffee machine. A true hero buys coffees two at a time, and only from the last mom-and-pop shop on 14th Street. A true hero is cherished among deliverymen because he always tips them five dollars. A true hero gets his suits at Brooks Brothers, but wears them maybe once a year. A true hero decides to take up piano at age 40, hiring a teacher who shows up the first day asking for little Patrick. 'That's me!' Paddy announced.

All of which is to say that a true hero is exactly himself, wherever he was, in all his adventures. Be he chatting with a countess at Da Silvano's, or standing with a soot-blackened face at Waterside Tower, saying how brave everybody else had been without mentioning his own courage. Or teaching karate to the blind, telling a student who had lost what little sight she had in a subway attack, 'You can't give up. You got to keep going.' Or taking 3 Truck to Tompkins Square to drink egg creams and watch the East Village parade go by. Or taking the same men to practice cutting a roof on a broiling summer day. Or suddenly turning to you in a trendy SoHo restaurant and saying how much it hurt to return home from Vietnam and be welcomed more like a criminal than a hero. Or inviting Vina and Father Judge to dinner at his Fifth Avenue mansion and uptown home, Engine 69. Or jogging into a happy sweat with James Remar. Or speaking with such pride about his brother Mike, the doctor, but never mentioning Mike is about two feet taller. Or telling you, 'My father was a big guy in the FBI. A President honored him or something.' Or, bouncing with excitement on the balls of his feet as he showed you the new thermal imager that let him peer through the smoke and for the first time really see the red devil. 'I never knew this was so dangerous!' And then—that Paddy Brown laugh. Or watching his four-year-old godson Dylan playing in Central Park on a sunny St.

Patrick's Day.

Or surprising yet another firefighter that the legendary Captain Brown was humble and even shy. Or laughing with his beloved Bobby Burke. Or giving you a little boy's grin from his boot-camp group picture, the Marine recruit nicknamed Calm Down Brown liking a camera even at Parris Island. Or mumbling that maybe there might be some little thing in Time *magazine—which turns out to have a picture of him looking like Douglas MacArthur. Or checking on John Drennan's kids. Or prompting Father Judge to tell him, 'God loves you, Paddy Brown, but you have to slow down.' Or telling Father Judge, 'Yeah, I know.' Or once again searching for life in a blazing building.*

At all times, in all circumstances, Patrick J. Brown was precisely Patrick J. Brown. The one and only. And just as being all things to all people makes you shallow, being ever himself made Pat ever deeper as he charted his own particular way through life. He is the only person I have ever encountered who could be profound by saying 'kinda' and 'sorta' and 'you know.'

His guide words were Semper Fi, and, as always, he had his Marine Corps pin on his chest when he was in this cathedral last May. The occasion was the Holy Name Society Communion breakfast, and as he filed out with the others, he once again proved nobody looks better in a uniform. I remember him saying, 'It's kinda nice to be here when nobody died.'

In June, I saw him again in white gloves outside another church, that occasion being Harry Ford's funeral. Ford had been one of the three to die in the Father's Day fire, and Paddy needed to say nothing at all for you to know how he felt. Just before the bagpipes played, Paddy spoke of something he called 'kinda beautiful.' He had helped firefighter Jeff Giordano rescue a young woman from a fire just down 13th Street from the firehouse, and they tried to resuscitate her twice with no luck. But they were not going to give up and they tried yet again. And then Paddy saw it, that most beautiful sight: the light of life coming back into Jessica Rubenstein's blue eyes. 'I just keep seeing those eyes,' Paddy said.

Paddy almost smiled and joined the formation outside the church and saluted Harry Ford's mortal remains as the bagpipes played. Brian Fahey's funeral was next, and then came John Downing's. Paddy Brown and all the others kept dashing to fires.

On the morning of September 11, Paddy arrived home at 3 Truck and wrote "0800 Capt. Brown RFD" in the journal. RFD. Reporting for Duty. That 'D' denoting the core of Paddy's life. Not an hour later, he and 3 Truck were racing to the World Trade Center. Paddy would not have had time to consider the poetry of pulling up right alongside Terry Hatton's Rescue 1. Paddy's thoughts would have already been in the tower, where more people needed help than at any single moment in the city's history.

'Don't go in there, Paddy!' somebody supposedly cried.
'Are you nuts? We've got a job to do!' Paddy said.
In they all dashed; more bold than any knights, as brave as any Marines,

climbing up flight after flight to meet the very devil himself.

Tower 2 collapsed, and Paddy understood Tower 1 would soon follow. He got on the radio as calm as ever. "Captain Brown, Ladder 3. Forty-fourth floor. Exit is proceeding orderly."

A chief ordered an evacuation. Firefighters have told Tim Brown that Paddy urged them on as they started back toward the street. 'Keep going, guys. Keep going.' They called for Paddy to join them, 'Come on, Captain, come on.' 'Keep going, guys. Keep going.'

By one report, Paddy and the rest of 3 Truck found themselves on the 40th floor with 30 to 40 severely burned people. Mike Moran has noted that all these firefighters were strong and fit and could have easily fled to safety in those final minutes. But Paddy and 3 Truck would no sooner leave those burned people than they would have left John Drennan. Those suffering, terrified people could have had nobody better to die with. I picture Paddy still calm, still precisely Patrick J. Brown at the instant the light left his eyes, he and his men showing with their very presence that there are greater things than saving your own life, you know.

When Tower 1 collapsed, anyone who knew Paddy Brown knew he was still in there. I was standing at the distance you stand when you are not a hero, and when I stopped running I was near the water's edge, where Paddy and Vina had stood seven years before, tossing in a fistful of change for her husband. As I walked back to the stunned, eerie hush of what would become known as Ground Zero, I encountered Tim Brown. Ricky Serrentino was alive, but the rest of the round table was gone: Terry Hatton and Dennis Mojica and Father Judge and Paddy Brown.

Today Paddy's mortal remains are still down in that smoldering pile. Perhaps he continues to fight the devil. He always knew that the devil is not just fire. The devil is also indifference and callousness and materialism and disrespect and anything else that hardens the heart.

To gaze upon that pile is to be challenged

to remember and honor Paddy and all those who perished with him, to live true to his everlasting example. You who are firefighters or police officers or paramedics or soldiers already do, and our debt to you is beyond paying.

I have wondered how Paddy could be happy in heaven with all of us grieving below. I then remembered what Father Mychal Judge used to say: 'My God is the God of surprises.' I think he meant that good always arises from the bad. I am hoping that the biggest surprise arising from September 11 is one the church teaches us should be no surprise at all.

I pray the day will come when we will arrive in heaven to see Paddy at a big round table with our priest and all those knightly firefighters...and, of course, John Drennan. There will be Diet Coke, not Pepsi. No ice. Maybe even a birthday cake. As Vina has predicted, John Drennan will say, 'Paddy, we're both brave, we're both tough, we're both true leaders, heroes who have done great things. But Paddy, I was married to Vina for 26 years, and there's no way I could have spent 40 days in a row with her.

Paddy, you're the greatest!'

Then we'll hear Paddy laugh once more. He will laugh even louder when Vina arrives to take a seat next to her husband for eternity. And Father Mychal Judge will say something else he always said— 'All is well.'

We can count on Paddy to make sure the table has lots of room for all of us who love and miss him so on this first birthday without him. We'll all be together.

And that will be kinda beautiful, you know?

With that, Daly was done. Thunderous applause followed as he walked off the altar.

He did it! Mike Daly said everything that needed to be said. I thought that maybe I wouldn't have to speak. I mean, what could I possibly add to that?

Then Mike Moran stepped up on the podium. Steve Brown had suggested at the W meeting that someone from Ladder 3 should speak. I said sure, and when he told me it would be Mike, I thought it was another perfect choice. He was a giant of a man in his dress uniform and ready to speak to represent Pat's men.

Cardinal Egan appeared a bit concerned about what might be said in his cathedral; Mike Moran's reputation to tell it like it is had preceded him. Most in the church already knew that Moran was a commanding speaker who had previous experience addressing a crowd slightly larger than the one in St. Pat's. Just weeks before, in front of a sold-out Madison Square Garden at the Concert for New York City—and right before The Who was about to play—Big Mike Moran boldly and fearlessly walked up to the microphone in the middle of the stage and declared: "All I can say, on behalf of my brother John and all the 12 members of Ladder 3 that we lost; and the 20 members of the New York City Fire Department football team that we lost; and all the people from my neighborhood, my hometown, Rockaway Beach, Queens, New York: Our friends, our neighbors, our relatives—they are not gone, because they are not forgotten. And I want to say one more thing, in the spirit of the Irish people: OSAMA BIN LADEN, YOU CAN KISS MY ROYAL IRISH ASS!"

When Moran started speaking in St. Patrick's Cathedral, his voice was as strong and resolved as it had been in Madison Square Garden:

> *On the morning of September 11th, enemies of the United States attacked the World Trade Center. Their followers rejoiced—they even danced in the streets. They thought they had achieved success,*

but they did not. They made the mistake on the morning of September 11th, when all they saw when they looked at the World Trade Center was two buildings. What they failed to see was the nation that stood behind them. What they failed to understand was the terrible resolve they had awakened.

And if there is justice in the afterlife—and I believe there is—those fanatics who crashed those planes into the World Trade Center did NOT get to meet Allah. They did NOT get 70 virgins. Instead, they met Patrick J. Brown. And they discovered they'd messed with the wrong Marine. Because you don't mess with 3 Truck. You don't mess with Paddy Brown's guys. Not when HE's working.

When Paddy first came to 3 Truck, he earned our undying respect when on two different occasions tough guys thought they could push Paddy or his guys around. They found out the hard way that Paddy was not only a black belt in karate, but also a heck of a boxer. He was what my father used to call 'good with his hands.'

We used to joke around in 3 Truck and tell the officers that they were not in charge, they were just responsible. Well, we never, ever whispered that about Paddy because we all knew he was in charge. And not because he yelled, but because he spoke softly. He was humble. He led by example. He was bigger than life. Therefore, a simple request from him was like a shouted order from another. Late at night, you could usually find him in the kitchen talking with the guys. He liked to shoot the breeze with the men. It is a testament to his character that with all the famous people he knew, all the mayors that pinned medals on his chest, all the big chiefs that were relieved when they saw his familiar visage enter the fire ground, that Paddy liked nothing better than hanging out with the men. Because Paddy never stopped being a fireman. He only cared if you showed enthusiasm, if you were willing to learn. He didn't care how many bars you had on your collar. He only cared about the content of your character.

Guys that had had problems in other houses wanted to come to Ladder 3, not because the captain was soft, but because he was strong. He didn't prejudge you, he let you prove yourself to him, and the great thing about him was that you didn't want to let him down. We were becoming the Oakland Raiders of the Fire Department. And I will tell you this, we loved having him. He was not only a great storyteller; he was also a great listener. He took tremendous interest in the guys' lives and well-being. The funny thing is, most of us never realized that in those informal chats, the captain was teaching us. That's what he was doing. He was teaching us the fire department way, the 3 Truck way, and most important, the Paddy Brown way.

He was respected and loved because he lived his life so well. I am reminded of the movie Braveheart *when the men saw William Wallace for the first time. It wasn't much different from when the captain first walked through the doors of 3 Truck. It was whispered, 'This can't be the man they call Paddy Brown, he's not big enough. Paddy Brown is eight feet tall.' Well, he wasn't that big, but his heart was. That is the burden of being a legend, one that Paddy carried with tremendous grace and humility. To hear*

*the stories and legend of Captain Brown
was to be inspired. But to actually meet
the man, to be led by him, to follow him
down that long, dark, smoky hallway, was
to be blessed because Paddy's strength,
courage and experience were a
tremendous comfort in tough times.*

It was at this point in his eulogy that Big Mike Moran
started to choke up. Swallowing the tears before they
could spill out, and with a crack in his voice, he pushed
forward:

*When you went to Cap with a request or
a problem, his usual reply went along the
lines of, 'Don't worry, we'll see what we
can do, we'll take care of it.' Anything for
the men.*

*So I can only imagine how it was in those
final moments of September 11th.
Captain Brown leading his men. Helping
30 to 40 severely burned people down
those dark stairs. Paddy giving
'maydays' that saved many other
firemen's lives—but he and his men
refusing to leave those people behind. I
can see the guys from 3 Truck turning one
last time to Paddy and being comforted
by a nod of his head, a shy smile. 'Don't*

*worry, fellas, we'll take care of it.' And
they were inspired.*

*So this marks the 12th and final funeral
for the men of Ladder 3. And it is fitting
that Paddy go last. The last man out.
Paddy never would have left any building
until all his men were out. He couldn't
leave the scene or firehouse until all his
men were accounted for. He would even
come in on his off days to take care of
things for his guys.*

Mike Moran then lost the battle with the tears. They
overtook him as he finished:

*So on behalf of the surviving members of
Ladder 3, you can take up now, Cap. All
your men have been cared for. And they
have gone home. You should join them
there and rest easy. Any problems that
come up, don't worry, we'll take care of
them. For you taught us well. You taught
us the Paddy Brown way.*

Deafening applause and a standing ovation followed as
Mike walked down the steps of the altar. This was it—
the final memorial for 3 Truck. Time for their
courageous captain to go home, time for the surviving
members of Ladder 3 to take up. They had taken care

of 13 funerals and memorials—one for Mike's own brother, a chief in Special Operations. They had stood as honor guard, marched in formation, comforted the devastated families, tried to answer unanswerable questions, held their lost brothers' kids, and they had done it all with patience, professionalism, compassion and class. "Whatever you want, Mike" is what I was told over and over, and despite the hundreds of services, Ladder 3 made me feel as if Pat's had been the only one. I'm sure they did that for every family. I looked around St. Patrick's Cathedral, at all the grandeur fit for a President or Pope, filled with palpable love for my brother, and all the love that went into the planning. Pat's close friends, both in and out of the fire department, made sure that this event was going to be perfect; they knew that Paddy Brown's wishes were fulfilled. I could hear Pat say, "Yeah, guys—this is exactly what I wanted."

Before Mike Moran could make his way back to his seat, Cardinal Egan intercepted him and brought him back up to the top step of the altar. The Cardinal said something about Mike representing the best of the best, the New York City Fire Department. When I saw this, I thought that we'd passed our maximum number of speakers and the Cardinal was putting an end to the eulogies. I felt bad for Jim Ellson, who was ready to deliver his tribute to Paddy, but I also felt like a kid who didn't do his homework and, as I was called on to show it, the bell rang to end the class. The Cardinal's reprise only lasted a moment. Jim and I were escorted to the altar to wait our turn at the podium.

Jim was wearing his fire department uniform with a chest full of medals and commendations. He was close to Pat, and by the look of that uniform it was obvious that Jim knew the meaning of being a hero. He did a fantastic job speaking about Paddy's life on the job. Unfortunately, I was too preoccupied with rising panic and was still trying to figure out exactly what I was going to say to remember much of what he said. I heard the loud applause. Jim had done a great job—and now it was my turn.

I slowly moved to the lectern, gripped both sides, and looked out into thousands of pairs of eyes. I took a slow, deep breath and started:

> *I know what I want to say but don't know how to say it. I tried to write it, but only got through the first line—I couldn't make it. I got advice from people—from the family in the limo coming up here— and they said, 'Mike, speak from your heart.' So that's what I'm doing. My father gave me advice. He said, 'Hey, Mike, keep it short.'*
>
> *Pat loved Dad and Carolyn very much. But to me—he was my older brother and always took care of me. He would call me in Vegas, ask me medical advice.*

Sometimes strange medical advice like, 'Hey, Mike, how does Advil work?' He always returned the favor by helping me with life, helping me choose the right thing to do.

When all this came down, I found myself in New York City wandering around, not knowing what to do. I ended up going to 3 Truck; they brought me into the back. Bobby Burke was waiting there. They said, 'Mike, what do you need?' I realize today, through Pat's close friends, family, the fire department—he is still taking care of me.

When I was back in medical school, we had a discussion about Chernobyl and all the horrors that the Russian firemen suffered. One of the other medical students kept asking, 'Why did they go in there?' I said, 'Because they are firemen, and that's what they do.' When you look at what happened on the 11th, the horror, and wonder how could anyone possibly go in there, it's because our firemen are the best firemen in the world. And there was no one better than Paddy Brown.

And that was it. I released my grip and pushed off the podium like a fireman pushing off the back step on a fire truck. By the standing ovation, I was confident that I did not screw the pooch.

I returned to my seat and the two Marines serving as honor guard folded the flag. Father Rutler gave the final blessing, and the angels' voices started to rain down on us once again from the choir loft. The procession made its way out of the church while the American Boychoir and Officer Rodriguez sang *The Battle Hymn of the Republic.*

It was twilight now. Outside the church, we were greeted by the silence of the thousands for whom there had been no room in St. Patrick's. Two buglers played Dueling Taps, followed by a flyover of three NYPD helicopters. Then, with shadows falling over Fifth Avenue, the Marines presented the folded flag to my father—which almost killed him.

We loaded into the limo for the short ride to the collation at the Hilton Hotel. Bobby and I were exhausted—but very proud of how things turned out. In fact, we had a laugh when I announced, "I'm never, ever, ever going to speak in front of anyone ever again." The limo pulled up in front of the Hilton and we were greeted by a frantic Gonzo.

"Mikey, Mikey, how many people do you think will show?"

"I don't know."

"There must be 7,000 people. We only planned for 4,000!"

By then, all my major worries had passed. With a shrug I told him, "Hey, 4,000…7,000…who's going to count? Let them all in."

Gonzo realized that I wasn't going to be much help and took off to find a more sympathetic ear.

JUST OUTSIDE THE ENORMOUS ballroom where the collation would be held, the guys from 3 Truck were selling Paddy Brown memorial T-shirts to offset the cost of the event. On the front of the shirt was the Ladder Company 3 Maltese cross with RECON underneath it. Written on the back was CAPT. PATRICK J. BROWN—A TRUE AMERICAN HERO. It also had representations of the faceplates of all the fire companies Pat had served with. They were selling like hotcakes, with most guests buying more than one.

Soon the ballroom was filled, and my family was once again shaking the hands of thousands of people. This was a true Irish wake for a true American hero. I met many more people whose lives had been touched by Pat. One of them was a woman who handed me two pieces of paper: on one was a poem that she'd written, and on the other, which is now hanging in my office, were the following words:

> *The night I met Paddy Brown, he quoted
> the composer Schumann:*
>
> *'When I tried to write a song about love,
> I wrote a song about pain.*

*When I tried to write a song about pain, I
wrote a song about love.'*

The poem that she'd handed me was too long to
read without my being interrupted by those 20-second
conversations. I placed the poem on a table, and when
I went back for it later, it was gone. To this day I regret
that I never got to read it.

Among the thousands of people there, I finally
had the opportunity to adequately thank the lieutenant
and the crew of Ladder 113, who had rescued a
drunken Donny and me from the New York City gutter
at 3 a.m.

Steve McCarthy asked me to introduce the short
film that he'd made to honor Paddy. Bobby used his
smile to remind me that I'd just said I was never going
to speak in front of anyone ever again. I took the stage.
A large screen descended from the ceiling just behind
me as I said a few words about what we were all about
to view. The lights dimmed and Steve's tribute began.
To accompany the visuals, Steve used the haunting
Irish melodies from *The Long Way Home,* the CD that
Keith McLaughlin had lent him. When my father saw
my brother's image on the screen, larger than life, he
let out, "That's Pat!"

By the end of the film, people were shaken. Tears
were flowing freely. I felt that something more needed
to be said. So once again I climbed up on the large
stage. After thanking Steve McCarthy for doing what

I'd asked him to do—which was to tear everyone's heart out—I lifted my Heineken and made a toast.

"To Patrick J. Brown, FDNY, who dedicated himself to saving the lives of the people of New York City and lost his life that day along with so many of the other true heroes of the world. We will never forget."

"We will never forget!" repeated the thousands of guests and workers there that evening, as everyone raised their glasses in a toast to Paddy Brown. I took a hit of my Heineken and escaped, stage right. Donny stepped up to the mike and invited everyone to the Turtle something or other bar—and with that, it was all over.

We were removing the photos and other memorabilia we had brought in, and I asked if I could have the large picture of Pat standing by himself at a fire scene. Someone said they would put it in a safe place for me. We didn't make it to the Turtle bar; the hotel bar was much closer. Janet and I were hanging out with Mike Moran, his girlfriend Donna, Steve Browne, Mike Daly, Ellin Martens, Bobby and wife Blair, when Janet suddenly spotted Daniele, one of Pat's ex-girlfriends, holding Pat's 3 Truck helmet.

"Mike, why does she have his helmet? Go over and get it from her."

Daniele was not just holding the helmet; she was cradling it as if it were priceless to her. I strolled away from Janet and started a conversation with Mike Daly when Gonzo came over.

314

"Mikey, I'm sorry. I shouldn't have given your brother's helmet to Daniele. Maybe you should ask for it back?"

"No, I can't ask for it back. Gonzo, look at the way she's holding it."

The three of us watched as Daniele, wrapped in her winter coat and still tenderly hugging Pat's helmet, headed out into the cold, dark streets of the city, her long blonde hair whipping in the wind.

I shrugged helplessly. It was out of my hands—for tonight at least. I turned to Gonzo. "So you think you going to make it to Central Park tomorrow night?"

"No, I can't," he said with real regret. "I have another commitment with some of the other family members."

Later that evening, I found out from Jim Carney that the members of Engine 69 and Ladder 28 had a wedding to go to Saturday night; they asked if we could do the tree planting in the afternoon. I had to say no. It would be impossible to get away with what we were planning to do in the light of day. I didn't even know if we could accomplish it under cover of night.

Chapter 30

THAT NIGHT JANET AND I experienced yet another silent cab ride back to the Hotel Delmonico. The driver appeared to be going out of his way to try and scare us, but his flying through traffic and cutting in and out of lanes didn't faze us at all. He was no match for Donny Brown. A reckless cab driver, city streets, traffic or noise could not have breached the wall that I'd put up between Janet and me. No, that wall could not have been breached, not even by Janet's righteous anger. And she was so angry. She was angry that a bunch of religious fanatics who did their praying at topless bars in Las Vegas killed all those innocent people just so they could go to their heaven and finally get laid. Angry that our government, fat and bloated, watched the terrorists get stronger and more organized—and did nothing. The U.S. responses to the previous terrorist attacks had been like a puppy exposing its underbelly. Is this what one should expect from the world's only remaining superpower? Janet was angry that her brother-in-law was killed and that she'd had lost a close friend. But mostly she was angry with me—and how I dealt with it all by cutting her out.

Trying to deal with this rage made it easy for her to get upset over anything and everything. She was upset that the garbage trucks woke her each morning, pissed off that she could not come plant the tree, angry that Marc was in town yet again. She told me in no uncertain terms that if she couldn't come plant the tree, then I'd better not allow Marc to go either. She was also quite upset that Daniele had, as she put it, "absconded" with Pat's helmet. I had been giving Pat's stuff away ever since I'd finally admitted to myself that Pat would not be returning. All I cared about was that whoever got whatever would appreciate it.

"Bobby was supposed to get Pat's helmet!" she fumed. *"You* should have kept that helmet! You didn't even ask me if *I* wanted it!"

Even my great wall couldn't keep out the truth. If there were a hierarchy of my brother's possessions, the 3 Truck leather helmet was on top. No one else but Bobby should have it. I was so tired of hurting people's feelings that I just wanted to leave things the way they were, but on this matter I realized I couldn't.

With a sigh I said, "Janet, I'll make the calls in the morning."

"You'd better!" was her reply. End of discussion. Saturday morning, after being awakened by the hungry garbage trucks, I called Marc and told him that he couldn't come to Central Park. He understood and said something about spending the time shopping. Then I called Daniele and told her that I needed Pat's helmet back. She offered to come uptown to drop it off, but I didn't think that was such a great idea. Since I was going downtown anyway, I could pick it up before going to 3 Truck.

Not much more was said in that hotel suite the rest of the morning. I was thrilled once the afternoon came so I could run away from our problems. With my backpack and cell phone, I headed for the subway to go downtown. The cold gray rain didn't bother me—I thought it was a beautiful New York City day. I was off on an adventure to grant my brother's final request.

DANIELE WAS TO MEET me at a bar a few blocks from 3 Truck. It was located on a corner, in an older building with large windows and a small, table-like inside ledge where you could eat or drink as you watched the world go by. I stopped in front of the building so I could see her approaching. The rain had flattened her blonde hair, and she was holding Pat's helmet in her arms the way she had the night before. Handing it to me, she said, "I knew I couldn't keep it. But thanks for letting me have it for the night."

We went inside and sat next to the window with Pat's helmet on the ledge between us. As Daniele started speaking, I saw a woman who had been walking past the bar notice us sitting there. She ran into a store across the street and came out with a camera. Then she came into the bar, walked up behind me and said, "Hey, I'm doing this thing about New York. Can I take your picture?"

Without turning I said, "No!"

The woman walked away, wet and insulted.

Daniele told me that she always felt she and Pat would get back together. The two of them would break up and not see each other for a month or two; then she'd be walking down the street, and there he was. "Hey, Blondie!" he would call out, and soon they'd be dating again. She started to cry.

"Even now, there are times when I'm walking down the street and see someone who resembles him out the corner of my eye, and just for an instant I'll think it's Pat," she said. "Then it hits me, and I remind myself that I'll never see him again." She told me that the happiest she'd ever seen him was when they were at Fire Island with Bobby, Blair and the Burke kids; the saddest was after Peter McLaughlin was killed in 1995. Pete had been his protégé. She noted that Pat started to go gray almost immediately after Pete's death. She would frequently accompany Pat and Terry Hatton to the trial of the arsonist who had started the fatal fire—the blaze that removed Pete from the Round Table that Michael Daly had spoken about in his eulogy.

The rain stopped, and she needed to go home and get ready to go out with friends. It was her birthday. And I needed to plant a tree. So I took the helmet, stuffed it safely in my backpack, gave her a goodbye hug and continued on.

IN MY JOURNEY TO Ladder 3, I walked past St. Vincent's Hospital and the now weather-beaten pictures of the people who had never returned from work on September 11. You could still make out the messages from the families. But the faces on the printouts were faded from the sun, and as a result of the rain, the words were running together like their incinerated remains and the washed-out hopes of the families. I felt the sadness and choked back my tears before they could escape.

The hell with it. I'm calling Marc. Marc was supposed to be shopping. I knew he wasn't shopping and was just wandering around New York. I called his cell.

"Hey, Marc, what are you up to? Good, want to come with us? Good."

He met up with me a short time later and we continued on to the firehouse.

This was the last of Pat's last requests. There were no ashes, but at least there would be a tree and a stone. It was almost 10 p.m. when Marc and I arrived at Ladder 3. Bobby, Steve Browne and Steve McCarthy were waiting outside for us.

Steve Browne said to me, "General, your troops are waiting for you in your basement." He then told me that Jimmy Brown was on his way in from Long Island with the tree in the back of his Dodge Ram.

On the pool table in the basement, I spread out the map that Pat had given me as I laid out the plan.

"We will meet here at the Met and park our vehicles. A few guys will stay with the tree. The rest of us will walk into the park and dig the holes. Then we'll call for the stone and the tree. Jimmy will drive into the park, and we'll plant the tree and cement-in the stone to secure it. Then we'll get out of there fast. It should take about half an hour. Now if we run into any cops, we have Keith and Donny. If we run into any Parks Department personnel, well, we're screwed."

As if we were coming out of a football huddle, with all hands on one, Mike Moran pronounced: "May God bless us and keep us safe."

With that, the 20 of us headed up the stairs.

I EXPECTED THE TREE to be a sapling and sitting upright in Jimmy's pickup. So I was a little taken aback at the sight of a maple tree lying down and extending another six feet or so out the back of the Dodge Ram. Tied to the tip of the tree was a strobe light. We loaded shovels, a pick and other implements of destruction into our vehicles and headed out into the Manhattan night. The strobe light was blinking its little heart out and the top of the tree waved it wildly with every city bump as our convoy flew uptown. I was in a car with Ray Trinkle, Chris Tighe, Steve Browne, Marc and Bobby, and we all shared the same thought: we had no clue how this was going to turn out. We met up as planned at the Metropolitan Museum of Art and, wearing our FDNY shirts and carrying garden tools, marched into the darkness of Central Park.

The few people we passed who were exiting the park were a bit curious seeing 20 firemen on their way in, in the dark of night, carrying a pick and several shovels.

"Hey, guys—what's up?" asked a late-night dog walker.

One of the men responded, "Von Essen detailed us to pick up dog shit."

Another comment: "We're looking for land mines."

Steve Browne answered one couple's question with a deadpan, "We are ninja gardeners."

Walking through the park, I was reminded of the first time I'd carried a shovel into the night with the men of Ladder Company 3, but this time the air was clean and the mood was positive. Well, that was, as long as we didn't get arrested.

Unmolested, our detail made it to the northernmost stretch of the Great Lawn, and it became obvious why Pat had picked this particular spot. Looking downtown, the dark, vast lawn was framed on three sides by the lights of the Manhattan skyline. Looking uptown, there were a few softball fields; behind them was a green building with the letters NYPD written on the side. In front of the building was a car that had its lights on—and the same letters painted on its side. We stopped in our tracks. Like a bunch of kids playing combat, we headed for cover in some nearby shrubs. *Now what do we do?*

Donny whispered, "You guys wait here. I'll be right back."

Donny headed off to the car while some plotted their escape, and the rest of us thought that this might be as far as we'd get. We could see Donny in the distance talking to the officers sitting in the car and, just like the kids we were that night, we started to joke around.

After a few minutes Steve Browne turned to me and said, "I've done worse things in my life than plant a tree for my captain." He then walked out of the bushes, looked up at the magnificent illuminated skyline, and drove his shovel deep into the grass, proclaiming, "This looks like a good spot!"

So what did we do? We started to dig. Steve McCarthy started filming, and the light from his camera turned out to be very useful. I kept waiting for the cops to drive over and say, "No, no, no—sorry, guys. You can't just come here and plant a tree. You need permits and such." But they didn't. In fact, after hearing why we were there, they told Donny to let them know if we needed them to drive over and point the headlights of their patrol car at where we were digging.

The preparation of the ground for the tree was progressing very slowly. The ground was cold and hard, and we took turns in the hole with a pick. Whoever happened to be down there would swing the pick with all the power and passion that was left in his soul. This was it: The last thing they would have to do for one of their guys, and they were going to do a great job. Of course, in the great tradition of the FDNY, the rest of us who were waiting to get in and shovel out the loose dirt had nothing better to do than bust balls. They made fun of Marc's loafers, Moran's determination, McCarthy's technique. While Bobby was in the hole, he stopped mid-swing and announced, "Gee, I never thought joining the Mob would be this much work!"

The hole was progressing much more slowly than we had expected. It must have been pushing midnight when out of nowhere a black man with a boom box walked up to our group.

"Yo, it's good to see some white niggers digging in a hole for a change!" he greeted us. He hung out and watched us for a while, and someone explained what we were doing.

He said, "That's cool, that's real cool." He thanked us for protecting the city and disappeared into the night.

I guess Jimmy Brown and Keith got tired of waiting in the parking lot of the Met. The truck suddenly appeared with the tree sticking out the back and the strobe light still holding on, bouncing and blinking its way into the park. Keith opened the doors and blasted the same beautiful music that had been such an important accompaniment to Steve's film the night before. The atmosphere became festive, with the Irish songs playing, the "white niggers" digging, busting balls, and all feeling that we were exactly where we were supposed to be. Jim Wind, the big man from 3 Truck with the deep voice who didn't waste words, turned to Bobby and smiled.

"This is the first good day," he said.

Jerry Brenkert—he originally had the idea for the tree at the October meeting at the W—was maybe the only one among us who had actually planted one. He was supervising the digging when he came over to me and said, "We got a problem. We need more water."

There were about four gallons of water on the truck, and we needed most of that to mix the cement to set the stone. This could be major. The tree could die. The answer soon came to me: fire trucks carry water! Dan and Steve Browne were in conversation when I came over.

"Do you think we can get an engine company to come out and give us some water?"

A discussion followed and a call was made to an Upper West Side firehouse; turned out the men there already knew all about our mission. I guess Donny told them in Campbell's or they heard it from other firefighters; actually, on that night every firefighter in New York City knew what we were up to. A short time later, Engine 74—a huge 1,500-gallon-per-minute pumper—pulled up in front of us on the walking path. The doors flew open and Captain Loeb and his men jumped out in their bunker gear. There was still more digging to be done, and soon these men were taking their turns in the hole. When the hole was about five feet deep, it was time to move the tree into it. Jimmy Brown backed his truck up to the hole, and it took most of us to maneuver the heavy maple. At its base was a huge ball of dirt held together with thick steel mesh. It must have weighed over a thousand pounds. Next to the tree was some kind of a tree-lowering ramp, which we braced against the tailgate of the truck.

We were slowly sliding the tree down the ramp when Jim Wind yelled to me.

"Mike, get in the hole!"

So I did. I was a little concerned to see the tree coming my way.

"What the hell are you doing?" yelled Ray Trinkle.

Jerry turned to see me and called out, "Are you nuts?! Get outta there!"

I thought that was an excellent idea, and quickly did a little dirt dance to get out of the way of the approaching tree.

Mike Moran jokingly asked, "Mike, are you always this gullible? I thought doctors were supposed to be smart!"

One thing was for certain—once that tree was planted, there would be no way to move it. It dropped in place. While the dirt was filled in around the tree, I prepared a small area for the stone directly in front of the tree. Donny mixed the cement and we drove rebar into the hole. Donny and I carefully placed the stone, Pat's stone, over the cement and rebar and secured it. Engine 74 took the booster line and soaked the dirt around the tree. We were almost done when I saw lights from a car driving through the park coming directly toward us.

Panicking, I said, "Shit. It's the Parks Department."

The brown Parks Department car stopped in front of the fire truck. The Central Park night supervisor walked slowly toward us. Here we were covered with dirt, holding shovels and such, caught with our hands in the cookie jar.

Keith said, "Hang on. I'll take care of this."

He intercepted the park supervisor and walked him back to his car. The rest of us silently watched them for a while then went back to work. We found out later what happened.

Keith shook the supervisor's hand and said to him, "Hello, I'm Jim McFabin. I think we may have spoken over the phone? We really appreciate your input on planting the right tree. Remember, you gave us two choices—and we picked this one. What do you think? Looks good?"

Dumbfounded, the supervisor said, "Looks very nice."

Here was this poor guy in the middle of a terror alert, patrolling his park in the middle of the night, looking for any suspicious activity. He comes upon all these firemen, a huge fire truck, and some guy with a large video camera filming the planting of a tree. Add in the fact that Keith was selling him down the river by telling him some bogus story, and we can understand why he was very confused.

We all stopped what we were doing and watched Keith and the Parks Department supervisor slowly walk back toward us. We had no idea what was about to happen. Was he going to call the cops? Was he going to make us dig up and remove the stone and the tree? After all this effort, was the night—this perfect, important night—going to end in disappointment and frustration?

There was dead silence. He stopped in front of the stone and read it. Slowly, he looked over at Engine 74 in their gear, standing in front of their fire truck, then at the rest of us wearing our fire department T-shirts, holding our shovels—and our breath. He understood. He said with emotion and sincerity, "You people, all of you, are true heroes. God bless you. And God Bless Paddy Brown."

He then got into his brown car and drove off. *Whew.* We thanked Engine 74 for coming out and saving us. The men got back into their fire truck and, with two blasts from the air horn, they disappeared into the Central Park night.

It was now quiet again. The music was off. It was time for a few words. We all gathered around the tree, and I read one more time the words from the stone: "To Captain Patrick J. Brown, FDNY, who dedicated himself to saving the lives of the people of New York City and lost his life that day along with so many of the other true heroes of the world. We will never forget."

Everyone else responded, "We will never forget."

Steve McCarthy then loudly proclaimed, "From this night on, when any of us walk past this spot, we will yell 'God Bless Paddy Brown!' " And in unison, with the words seeming to echo off the majestic Manhattan buildings, we all yelled, "GOD BLESS PADDY BROWN!"

Steve Browne grabbed my shoulder and pointed to the night sky above the Great Lawn. "Mike, you know all our guys are up there watching and smiling. You can feel it. And Paddy is telling them, 'That's my brother who did this.' "

He turned to face me and said, "I don't know about this Master of the Universe stuff, but to me you'll always be my general."

We loaded the ninja gardening tools in the vehicles and started to make our way out. We planned to return to the spot in one year and place a stone for each of the guys. I was one of the last to leave, and I turned around to see Bobby standing alone in front of the tree. He was playing a sad Irish tune on a tin whistle. This was a night I would never forget.

WE ALL ENDED UP at Finnerty's on Third Avenue for one, maybe two, but ended up drinking as if we'd won the war. I gave Bobby the helmet. He was very touched. He handed me three small Buddhist charms and told me that Pat had given them to him years ago to keep him safe.

JANET WAS UP AND waiting when I made it back to the hotel. She was more than upset to find out that Marc had been with us in the park. An argument followed, but it no longer mattered. We were in two completely different worlds.

Chapter 31

November 12, 2001: The Flight

DONNY AND JIMMY DROPPED us off at JFK early Monday morning. After check-in, Janet and I joined the long line at the first security checkpoint. Approaching the x-ray machines, we exchanged glances as we realized that broken English was the language of the day, spoken by most of the security personnel. The majority of these employees were obviously not native New Yorkers. They grunted and used their magnetic wands like conductors of an airport symphony, making us do whatever dance pleased them. Once satisfied with our performance, they grudgingly allowed us to pass through to the gates. The nurses from the ER who had been in New York for Pat's memorial—Troy, Ellen and Lois—were waiting for us in the terminal. They had already done their dances. We were exhausted and moped around a bit wasting time waiting for our flight. There would be no food service on the plane—perhaps they did not want anyone to use those stale rolls as weapons. So I was forced to buy one for eight bucks.

We boarded our plane at about 8:15 a.m. Janet and I settled into our seats and waited while the other passengers boarded. We sat quietly, both absorbed in our thoughts and memories of the past few days. We were glad to be heading home to our everyday life, yet I had ambivalent feelings about leaving my family and friends in New York.

An anxious young man boarded and took a seat in the row behind us. We could clearly hear him speaking to himself, saying something about not wanting to fly.

"Janet," I muttered, "is this guy going to do this all the way to Vegas?"

Janet answered, "God, I hope not. The plane is pretty empty, so if he doesn't stop we'll move."

He went on. "No, no, I don't want to fly—just too dangerous." Maybe he was worried about my stale-roll weapon that I'd smuggled aboard. He continued. "Planes are crashing and this one could be next. No, this is all messed up. I don't know what I'm doing on this plane. This is crazy."

I assumed he was talking about the planes on 9/11, and also thought Janet was about to tell him to get the hell off the plane if he were that worried. Then he burst out with, "Crashed right into Rockaway! Just took off and crashed!"

Indeed, there had just been a crash. American Airlines Flight 587 had taken off moments before from Kennedy, and the incident happened while we were boarding. The flight attendant informed us that our flight was canceled. We all deplaned and headed back into the terminal. Lois, Ellen and Troy joined us, and we gathered behind a large crowd huddled around a TV in one of the bars. The flight crashed in the neighborhood of Rockaway Beach, home to many police and firemen, including Mike Moran. The footage of houses burning and firemen rushing to the scene to set up hose lines was played over and over. Everyone stood there very quietly, speaking only when necessary and in hushed tones. No one panicked and we heard not one complaint about the delay. New Yorkers now dealt with tragedy in a different way—proficiency during crisis. Unfortunately, we all had experience.

For now it was being considered a terrorist attack, and everyone wondered if there would be news of more crashes to follow, as on 9/11. The powers that be closed down New York. All bridges, tunnels and airports were closed; all flights were canceled. Now I *really* didn't want to go back to Vegas; we were at war, and New York was the front line. But there was nothing we could do for now except pick up our luggage. Janet called her sister Karen in Queens and told her we were all coming over. Karen lived in Bellerose, about 20 minutes from the airport. Since we couldn't get back into Manhattan, this was the logical place to go. Troy got on her cell phone and arranged seats for all of us on a possible 8 p.m. flight. At least we were booked if they reopened the airport.

WE ARRIVED AT THE house and I gave my $8 roll to Lois; we borrowed Karen's car and drove to Westbury. I left the car at my dad's house and exchanged it for my big white truck, which I'd left there. I drove down to Jones Beach and sat on the boardwalk for a while and watched the ocean—the one thing I couldn't do in Las Vegas. After a while, I got back in my Tundra and, as if my truck knew where to take me, I ended up in the basement of the Westbury Fire Department. There was a full crew waiting to respond if need be. For more than 16 years that basement had been my second home, and I'd always thought of the members of the WFD as family.

Since 9/11, everyone had treated me with the utmost deference. But as soon as I got to the basement of the firehouse, they started busting my balls. It was as if I'd never left.

"Doc, we thought you were going to collapse at St. Pat's!" said Pat Hyland.

"We were taking bets," Doug Ingram laughed.

Someone else yelled, "Hey, Brownie, you looked like you had freaking Parkinson's!"

I loved it. I had no quick-witted comebacks. Only one thing came to mind. *Yup, this is my family all right.*

THAT EVENING NEW YORK City reopened. The five of us grabbed cabs from Karen's house back to JFK. We did the same idle roaming around the terminal, which was now packed with people trying to get to their various destinations. I was lucky enough to find room on a cement ledge to lie down while we waited to board our flight. The girls met a few out-of-state firemen who had attended Pat's memorial; they said they would remember the event for the rest of their lives. Thrilled to find out who we were, Janet gave each of them a Paddy Brown prayer card, for which they were very grateful. They were so grateful, in fact, that they wanted to give us their fire department shirts right off their backs—something, I think, one or two of the nurses would have enjoyed getting. I looked at my watch. "Let's go, guys. Time to board."

The plane was not full. To fly that night, after seeing what had happened that day, took some degree of bravery. As we took off, it seemed that everyone on that plane was in the same frame of mind—a bit apprehensive, but wanting or needing to get somewhere. Troy wanted to talk with Janet, so she and I switched seats.

I found myself in an empty row and planned to take full advantage of it. I laid across the three seats, got as comfortable as I could, and fell asleep to the sweet white noise of jet engines taking us home. When I woke to an announcement over the PA system, I thought I must have been dreaming.

"Are there any medical personnel on board?"
Slowly I stood up—to find Lois in the aisle holding a passenger's head. He was unconscious.

Approaching them, I asked, "Lois, is he breathing?"

"Yes, but he's out like a light."

The passenger was lying with his feet facing the back of the plane, the direction from which I was coming. I walked up and started to do my doctor thing; he was coming around, and I began asking him questions. Then, from behind Lois, a somewhat intoxicated woman pushed through. In a loud, booming voice, she announced, "I AM A DOCTOR."

I was not in the mood nor did I have the patience for any bullshit. Looking her in the eye, I said, "Good. So then you are assuming care of this patient?"

This question stopped her in her tracks and she immediately backed away. Lois gave me a look that said it all—she's an IDIOT!

I introduced myself to the man lying in the aisle and told him I was a physician. Lois and I started to ask him about his previous medical history and any recent occurrences that might explain this episode. He was intelligent, a gentleman. His wife was sitting in the aisle seat next to where he was lying. We all discussed what could have happened and what would be the best course of action. The flight attendant appeared and tried to pass a stethoscope to me. Out of nowhere, the intoxicated lady grabbed the stethoscope out of the flight attendant's hands. Lois gave me that look again and we watched as the woman placed the stethoscope on the man's neck. This procedure is used to listen for a disruption of the flow in the carotid arteries and is appropriate in a doctor's office or during an ER visit, but on a plane? It was just silly.

So there we were, trying to help this guy—and this doctor, who did not want to be responsible, kept getting in the way while listening intently to his neck. In my best Donny Brown voice, out of the side of my mouth, I said, "Hey, lady, what are you going to do—a fucking endarterectomy up here?"

It turned out the man had orthostatic hypotension. He could maintain his blood pressure while lying down, but as soon as he sat up or stood, the pressure dropped precipitously. Every time he would try to get up, his blood pressure would tank—and so would he. Another passenger, identifying himself as both an emergency medical technician and an FBI agent (and, I assumed, a sky marshal too), asked me if we needed help. I thanked him but said we had things in hand. Returning a short time later, he told me that the pilot wanted to speak with me. I positioned myself in the threshold of the cockpit and spoke over the radio with an airline doctor on the ground. I had an uncomfortable feeling that this FBI agent had a gun pointed at my back. We were discussing the best course of action when word reached the cockpit that there was a doctor in the cabin stating that it was safe for the patient to fly another three-plus hours to Vegas, and that the patient himself wanted to go on. It was easy to figure out who the other doctor was, but I needed to see what was happening. When I got back to my patient, he was still on the floor with Lois leaning over him.

"Lois, what's up?"

"What do you think?" Lois replied, obviously irritated by the inappropriate actions of the female who claimed to be a doctor. "He can't sit up without passing out."

I spoke to the man and explained what could be causing the drop in his blood pressure— mentioning a GI bleed among other things. I stressed the need to get him to an ER. He argued some. "Doc, I'm fine. Really, I can make it to Vegas without any problems."

I said, "O.K., it's ultimately your call."

He tried to get up and passed out again. When he regained consciousness and found that he was back on the floor, I looked down at him and said, "See?"

I returned to the cockpit and the pilot asked me, "What do you think? The guy wants to continue on."

"The bottom line is that when he stands up, he isn't getting enough blood to his brain," I said. "The last thing we need up here is a cardiac arrest."

With those words, the beautiful airliner made a steep, banking turn to the left, and we were on our way to the closest airport. A few minutes later we were on final approach into Columbus, Ohio. I was sitting in an aisle seat next to my patient with my seatbelt on and my right hand on his chest to secure him for the landing. His wife, looking very concerned, sat in the aisle seat across from me. The plane made a perfect landing. After we arrived at the gate, paramedics came onboard and took the man, accompanied by his wife, to the hospital.

WE WERE ON THE ground for some time while the pilots charted a new flight plan. It was getting pretty late and everyone on that plane was totally exhausted. I made it back to my row of empty seats and the plane once again took to the air—and I took to trying to fall asleep. With the engines cranking, we continued on. Then I felt someone shake me. I opened my eyes to find the flight attendant with a concerned look on her face.

"Sorry to disturb you, but where are your nurses sitting?"

I sat up as the attendant told me that there was a woman in the bathroom who had passed out. I pointed out Janet and Troy. They got up quickly and the three of them walked to the back of the plane. I resumed my position across the seats and thought—no, I prayed—that the lady simply fell asleep on the bowl. The girls would go back, wake her up, all would be well, and I could go back to sleep. My eyes closed, then opened to Janet's voice. With her face about four inches from mine she whispered, "Mike, I think she's dead!"

I scrambled from my seat and, in a few long strides, I was at the door of the lavatory where I found the elderly woman slumped on the toilet. I turned to Janet and Troy and said, "Wow. She does look dead."

"What should we do?" Troy asked.

"Let's work her. Come on, help me."

As best we could in the tiny cramped lavatory, I took hold of her collar and Troy grabbed her legs. We maneuvered her out of the stall and laid her in the aisle outside the lavatory, perpendicular to the rear galley. The three of us checked for a pulse: nonexistent. As I started chest compressions, the flight attendant handed me a first-aid kit. In it, I found a resuscitation mask that I handed to Janet, who had positioned herself half-in and half-out of the bathroom. She started rescue breathing but was having difficulty maintaining a good seal with the mask. Troy took over the chest compressions so I could use my left hand to hold a seal for Janet and examine what was in the first-aid kit with my right. There was an IV setup and some medications; I handed the IV setup to Troy and, with skill and efficiency, she had the catheter in place and we had intravenous access within seconds. A flight attendant handed us an automatic defibrillator, and I placed the pads on the woman's chest. I slid the defibrillator under my legs; in the cramped space we had to work in, that was the only place it could fit. The machine had a small cardiac monitor screen that I needed to raise my right leg to see so I could follow her heart rhythm. Lois saw what was going on in the rear of the aircraft and came charging back, stepping over us to get into the galley area and, in doing so, kicked Janet squarely in the head.

"HEY!!" Janet cried.

It was quite a scene. Lois was down at the patient's feet opening supplies and drawing up medications; Troy was straddling the woman's legs, leaning forward to do chest compressions; Janet was kneeling out from the lavatory performing rescue breathing every five seconds. I had my right leg up against a seat and my left hand holding the mask to the lady's face—and all of us five miles in the air.

The patient was in pulseless electrical cardiac activity and needed epinephrine. With my right hand, I passed the epinephrine that I found in the kit over to Troy, who passed it on to Lois, who pushed the drug through the IV line. All of a sudden, the defibrillator started talking in a mechanical woman's voice. *"Stand clear of the patient. Stand clear of the patient."*

341

Not wanting to get shocked by this thing, we did what it told us. The mechanical voice continued. *"Analyzing rhythm...not a shockable rhythm, continue CPR."*

Yeah? No shit!

Another dose of epinephrine was given. A minute later, I saw the cardiac rhythm change on the monitor and said, "Hold on. Check for pulses."

Troy said excitedly, "I got a pulse!"

"Me too, Mikey!" Lois announced.

We all stopped and leaned back a little, grateful for the break—except for Janet, who needed to continue to breathe for the patient. Our reprieve lasted only a few minutes. The rhythm changed again and I called out, "Check for pulses."

We found none, so we resumed CPR. The robot voice sounded. *"Stand clear of the patient, stand clear of the patient."* Not again!

We performed our ER magic and again got a pulse. Unfortunately, we had exhausted our supply of epinephrine. A few minutes later, we lost all pulses again and I saw the same ineffective cardiac rhythm on the monitor. *Now what?* We did what we had to—started CPR again. We had been resuscitating this woman for more than an hour and, to her credit, Janet never stopped rescue breathing. She never even asked for relief.

I asked the flight attendant, who could not have been more helpful, if there were any other first-aid kits around. She returned with another type of kit.

It contained supplies for treating anaphylaxis—a severe allergic reaction—but it did have epinephrine in it! It was in a lesser concentration but it was epi just the same, and that's what we needed. And it worked. We all leaned back—except for Janet—and I gave a report to the EMT/FBI agent. During the resuscitation, he was keeping the pilots updated about what the hell was going on in their aircraft. Vegas was the closest airport and, by God, that's where we were going.

The FBI agent leaned over to me. "Hey, Doc, see that old guy sitting in the seat, over my right shoulder?"

I looked to where he had indicated and noticed an elderly man, worried and exhausted. "Yeah."

"That's your patient's brother. He told me that she wanted to see Las Vegas before she died, and that neither plane crashes nor terrorists were going to keep her from going."

Then the patient's brother and I made eye contact. No words were needed—we were reading each other's mind.

"Mikey, Mikey!" It was Troy. "No pulses!"

No more epinephrine, and no more hope of finding another supply of it on the plane. We were screwed. I asked the FBI agent to radio ahead and, as soon as we landed, have paramedics come onboard with a dose of epi, a laryngoscope and a 7.5 endotracheal tube. This woman needed to be intubated and desperately needed epinephrine.

An hour and a half after beginning resuscitation on our patient—90 minutes that seemed like an eternity—an announcement was made over the PA system. *"Everyone please prepare for landing. Make sure your seatbelts are firmly secured, and lock your tray tables into their full and upright position."*

We all just looked at one another. All of us would be unrestrained, sitting or kneeling on the floor, performing CPR during the landing. I braced my foot on the seat so I could hold Janet by her belt; she had to continue to ventilate the patient's lungs. We bounced around a bit on the landing, but we finally touched down on terra firma and, best of all, we were in Las Vegas.

The flight attendant spoke in an exhausted and relieved voice over the PA. *"Welcome to Las Vegas. We have a medical emergency going on, so please remain in your seats."*

Most of the passengers had slept through the entire incident; now, curious, they were turning around to see if they could catch a glimpse of what was happening in the back of the plane. Word was spreading through the passenger cabin of the drama that had taken place over the last 90 minutes of the flight. We continued to do CPR as the plane taxied and finally arrived at the gate. We expected a paramedic or two to rush in with a stretcher, the equipment I'd requested and more cardiac drugs.

This patient was not going to die before seeing Vegas—not if I had anything to do with it.

The door opened and, to the credit of those onboard, not one of our fellow passengers got up out of his or her seat, keeping the aisle clear for the rescue workers to reach the patient. Down the long aisle strode one cocky fireman. He loudly pontificated that they would *not* work the patient where she was lying, but that this would be a "scoop and go"—which meant that my patient would get none of the treatment that I'd requested here on the plane and would have to wait until she was in an ambulance.

Rage like I never felt exploded out of me—a Paddy Brown rage. If anyone would be in need of a "scoop and go," it would be that fireman. A second paramedic from the ambulance crew saw what was about to happen, reached into his equipment bag and immediately gave me what I needed. I quickly intubated her and administered a life-saving dose of epinephrine. In about 30 seconds, the patient's heart was beating effectively and she'd made it to Las Vegas. While this was going on, Janet had straightened up for the first time since the episode began and went up to the front of the plane. She gave some requested information to the flight attendant. I was following my patient, who was being carried from the plane on a thin stretcher, just as the flight attendant said over the PA system, *"I want to thank Dr. Brown and his nurses Janet*

Brown, Troy Repuszka, Lois Hale and Ellen Garcia. " The other passengers started to applaud, and we were almost off the plane when the voice over the PA issued one final directive: *"And God Bless Paddy Brown. "*

Chapter 32

HOME, HOME AGAIN. LIFE would never be the same, so there was no need to attempt normality. Janet needed to get back to school and I needed to go back to work. And we both needed to communicate. That's what *we* needed to do. But what *I* wanted to do was move back to New York and rejoin the Westbury Fire Department.

After a crisis, conventional wisdom dictates waiting at least two years before making any life-changing decisions. So we remained in Las Vegas for the time being. But as the reality of my new life took shape, I started to slip from grief and sorrow into clinical depression. Little by little, I found myself spending more and more time in that black hole of despair that Ernie seemed to live in. The journey back to the living was going to be long and slow—and I was going the wrong way. And to make things worse, I didn't much care.

It was all over. Paddy Brown's wishes had been granted in a grander fashion than anyone had expected, even him. But it was over. There would be no more eight-hour days spent on the phone planning with the Inner Circle. There would be no more final decisions that only I could make, no more urgent trips to New York. The tight bonds that existed among those of the Inner Circle were no longer needed, and they slowly began to unravel as we headed in separate directions. Just as on 9/11, I sat stranded in my backyard. But this was different—there was nothing that needed to be done.

I knew I wasn't the only one feeling this way. Back in New York, the word of the day in the FDNY was *divorce*. It would have been easy for Janet to give up on me and follow suit. She didn't. I realized that I was the one who had transformed us into two raving maniacs. I had put up that wall between us. Once it was in place, we couldn't have an intelligent, reasonable conversation. The wall was so high and so thick now that we felt we had to scream to be heard, and the heated words went in circles, they made no sense. We didn't fight over a particular situation anymore; we fought round and round about the wall. It was stronger than either of us, and we existed on opposite sides, in silence, until the next argument.

Janet thought our friends should know about the adventure we'd had on our flight back to Vegas. What had happened was more than a coincidence. Two people going down on the same flight? It could only happen to someone like Pat. Michael

Daly agreed with Janet and wanted to interview me. Over the phone I tried to tell him that I didn't think it was that big of a deal, but he wanted to interview me anyway.

On that same day, just after I hung up with Mike Daly, the phone immediately rang again. It was Pat Hyland calling from New York.

"Brownie, I don't know how to tell you this...but the tree and the stone are gone."

It seems the ninja gardeners did two things wrong: 1.) We planted the tree and placed the stone too neatly and professionally and, therefore, made this new addition to Central Park much too obvious; 2.) We put a young maple in the middle of the world famous Arthur Ross Pinetum. What did we know? We're a bunch of firemen. After I hung up with Pat, I immediately knew the right person to call. I dialed the now familiar number.

"You must be fucking kidding me! Listen, Mike, I'll get back to you." Donny was on the case.

I made calls to the Inner Circle about the disappearance of Pat's tree and stone. This disturbing situation was making the first good day just—a day. Just another day to try and get past the grief of 9/11. Everyone was outraged and wanted to do something, but there was nothing that could be done. Pat's tree was probably cut at the base and thrown into a dumpster. And his beautiful black granite stone with those powerful words carved into it—the stone that took on a far greater meaning than

I could ever have imagined, the stone that caused me to lose a good friendship and almost my marriage—was gone. The way that Donny and I had cemented it in place that night made it impossible to remove without using a jackhammer. The shattered granite was probably in the same dumpster as the tree. For the hundredth time in the last three months, I was both heartbroken and angry.

A short time later Donny called back with an update.

"This is the deal. They transplanted the tree to another area and dug up the stone. It looks like they took great care to move the tree. They did an excellent job."

"What about the stone?" I asked.

"Not a scratch on it."

I was both relieved and astonished. "What?! It's still in one piece? Donny, you saw it?"

"Saw it? I'm driving with it! It's in the back seat of my patrol car. Now what do you want me to do with it?"

What do you do with a hundred-pound black granite stone in the middle of Manhattan? I asked him to take it to 3 Truck. Other than Central Park, where else would it belong?

MY SOUL WAS STILL on a slow, descending spiral when Michael Daly's column was published. The story of our trip home was in the New York *Daily*

News on Sunday, November 18, and read by a few million people. Mike, being the incredible writer that he is, took the events of the flight and wove them into a great story. The next day I got a call from producers at the *Today Show*. They wanted to interview me. I told them I needed to think about it and I'd call them back.

Later that day Bobby called me. "I just read Mike Daly's column. That was amazing!"

"No, no, Bob, not really. That's everyday stuff in the ER. I'll tell you what's amazing—the *Today Show* wants to interview me."

"Wow! The *Today Show!* You're going to by interviewed by Katie Couric? That's great! When are you going to do it?"

"I don't think I am. You know how much I *love* talking on camera."

Bobby quickly replied, "No, no, Mike, you have to do it! It's the freaking' *Today Show*. It will be fun!" *Here we go again.*

"Bobby, your definition of fun is not even close to mine."

Bobby was enthusiastic when he said, "You know your brother is doing this to you. Don't worry, Mike. There'll only be about 12 million people watching."

"Oh, is that all? Thanks a lot, Bob!"

Everyone else was excited at the prospect of my being on the *Today Show*. Janet also wanted me to accept their offer to tell our story on national TV, but her motive was different. She was worried about me dropping out of life and jumped at any opportunity to get me excited about something and back in the game.

WELCOME TO THE TODAY Show. It was Tuesday, November 20, but Janet and I were not at NBC studios in New York; we were in a small dark studio in an industrial park in Las Vegas. It was 5 a.m. and I was about to be interviewed, live via satellite, by Katie Couric. I sat on a thin, cold metal chair that was slightly elevated and bent uncomfortably forward. The backdrop behind me was an outdated and somewhat faded picture of the Las Vegas Strip. The only thing that I could see through the blinding spotlights was a big, black, cold camera lens. This was not going to be easy. I expected a monitor to view so I could get those all-important nonverbal signals from my interviewer. Steve McCarthy was a master with these signals. When he had interviewed me, he'd used very subtle expressions that would guide me through any obstacle that might arise.

A technician at the studio handed me an earpiece. "Here, put this in your ear, and when Katie comes on, talk to the camera like you're talking to her. And whatever you do, don't look around. If you do, you'll look like a fool."

What! Pretend to see someone I'm only hearing through a tiny earphone?! And don't look around? How do people do this stuff?

The earpiece was put in place, and I was instantly hooked into Rockefeller Center and listening to the *Today Show*. There was an interview going on, an incredible story of a journalist who'd escaped from Afghanistan. *Why the hell would they want to talk to me?* Then I heard an annoyed Al Roker speaking to those happy people outside the studio on 49th Street who, apparently, were grabbing at him. Next, a voice in the earpiece: *"O.K., Dr. Brown, you're on in about 30 seconds."*

I started to sweat. The voice disappeared and Al Roker was back again. He was speaking to Mimi, whose daddy was a pilot in Saudi Arabia. Then I heard the voice of Katie Couric talking about me. *Who the hell would think this is fun?*

"Thank you, Al. As he was flying home from attending a service for his firefighter brother who lost his life saving others after the World Trade Center attack, Las Vegas Dr. Michael Brown was also called on to save two lives himself. Dr. Brown, good morning."

And I was on! I was peering at that black hole in front of 12 million people and not feeling like a hero at all. Contrary to the studio guy's warning, I was looking around—looking around like a deer caught in the headlights, looking around like a man in the electric chair waiting for the juice to flow, looking around for any route of escape whatsoever.

Katie was a sweetheart, and I didn't die. But for Lois, and in my best Brooklynese, I did manage to pronounce the word *toilet* as *turlet*—like Archie Bunker. And that is the only thing anyone remembers about that interview.

Chapter 33

IT WAS IRONIC THAT I was being touted as some big hero doctor back in the ER—ironic because not only was I convinced I was *not* a hero, but also because my depression had become so entrenched that I didn't even want to be a doctor. Everything, everything was so goddamned sad. I had always possessed a healthy fear of going to work in the ER, but now I just hated going to work, period.

As with every other job, there were good days and bad days; now every day was a bad one. Most of the patients seemed to be there for ulterior motives. Many were drug seekers wanting a narcotics prescription for their own addiction, to sell on the street, or both; some wanted attention from their families; still others simply wanted a day off from work. A lot were trying to sue someone, anyone. I was progressively becoming more cynical, and I carried my mood like a layer of thick, heavy flesh that weighed me down. Unfortunately, I was taking everyone else down with me.

The people I worked with had nothing but support and love for me. That's what made this so wrong. During one particular night shift, I realized just how much this problem was affecting me as well as my coworkers, and why I hated to go to work. That night I wanted to be anywhere but in the ER. A patient with full-blown cardiac arrest was brought in, and I started to yell at a nurse when a piece of equipment I needed was not where it should have been in the crash cart. Even though someone ran to get it, the equipment not being there didn't make one bit of difference in the outcome. The patient was dead when he came through the door. One difference it did make—one of my ER nurses was very upset. When I passed her sobbing in the hallway, I knew that I had morphed into something that I'd feared becoming for most of my professional life. I had become "that asshole doctor." I knew then why I hated work. I hated work because I hated myself.

And when I returned home, I would take my self-hatred and retreat behind the wall. Obviously Janet was getting tired of the situation. She broke through with a suggestion that I speak to a psychiatrist. *What would a psychiatrist be able to tell me? Maybe he could start me on antidepressants?* But I knew the reason for my depression. Medication was not the answer. I also didn't want to turn into a smiling ping-pong ball like the one in that TV commercial for Prozac.

Self-medicating with alcohol was becoming sociologically unhealthy. Back in New York during that perpetual Irish wake, alcohol had its place. Life was on hold. Being surrounded with people who were hurting as much as I was and had nothing to do but wait—drinking was something to do to pass the time. Back in Vegas, there was no Irish wake. There was something important to be done: Getting on with life.

James Remar called to remind me that Pat wouldn't want us grieving forever. Michael Daly said how much he missed his close friends, Pat and Father Judge, and commented on the close, almost spiritual friendship they had.

"Mike, with all the death in the world, we are sure ill-prepared to handle it."

Keith called and told me how difficult it had been to deal with his brother Pete's death in that fire six years ago, and how Pat had helped him get through the toughest times. Bobby called, and I brought up what Keith had told me. Bobby said actually it was Pat who had been in a major depression after Pete's death, and it was Keith who pulled Pat out of the hole. No matter who helped whom in the process, friends were helping one another. And now, using that same process, the members of the Inner Circle were pulling each other out of the hole. Calls were coming in from Pat's—now my—friends with increasing frequency. I think Janet had a lot to do with that.

There were those late nights when I would sit up alone scanning the TV channels and drinking beer. Depression and alcohol are a bad combination: alcohol is known to make normal people depressed; depressed people, suicidal. And there had been way too many funerals already.

There were other things that seemed to help, and Janet encouraged them whenever she could. One of these things was weightlifting. I did some of my best thinking when I was picking up heavy things and putting them back down. During one of these sessions, a particular memory of my brother filled my head—from out of nowhere, seemingly for no reason.

It was in my first year of medical school. Pat called to tell me he'd just enrolled me in a mind-control seminar. The course was in a small classroom in a small store in Manhattan and took place over two consecutive weekends, 10 hours each day. Pat insisted that I go. He paid the $600 tuition for me, so there was no backing out. "Mind control" turned out to be a class on meditation. So on my only days off, I would drive down from Albany and meditate for 10 hours a day. Back then, the only thing I wanted to do on a day off was meditate all over my girlfriend.

It's hard for me, a medical doctor, to admit that this 40-hour seminar helped me—but it did. It was about to help me again. The course had a lot to do with positive thinking and controlling your own thoughts. With Mark Knopfler's music blasting from my stereo while I picked up heavy things and put them down, I came up with a plan to fix my mood and make me less of an asshole.

Even though my insides were being eaten away with grief and sadness, I decided to act as though I were just fine. Years ago I'd read a book about public speaking. If you acted as if you weren't nervous when you were in front of a room full of people, the book advised, no one would notice that you were. Soon you'd no longer be anxious. So I lived only on the surface. It wasn't an instant cure, but the idea seemed to work. It was simple—if I continued to live in a pit of gloom where everything had a deep, dark and painful meaning, I wouldn't get a goddamned thing done. Therefore, I would act as though I were a successful, productive person…and maybe, just maybe, that's what I'd become once again. If I needed to fall apart, I would try to do it when I was alone. If I really needed to think, I would work out or go for a run. If I needed to get away from it all, I would swim—because I can't do much thinking in the water. All my attention has to be focused on staying afloat. I swim like a rock with arms.

Ernie too was trying to dig himself out of his hole of despair and anger. He called me one day and asked if I would like to get together with Mike Kramer, another ER doc, and play some music. *Music! What a concept!* Music had always been very important in my life and, before Ernie's call, I hadn't even thought to turn to my guitar for distraction and healing.

"O.K., Ernie, but I don't know many songs. In fact, I don't think I know any songs."

We decided to have our jam session at Mike Kramer's house. Mike would play the bass guitar and saxophone; Ernie, the drums; and I'd be on guitar. That night when we got together, the beer was cold, the pizza was hot, and the music...Well, Ernie said it the best. "You know, the more I drink, the better we sound!"

After an hour or so of a mixture of jazz, blues, Cream, Doors, Hendrix, blue grass Arabian-sounding stuff and anything else that happened to drift out of our instruments, we decided to try a real song. Mike got on his homemade computer and borrowed some charts from the Web. We tried a few songs that went belly up until we hit upon *Wish You Were Here* by Pink Floyd. I don't know if it was the straightforward guitar part, the simplicity of the music or the beer kicking in, but it didn't sound too bad. Ernie and I even sang. That night, Mike Kramer's blissfully undisturbed neighbors never knew how important it was that he'd installed extra insulation in his house:

> *So you think you can tell...Heaven from hell...Blue skies from pain...Can you tell a green field from a cold steel rail?...A smile*

from a veil?...Do you think you could tell?...Did they get you to trade...Your heroes for ghosts?...

We were innocently fumbling our way through the words. This was followed by a little rest for our brains, as our instruments seemed to play themselves. Then, in a moment of revelation, the chorus and the meaning of the song fell together. Before that night, I'd heard this song hundreds of times and had tried to figure out what the hell they were talking about. Right then and there, for the three of us, it had a meaning. It meant the world:

How I wish...How I wish you were here...We're just two lost souls swimming in a fishbowl, year after year...Running over the same old ground...Have we found the same old fear?...Wish you were here...

The instruments seemed to finish the song without us. Yes, it meant the world. It was not just about close friends playing music together to help get past the horrors of the past few months. It was more than that. It meant the world because, for a brief moment, the music cut through the haze of our grief. It showed us that there is life after death.

BACK HOME, I TRIED my best not to think about what was going on in New York—I tried to shrink the elephant in the living room. Just as he'd promised, Steve Browne was checking in and giving me daily updates on the progress downtown. They were starting to find the remains of some of the guys from Ladder 3; the elephant was becoming more and more intrusive. Steve reiterated that he wanted to be the first to tell me when they found Pat.

My father had been released from the rehab facility and was now back at home with my sister. After I spoke to Steve each day, I'd call and give my dad any updated information. There was nothing else that he could think about, and he knew the inevitable as well as I did. He knew that soon he would be going through a second service for his son. After I told him that they were finding some of Pat's guys, he gave me the number of the military cemetery out in Suffolk County where my mom and infant brother John were buried; my father had the plot next to them reserved for himself. He said, "Mike, I don't know what you're going to do, but remember Pat was a veteran, you know?"

Steve and the other members of 3 Truck were concerned about how I was holding up. I was concerned about how *they* were holding up. Here they were—Ladder Company 3, Recon—who in two months went through 13 memorials for their best friends, brothers and fellow firefighters, always making sure that the families and all arrangements were taken care of. And now they had to go through it all over again. There had been 13 memorials, including the one for John Moran, Mike's brother, and now there could be as many as 13 funerals. How could anyone expect anyone to go through something like that and, when it's finally over, still be sane? Neither Steve nor anyone else in the FDNY ever showed weakness or reluctance to do the right thing.

It was the inevitable shot at my superficial existence. It was as if Pat were warning me, "Hey, Mike—you ain't done yet."

A few weeks before Christmas, on a cold and rainy morning in New York, Bobby got the call from Bill Ells, a city fireman and a close friend of both Pat and Bobby.

"Bobby, you are not going to *believe* what I'm standing over." Bill had been searching the pile since 9/11 and was, rightly so, the person who found Pat.

Bobby arrived with 3 Truck in the pouring rain and, with great respect and tenderness, they placed Paddy Brown's mortal remains on a stretcher, draped it with an American flag and carried it to the waiting ambulance. Bobby called Keith. In a matter of minutes, the ambulance and Ladder 3 had a police escort to the morgue. Bobby told me that 3 Truck had a covering lieutenant who gave Bobby his seat in the rig. Bobby protested, not wanting to remove the officer from his position in the truck.

"No, you sit here in the front," the lieutenant insisted. "You deserve it."

IGNORING MY PROTESTS, JANET refused to skip Christmas. We were doing some shopping when my cell phone rang. It was Bobby.

"Mike, I think we found your brother." These were words I'd both hoped for and feared.

"Bobby, how do you know it's him?"

I heard him take a long, deep breath. "He's intact from the shoulders down and is wearing a 3 Truck turnout coat and Engine 69 boots."

My hands were shaking as I checked my voice mail. Doug Ingram from the Westbury Fire Department had left me a message.

"Doc, I got some very important news. Call me as soon as you get this."

A second message was from my cousin Jay, the California fire captain.

"I heard they found Pat. Call me."

News certainly did travel fast.

Then Steve Browne called. He told me that they found a body that was probably Pat's, and he would keep me posted. He said that usually the medical examiner needed between four and six weeks to make a positive ID.

It was only two days later, December 14, when Steve called again. "Hey, Mike, we just got word. It was Paddy that they found."

Apparently a positive ID was made without having to go through all the DNA analysis. Steve and I spoke at length. He asked if he had been the first one to tell me. For a moment I didn't know what to say. I knew how important it was to him that he should be the first to deliver the news, but I couldn't lie to him. Paddy Brown was well known when he was alive; in death he'd become world famous. My sister received phone calls from France wanting to confirm the news that Paddy had been found.

Chapter 34

STEVE AND I DISCUSSED how to handle the funeral. Most families were keeping the services private and simple. True to form, Steve told me that they would do whatever I wanted. He agreed that what we did at St. Patrick's on Paddy's birthday was a once-in-a-lifetime event and could never be repeated. He also knew that I had some concerns about Pat's request for cremation and my father's wish to have him buried on Long Island. My sister left it up to me. Since Pat had left me that note instructing me to cremate him and dump his ashes in Central Park, I was torn about it. I wanted to fulfill Pat's wishes, but I didn't want to hurt my father. One thing was sure—nothing was going to be done until after Christmas. I would have to think long and hard about this.

Later that afternoon I tried to take a nap before going in to work the graveyard shift. This shift is appropriately named because during the graveyard shift in Vegas, the waiting room is inhabited by the living dead. The TV was on while I was lying on the couch trying to get a few minutes of shuteye, and I fell asleep thinking of another important decision I'd have to make. *O.K., if I do have Pat's remains cremated, what would be the procedure to "dump" his ashes? Do I dump them in a pile? That doesn't sound right. Do I spread them out in a large area? Or should I forget about it and bury his remains next to my mom?*

I wasn't asleep for very long and awoke to a movie on the TV. I have no idea of the title to this day, but in this particular scene, there were three people standing at the edge of a cliff. They could have been on the Irish coast. One at a time, they reached into a container and took out a handful of what appeared to be dirt. Then, in unison, they threw the dirt up in the air and the wind carried it away from the cliff and toward the ocean. I sat bolt upright when I realized what I was watching—Pat was showing me exactly how he wanted it done.

JUST AFTER CHRISTMAS, JANET and I flew back to New York yet again. I had a few days to finalize Paddy's funeral arrangements. The funeral was going to be small, and Dominic allowed us to use the chapel at Campbell's. A private service would be held the night of December 29.

On December 27, James Remar called and asked me to meet him in front of what was now known as Pat's Tree. It was the first time I would be visiting the tree since it was transplanted and I had a difficult time finding it. Mike Daly told me that it was located just behind the statue of Alexander Hamilton, but where the hell was the statue of Alexander Hamilton? It was a cold but sunny day, and I wandered around the Great Lawn until I found James sitting on a bench. We greeted each other with a handshake.

"James, where's the tree?"

We walked across a pedestrian pathway and there it was. The tree was surrounded by a small, protective fence. There were flowers at its base, cards hanging on its branches, and a few pictures that a child had drawn. They all delivered the same message. "We miss you, Paddy."

Referring to the tree, James said, "You did a great job. Your brother would be proud."

I was nervous meeting James, especially at the tree; I'd denied him the opportunity to participate in the planting. But soon it was as if we'd known each other a lifetime. James and I had lives that went in totally different directions—he was an actor and I was a doctor—but our attitudes toward important subjects were surprisingly similar. It was obvious why he and Pat were such good friends. We talked a lot about Pat and how much we missed him. Even though I disagreed, James said I was right in not inviting him to the tree planting.

"I know that's been bothering you. I also know of another decision that's been tearing you apart that I might be able to help you with," he said. "You know, this past summer, I was working on *Sex and the City* and spending a great deal of time in Manhattan. Your brother and I ended up hanging out together a lot. We would go for a run, or he would have dinner with me and my family, or we would spend the afternoon with my kids here in the park. I remember one beautiful summer day, we were walking near here talking about nothing and everything. My kids stopped to play with a Frisbee right over there on that lawn..."

He paused, savoring the sweet, wonderful memory. After a moment, he shook his head and continued.

"Suddenly, completely out of nowhere, Pat turns to me and says, 'Whatever you do, James, don't let them bury me on fucking Long Island.' "

PAT'S WAKE TOOK PLACE, as scheduled, on the night of December 29. Janet and I arrived at Campbell's on that cold, blustery night and found Bobby and James waiting outside for us.

"Hey, guys, how are you holding up?" Bobby asked in a melancholic tone.

James opened the door for us and said, "Well, this is it."

We all took a collective breath and went inside. Dominic came out of his office and escorted us into the chapel. He said, "Mike, I think you're doing the right thing having him cremated."

I turned to Dominic, smiled and replied, "It really wasn't up to me after all."

My brother's coffin was draped with an American flag, surrounded by beautiful flower arrangements and huge pots of poinsettias, and there were large pictures of Pat on either side. Janet went to the front of the room, knelt down in front of the casket and said a prayer while I stood with Bobby and James. I noticed how each person arriving was brought up short on seeing the coffin; it was as if that last bit of irrational hope had been ripped away. Not much needed to be said as the seats of the chapel quickly filled. The members of Ladder 3, Engine 69 and Ladder 28 arrived wearing their Class A uniforms. I had forgotten all about an honor guard—but they hadn't. That night, all night, and two at a time, they stood tall and proud in honor and respect at each end of the coffin; Pat's men were taking care of their beloved captain. Nothing could have been more appropriate.

Steve Browne asked me how I was handling things. I told him that the tough part was the memorial at St Patrick's when we honored his spirit; now it was time to respect his body. Comparatively speaking, this would be easy. Steve gave me that clairvoyant look of his.

Sharon, the person who had suggested that we have a Buddhist monk at St. Patrick's Cathedral, arrived wearing Pat's dog tags and looking as if she hadn't slept for several days. Out of all the messages that were left on Pat's answering machine on 9/11, I will always remember Sharon's panicked voice: *"Pat, this is Sharon. I pray to God you're O.K. I don't believe this is happening. I just saw the second tower collapse. I know you're down there. I pray to God you're O.K. I love you. Buh-bye."* Her frantic message was then followed by the monotone voice of the machine calmly announcing the time of the call. *"Tuesday, 10:32 a.m."*

Jim Carney had arranged for a driver to bring my father from Westbury to the funeral home. The door to Campbell's opened and, accompanied by a blast of frigid air, in walked my dad. I hadn't seen him since Pat's memorial, and he didn't seem to be getting any better. Each step made him grimace in pain as he slowly made his way into the chapel. When he saw the casket, he tightened his grip on his walker and looked as if he'd been shot in the chest. The service was about to start, and I walked slowly behind him to the front row of seats. The chairs and pews on both sides of the small room were full, and people were standing along each wall. Daniele was kneeling in front of the coffin; Dan and Steve Browne, brothers who had helped me through the past three months with such selflessness and compassion, were taking their turn as honor guard.

The service was simple and appropriate. Keith provided the music; it was the CD that accompanied McCarthy's movie, the same one we'd played during our Central Park adventure.

New FDNY chaplain Father Chris Keenan—he'd taken the place of Pat's close friend, Father Mychal Judge, who had died in the lobby of the North Tower—gave a short but powerful talk and led us through prayers. Then Pat's friends and family, two by two, approached his coffin, knelt briefly, and said their quiet goodbyes. I waited until everyone left the room so I could be alone with my big brother and, just as Steve Browne knew would happen, I fell apart. This wasn't easy at all. Steve knew it wouldn't be. Alone in the chapel, with my right arm draped protectively over my brother's coffin, the last bit of my irrational hope was finally, painfully torn from me.

Chapter 35

THE NEXT MORNING, JANET braved the bitter cold to get us coffee from a sidewalk vendor on 18th Street. It was December 30. I stayed in our room at the W and made calls. I needed to do my best to ensure that Pat's Inner Circle had the opportunity to be with us later that night. For the hundredth time, I read the list of names on Pat's letter—James, Bobby, Tim and Rick would all be there. I called Ralph; he said he couldn't make it. The only person on the list that I couldn't call was Terry Hatton. He was already with Pat and would be with us in spirit. I asked Keith if I should call Beth Hatton, and he thought it was an excellent idea.

That night the weather lived up to the forecast: bitter cold and windy. It was brutal. There was no one waiting outside Campbell's that night when Janet and I arrived. Tim Brown and Bobby were in the foyer; more people started to arrive, singly and in groups, all dressed for the Arctic blast. One of the funeral directors approached me. "Dr. Brown, you need to sign a few things," he said. "Just take a seat in the office and I'll be right back."

Janet remained in the foyer while Bobby and I went into the office and sat down. There, sitting on the desk, was a cylindrical white cardboard container with a sticker on it that read CAPTAIN PATRICK J. BROWN. I picked it up and said, "Well, Bobby, this is it." I was surprised at the lack of weight of the container. The funeral director came in and sat behind the desk. He placed several forms in front of me.

I handed Pat's ashes to Bobby. He tenderly held his best friend's remains as I signed the papers one after another. "I have to ask you this," the funeral director said. "What do you want to do if they find any more of your brother's remains?"

At that point, I realized what Bobby had implied when he told me they'd found Pat "intact from his shoulders down." It would be cruel to do anything other than let whatever else they might find of my brother be cremated with the people he died with, and instructed the funeral director accordingly.

The funeral director knew of our occult tree-planting caper and was getting suspicious when he saw there now were more than 30 people waiting for us outside his office door. He warned me, "You do understand that it is illegal to spread ashes in New York City?"

I stood up, shook his hand, and Bobby handed me the cardboard container. With a big smile I said, "Don't worry. We're all going directly to fucking Long Island."

THE MOOD WAS SURPRISINGLY upbeat as our large group headed out into the icy wind. Just like the ninja gardeners that had marched into Central Park seven weeks before, we were marching into the park carrying Pat's ashes and were about to do exactly what he had asked. We stopped when we arrived at the north end of the Great Lawn and formed a long line. There was a problem. The brisk wind was coming from the south, downtown, where the Midtown Manhattan skyline faced the park. It was not going to work if the ashes were tossed in that direction. In front of everyone was an open area that had softball fields and behind them, the police building. High above this building, over the Central Park Reservoir where Pat used to run, shone the biggest and brightest full moon anyone had ever seen. Because of the cold and the wind, the night sky was crystal clear. I opened the container and walked down the line of people that meant the most to Pat. One at a time, we each reached in and took a handful of Paddy Brown. With my back to both the skyline and the wind, I stood and faced Pat's family. Then I quoted him. "This is kinda beautiful, you know?" With that, the line turned around and, rather than tossing the ashes to the frozen ground as

I expected, threw them up to the moon and yelled, "GOD BLESS PADDY BROWN!"

This magnificent cloud of what had once been Pat's bones, muscle and heart took flight and swirled magically toward the moon and over his city.

There was still a small quantity of ashes left in the container, so we headed in the direction of Alexander Hamilton's statue and to Pat's Tree. I stepped over the small fence that surrounded the strong, healthy maple and spread my brother's remaining ashes around its base. Someone handed me a dozen white roses and a votive candle to put beside them, and Janet stepped over and added one of Pat's prayer cards to our offerings. We stood in a circle around the tree, and Vina Drennan started to sing the *Marine Corps Hymn*. We all joined in; and when we finished, we softly sang *God Bless America*.

Then something truly miraculous happened. Since 9/11, flights over the city were severely restricted, and I hadn't seen a plane in the skies over Manhattan—until that moment, at the end of the song. Just as if it had been planned, a jetliner broke through the crystal clear sky and flew directly over us. Pat got his flyover.

Mike Daly grabbed me by the shoulder and proclaimed, "Michael, Paddy could not have had a better brother."

Chapter 36

AFTER PAT'S UNEXPECTED FLYOVER, we all stood in a huddle, not wanting to leave, until the pain from the cold forced us to move. There would be no 4,000-plus guests in a Hilton Hotel ballroom that night—just the 30 or so of us, and we needed to find a place to eat. Mike Daly suggested the Adriatic, a small, simple restaurant downtown within walking distance of my brother's apartment. Pat used to eat there several times a week, and it was an appropriate setting for our last meal together as the expanded Inner Circle. We took up two long tables in the back room.

Just before I sat down, the owner came over and told me a story about Pat. There had been a fire in the kitchen one night. Employees and patrons were running out of the building. Pat got up from his table, went into the kitchen and put the fire out. He then returned to his seat and resumed eating his dinner.

The Italian-accented owner said to me, "I was amazed. Paddy saved my restaurant! I asked him,

How did he know how to do that? He told me that he was a fireman, that's what he does. He had been eating in my restaurant for years, and I never knew he was a fireman!"

We ordered pizza, heroes, drinks. Marc, who was sitting across from me, said, "I'm worried about Tracy. She should've been here by now."

Marc's girlfriend Tracy did not go to the park with us and choose to stay behind at the W. Marc told her that she should take a cab to meet us at the restaurant, but I suggested that, since the place was only three blocks from the hotel, it might be easier for her just to walk.

"Marc, you wait for her here and I'll go out and look for her," I said, as I stood up and put my layers of clothes back on. I went outside, past the frozen smokers who had gathered just outside the front door of the Adriatic, and into the dark New York streets. With the wind off the East River, it was even more bitter here than in Central Park. The cold air took my breath away as I walked the cross streets thinking how dumb I was to tell Tracy, who was unfamiliar with Manhattan, to walk to the restaurant. I could still feel the grit of my brother's ashes under my gloves as I strained my eyes for the sight of Tracy. I didn't see her. To cover more ground, I started to run. My mind was racing too. This could end up as one of those New York nightmares, and it would be my fault. Then my cell phone went off. It was Marc. Tracy was smarter than me and took a cab. She was now sitting next to him eating a stuffed artichoke.

BACK IN THE ADRIATIC, I again peeled off my outer layers and, with the powdery grit of my brother still on my hands, sat down and started to eat the slice of pizza that Janet had passed to me. We were all eating with our hands, talking about the stuff that people talk about. Bobby was next to me. I leaned close to him and whispered, "Bobby, did anyone wash their hands?"

"No," he said, giving me a knowing look.

Then it hit me. I'd been referring to this group as Pat's Inner Circle. I realized now that I'd borrowed it from one of those cult classics I had read years ago—*Stranger in a Strange Land*. The ending of the novel was very similar, and we were truly, very much Pat's Inner Circle.

JANET AND I DECIDED to stay in Manhattan for New Year's Eve. We had no plans and figured that we would probably just have a drink at the Fish Bowl. That was until Tim Brown showed up at the W and gave us two tickets to Mayor Giuliani's "going out as mayor" party in Times Square. The TV news was full of information about the different terrorist weapons that could be set off in Times Square during the celebration. They were talking mostly about dirty bombs—biological weapons that could release substances like small pox or anthrax, and chemical weapons like mustard gas or nerve agents. I discussed this possibility with Janet and asked her what she wanted to do. Without hesitation and with a smile she said, "Are you kidding me? I want to go to the party!"

On New Year's Eve morning, Janet stayed at the hotel and I walked down to 3 Truck to say goodbye to the men. We would be returning to Las Vegas the next morning. The flowers were gone from the front of the firehouse. The signs that had been in the NYU dorm windows across the street from 3 Truck were no longer there. There was no one stopping by and, because of the cold, the big door was closed. I stood in front, took a deep breath, and pounded on it. The face of firefighter Chris Tighe appeared at the small window in the door.

"Hey, Mike! Hold on." The large door banged and cranked itself open, and I ran in as the heat of the firehouse ran out. The door creaked back down and banged to a stop when it reached the floor.

"How you holding up?" Chris asked as he shook my hand. "The guys are in the back. Why don't you go back and get some coffee? I'll tell Steve Browne you're here."

As he started to walk away, I asked him, "Chris, where's the stone?"

Pointing to the front corner of the firehouse he said, "It's right over there."

I started to walk over when Pat Murphy intercepted me. "Mike, I need to tell you something," he said, his voice low. "I felt like I needed to find out what really happened on the 11th. You know, that story that went around, that the 3 Truck guys were on the 40th floor helping those burn victims when the tower came down?" I nodded. "Well, it's true. I spoke to one of the guys who got out. He was very hesitant to say anything, but I kept on him. He and his company passed 3 Truck while they were evacuating the building. He said that Paddy knew that the South Tower came down, and that there was an order to evacuate the North Tower, but he refused to leave those victims behind—and the guys from 3 Truck refused to leave their captain behind."

Then Pat paused and looked at the battered sign on the ladder truck that read LADDER 3 RECON. The sign was the only thing salvageable from the old ladder truck that was destroyed at the Trade Center. He said softly, "I don't how it makes you feel, but it makes me proud."

Steve Browne then joined Pat and me. "Ah, Mike, how ya holding up? Chris said you were looking for your stone. It's over here."

And there it was, in the corner where it shared a space with other unwanted stuff. There was a broom head lying on top of it. Other than being dirty, it was in perfect shape. Not a chip or a scratch on it.

Steve was embarrassed and quickly removed the debris from the beautiful piece of granite. "Sorry about that. We were planning to make it nice, but haven't had the chance."

"No, Steve, don't apologize. You don't know how much I appreciate your letting me keep it here."

"That was some night at Central Park," Steve said with a smile. "I'll never forget it."

"Mike, what are you going to do with it?" Murphy asked.

"If it's O.K. with the guys, I would like to leave it right here until I can figure out how to get it back in the park."

Steve said, "Whenever you want, just give me the date. I'll meet you with shovel in hand."

"What I would like to do is get it there legally so it'll stay where it belongs. I'll figure something out."

Steve replied, "I have no doubt that you will, my General."

THAT NIGHT WAS ONE of the coldest New Year's Eves that I could remember. Because of the heightened security, there was no way to get near Times Square by cab. So Janet and I put on all the clothes we brought with us and headed for the subway. We were both excited as we headed into the Union Square station with other cold New Yorkers. We were holding hands, laughing and smiling at the prospect of going to the Mayor's New Year's Eve party in Times Square—when the sight of a picture on the wall of the subway station stopped us in our tracks. The photo was small, and among maybe a hundred or so others. They were pictures of some of the victims of the Trade Center. The one that jumped out at us was the one of my brother's face, big smile, in his Class A, the same photo on the front of his prayer card. Someone had placed a big red lipstick kiss on it. Janet and I laughed. And there he was, on that subway wall, smiling right back at us.

We had to wear our tickets on small chains around our necks to get anywhere near the party. There was a labyrinth of police barricades and police personnel surrounding Times Square. Only after we showed our invitation to the Mayor's party would the cops let us through. We quickly made our way through four or five of these checkpoints and arrived at the ESPN Zone restaurant, where the party was being held. We both handed over a pile of clothes to the coat-check girl and headed upstairs.

What a place for a New Year's Eve party! Most of the enormous TVs that usually show sports events were showing views of Times Square. Two of them were replaying Giuliani's appearance on *Saturday Night Live.* There was really no one that Janet and I knew, but we were very content just being together in the crowd. We found two seats at the bar and watched the TVs. There was a special area set up outside for the Mayor's guests to watch the ball drop, and people started to leave as it got close to midnight. Janet and I were in no hurry to leave our barstools for the cold waiting for us outside, so we waited until the last possible moment, ran down the stairs, threw on all those layers again and rushed outside.

The cold hit our senses almost as hard as the Times Square neon did. We kept our heads down and followed other cold-fearing people until they stopped at the area designated for the party's guests. I turned around, looked up and saw that we were about a hundred feet from where the ball would drop. There were rows of police officers lined up—which made me think of Tim, Keith and Donny, standing somewhere freezing their asses off, keeping the city safe. There was also a colorful sea of screw-the-terrorists-I'm-going-to-Times-Square-for-New-Year's-Eve people freezing their asses off. Noisemakers and horns were making their presence known as the excitement began to build. If someone had planted a bomb somewhere out there, now would be the time to set it off. I held my breath.

Hundreds of thousands of people began screaming in unison. *"10, 9, 8, 7..."* I held Janet close as the ball slowly descended and the countdown chant continued. *"6, 5, 4, 3, 2, 1—HAPPY NEW YEAR!!!"*

Tons of confetti were flying and raining down on us as *Auld Lang Syne* boomed out of the massive loudspeakers. No one, not even the cops, could hold back the tears. New York City had made it through.

Sinatra's *New York, New York* followed, and everyone sang along as if it were a battle anthem. Then it was over. The frozen crowd quickly dispersed, rushing off to find warmth and resume their everyday lives. Janet and I stood in place and clung to each other tightly like the two Nevadan icicles we were.

She looked into my eyes and said, "I think 2002 will be a better year."

I smiled. "It can't be any worse."

I gave her a kiss and, arm in arm, with no wall between us now, we left Times Square to start our journey home—back to our life.

———————

I started out writing a story about pain and ended up writing a story about love

About the Author

Michael Everett Brown, M.D., is a board-certified Emergency Medicine physician currently practicing in Las Vegas, Nevada. He was a volunteer firefighter in Westbury, New York, for over 12 years, a New York City firefighter at Engine Company 37 in Harlem for four years and is currently a member of Nevada Task Force One Urban Search and Rescue Team. In 2001 he received a United States Congressional Recognition Award for "selfless acts and commitment to his profession above and beyond the call of duty."